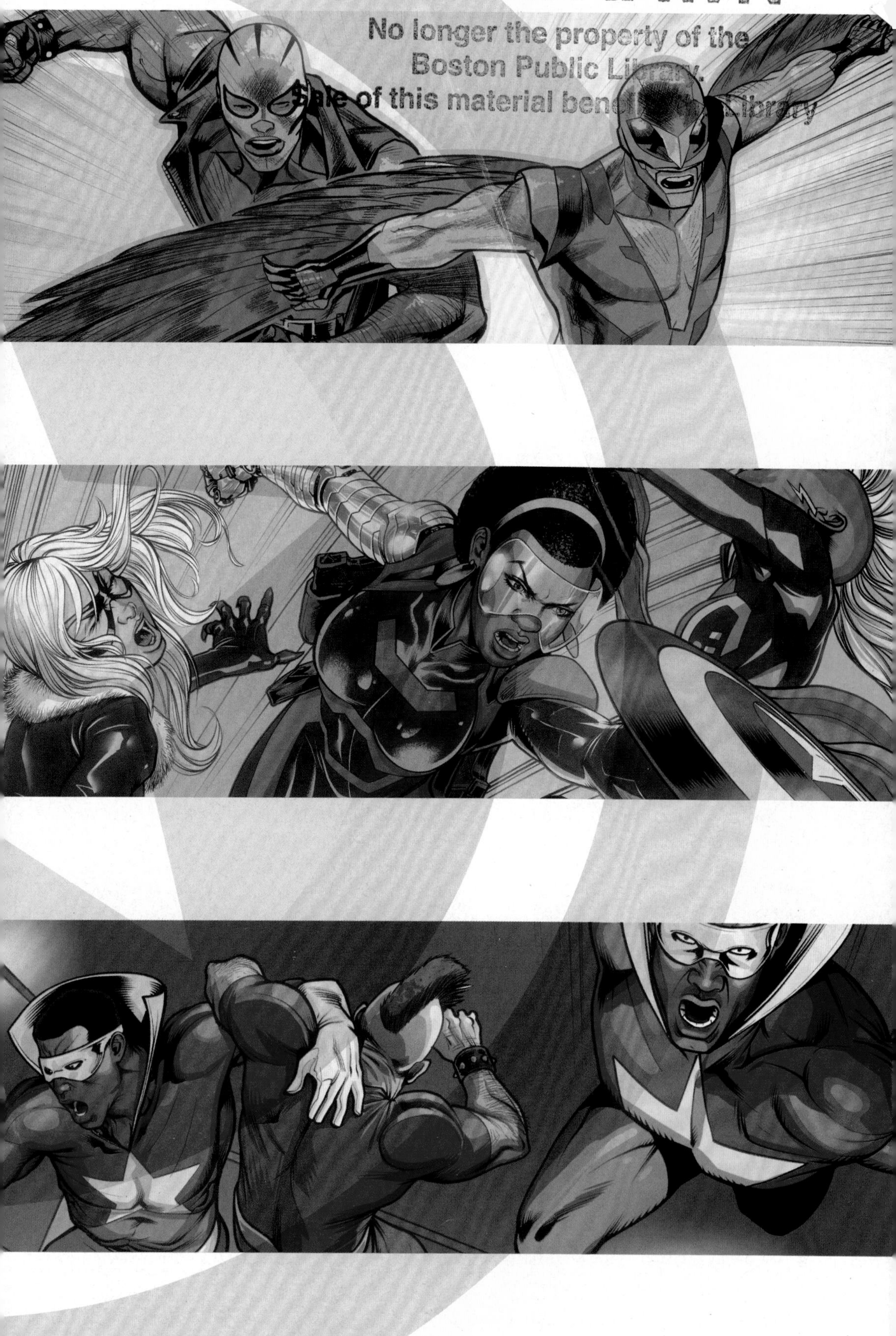

collection editor JENNIFER GRÜNWALD

assistant editor CAITLIN O'CONNELL

associate managing editor KATERI WOODY

editor, special projects MARK D. BEAZLEY

vp production & special projects JEFF YOUNGQUIST

svp print, sales & marketing DAVID GABRIEL

book designer ADAM DEL RE

editor in chief AXEL ALONSO

chief creative officer JOE QUESADA

president DAN BUCKLEY

executive producer ALAN FINE

CAPTAIN AMERICA: SAM WILSON VOL. 4 — #TAKEBACKTHESHIELD. Contains material originally published in magazine form as CAPTAIN AMERICA: SAM WILSON #14-17 and CAPTAIN AMERICA #344. First printing 2017. ISBN# 978-1-302-90329-9. Published by MARVEL WORLDWIDE, INC., a subsidiary of MARVEL ENTERTAINMENT, LLC. OFFICE OF PUBLICATION: 135 West 50th Street, New York, NY 10020. Copyright © 2017 MARVEL No similarity between any of the names, characters, persons, and/or institutions in this magazine with those of any living or dead person or institution is intended, and any such similarity which may exist is purely coincidental. **Printed in Canada.** DAN BUCKLEY, President, Marvel Entertainment; JOE QUESADA, Chief Creative Officer; TOM BREVOORT, SVP of Publishing; DAVID BOGART, SVP of Business Affairs & Operations, Publishing & Partnership; C.B. CEBULSKI, VP of Brand Management & Development, Asia; DAVID GABRIEL, SVP of Sales & Marketing, Publishing; JEFF YOUNGQUIST, VP of Production & Special Projects; DAN CARR, Executive Director of Publishing Technology; ALEX MORALES, Director of Publishing Operations; SUSAN CRESPI, Production Manager; STAN LEE, Chairman Emeritus. For information regarding advertising in Marvel Comics or on Marvel.com, please contact Vit DeBellis, Integrated Sales Manager, at vdebellis@marvel.com. For Marvel subscription inquiries, please call 888-511-5480. **Manufactured between 2/24/2017 and 3/28/2017 by SOLISCO PRINTERS, SCOTT, QC, CANADA.**

10 9 8 7 6 5 4 3 2 1

#TAKEBACKTHESHIELD

writer **NICK SPENCER**

artists **PAUL RENAUD** (#14 & #17) & **ANGEL UNZUETA** (#15-16)
WITH **SZYMON KUDRANSKI** (#16)

colorists **JOHN RAUCH**
WITH **PAUL RENAUD** (#17)

letterer **VC's JOE CARAMAGNA**

cover art **MARCOS MARTÍN** (#14),
PAUL RENAUD (#15-16) &
DANIEL ACUÑA (#17)

assistant editor **ALANNA SMITH**
editor **TOM BREVOORT**

Captain America created by Joe Simon & Jack Kirby

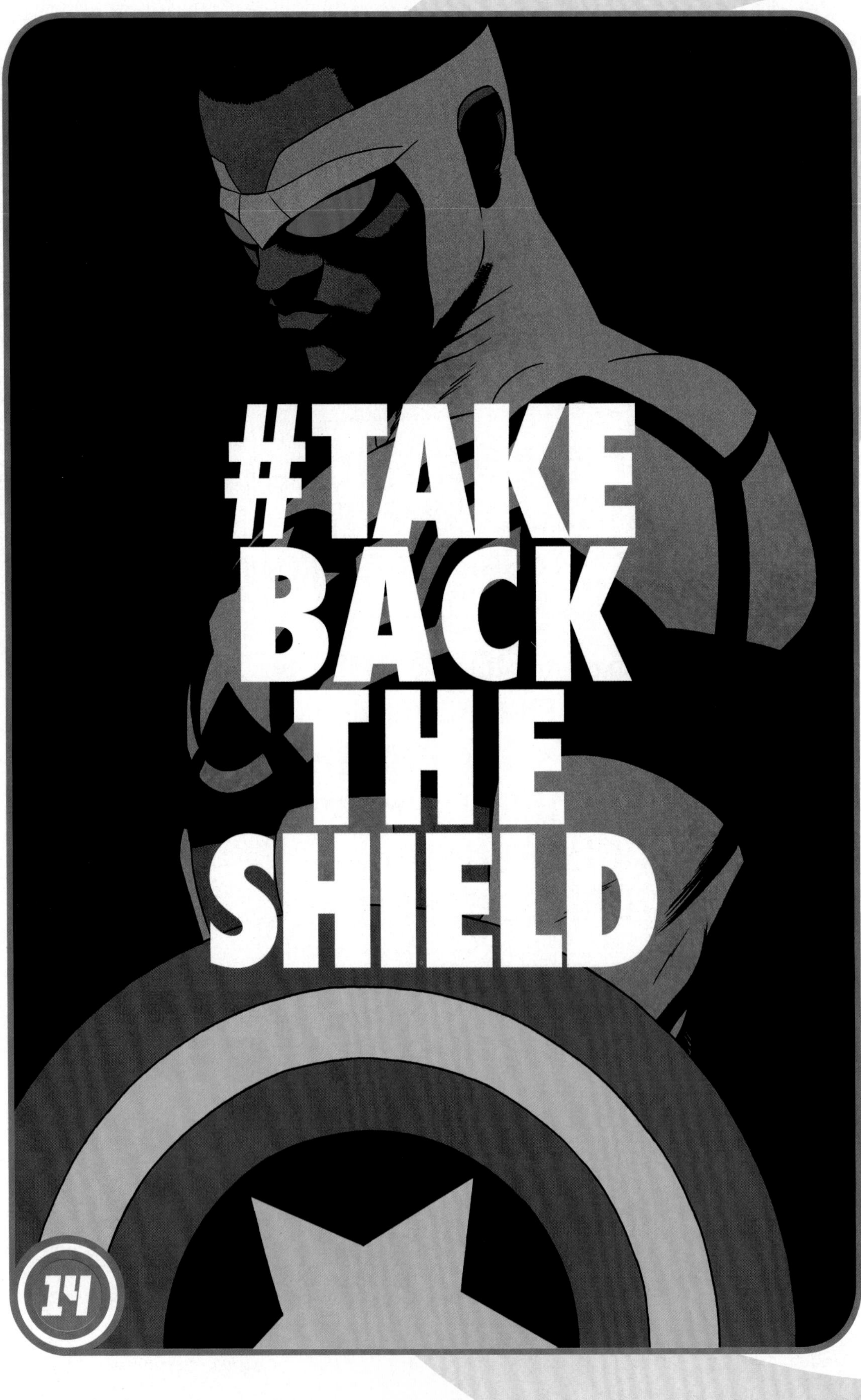
#TAKE
BACK
THE
SHIELD

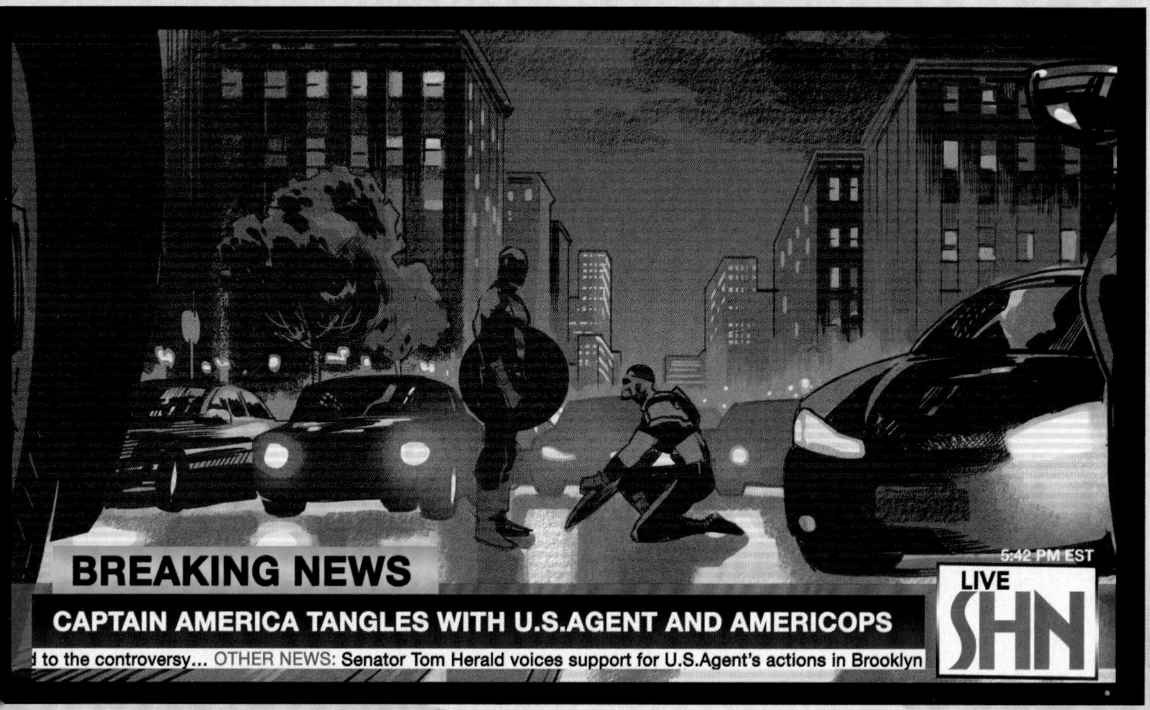
5:42 PM EST
BREAKING NEWS
CAPTAIN AMERICA TANGLES WITH U.S.AGENT AND AMERICOPS
to the controversy... OTHER NEWS: Senator Tom Herald voices support for U.S.Agent's actions in Brooklyn
LIVE
SHN

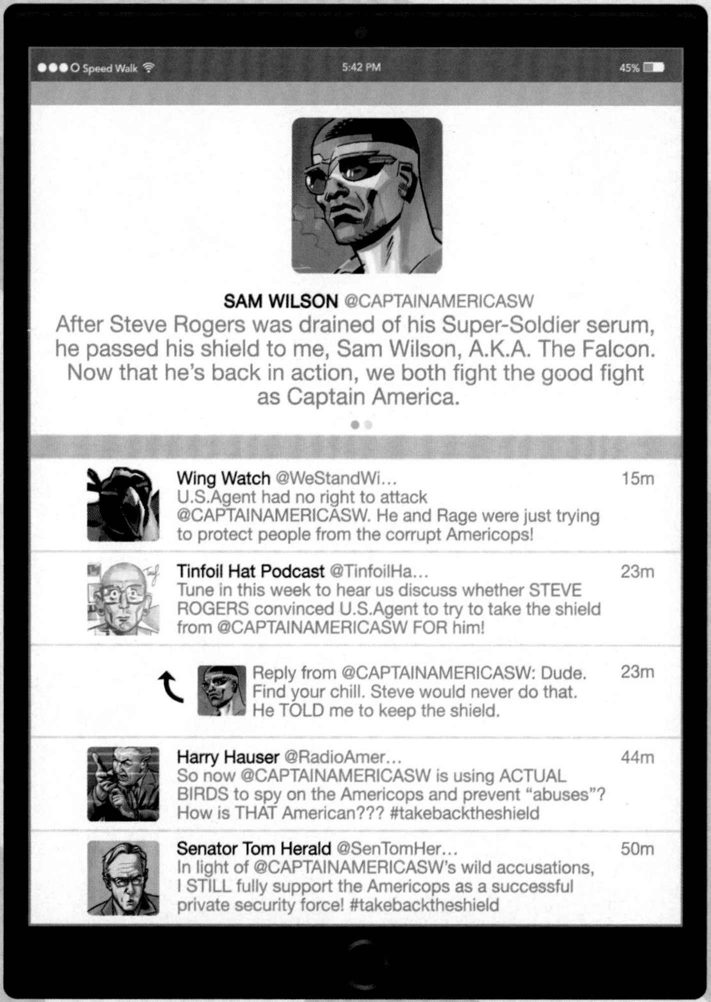
Speed Walk
5:42 PM
45%
SAM WILSON @CAPTAINAMERICASW
After Steve Rogers was drained of his Super-Soldier serum, he passed his shield to me, Sam Wilson, A.K.A. The Falcon. Now that he's back in action, we both fight the good fight as Captain America.
Wing Watch @WeStandWi... 15m
U.S.Agent had no right to attack @CAPTAINAMERICASW. He and Rage were just trying to protect people from the corrupt Americops!
Tinfoil Hat Podcast @TinfoilHa... 23m
Tune in this week to hear us discuss whether STEVE ROGERS convinced U.S.Agent to try to take the shield from @CAPTAINAMERICASW FOR him!
Reply from @CAPTAINAMERICASW: Dude. Find your chill. Steve would never do that. He TOLD me to keep the shield. 23m
Harry Hauser @RadioAmer... 44m
So now @CAPTAINAMERICASW is using ACTUAL BIRDS to spy on the Americops and prevent "abuses"? How is THAT American??? #takebacktheshield
Senator Tom Herald @SenTomHer... 50m
In light of @CAPTAINAMERICASW's wild accusations, I STILL fully support the Americops as a successful private security force! #takebacktheshield

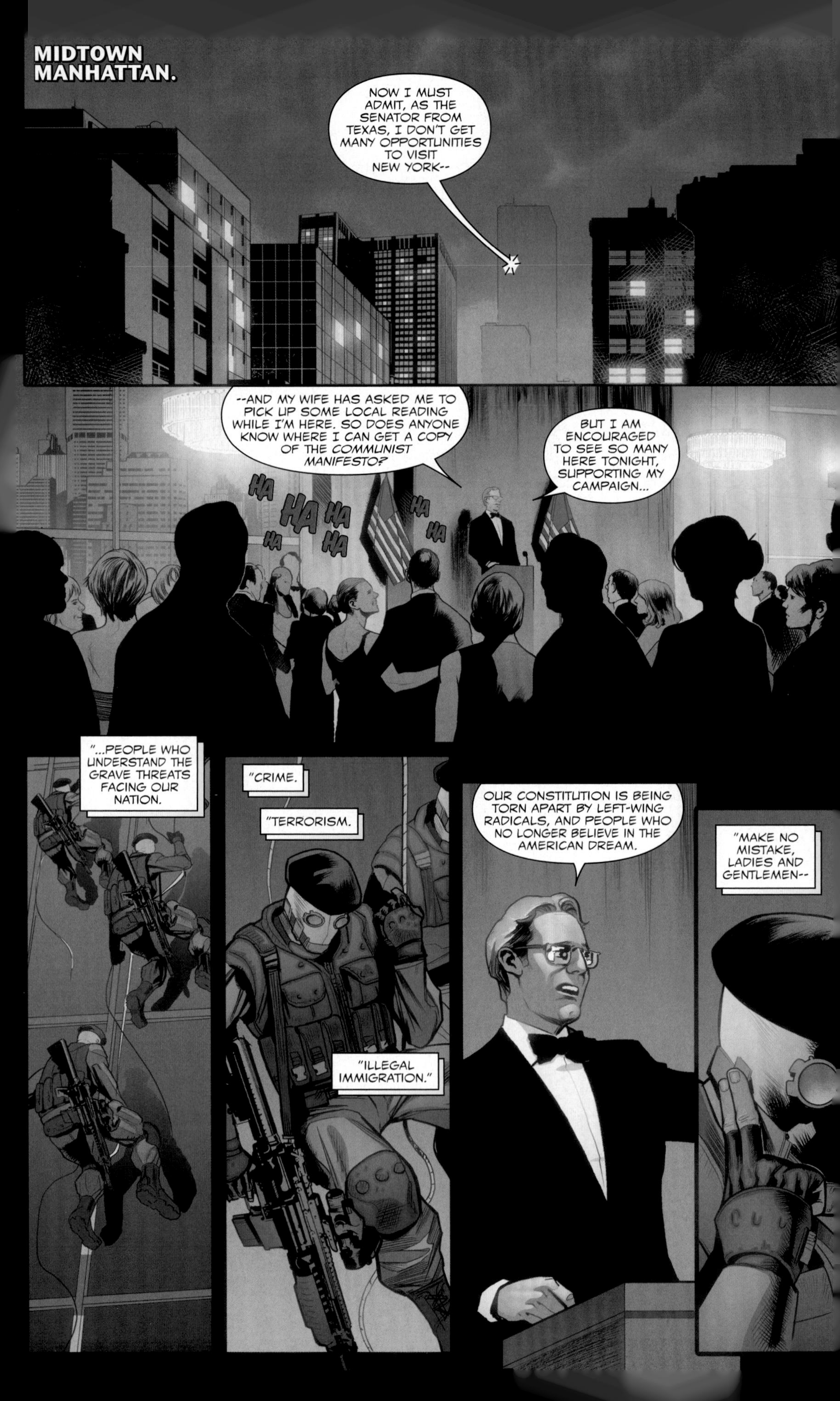
MIDTOWN MANHATTAN.
NOW I MUST ADMIT, AS THE SENATOR FROM TEXAS, I DON'T GET MANY OPPORTUNITIES TO VISIT NEW YORK--
--AND MY WIFE HAS ASKED ME TO PICK UP SOME LOCAL READING WHILE I'M HERE. SO DOES ANYONE KNOW WHERE I CAN GET A COPY OF THE *COMMUNIST MANIFESTO?*
HA HA HA HA HA HA HA HA
BUT I AM ENCOURAGED TO SEE SO MANY HERE TONIGHT, SUPPORTING MY CAMPAIGN...
"...PEOPLE WHO UNDERSTAND THE GRAVE THREATS FACING OUR NATION.
"CRIME.
"TERRORISM.
"ILLEGAL IMMIGRATION."
OUR CONSTITUTION IS BEING TORN APART BY LEFT-WING RADICALS, AND PEOPLE WHO NO LONGER BELIEVE IN THE AMERICAN DREAM.
"MAKE NO MISTAKE, LADIES AND GENTLEMEN--

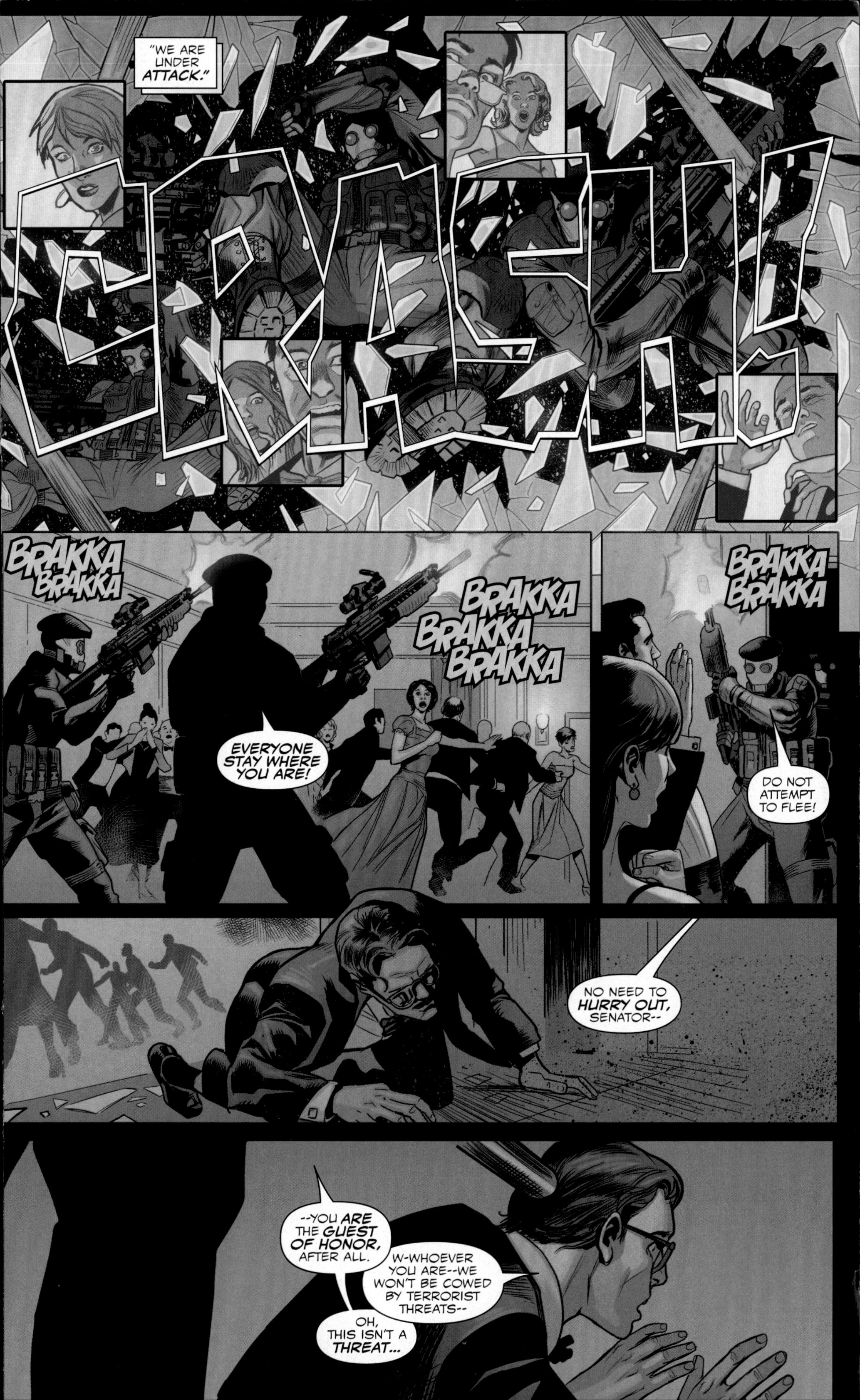
"WE ARE UNDER ATTACK."
CRASH!
BRAKKA BRAKKA
BRAKKA BRAKKA BRAKKA
EVERYONE STAY WHERE YOU ARE!
BRAKKA BRAKKA
DO NOT ATTEMPT TO FLEE!
NO NEED TO HURRY OUT, SENATOR--
--YOU ARE THE GUEST OF HONOR, AFTER ALL.
W-WHOEVER YOU ARE--WE WON'T BE COWED BY TERRORIST THREATS--
OH, THIS ISN'T A THREAT...

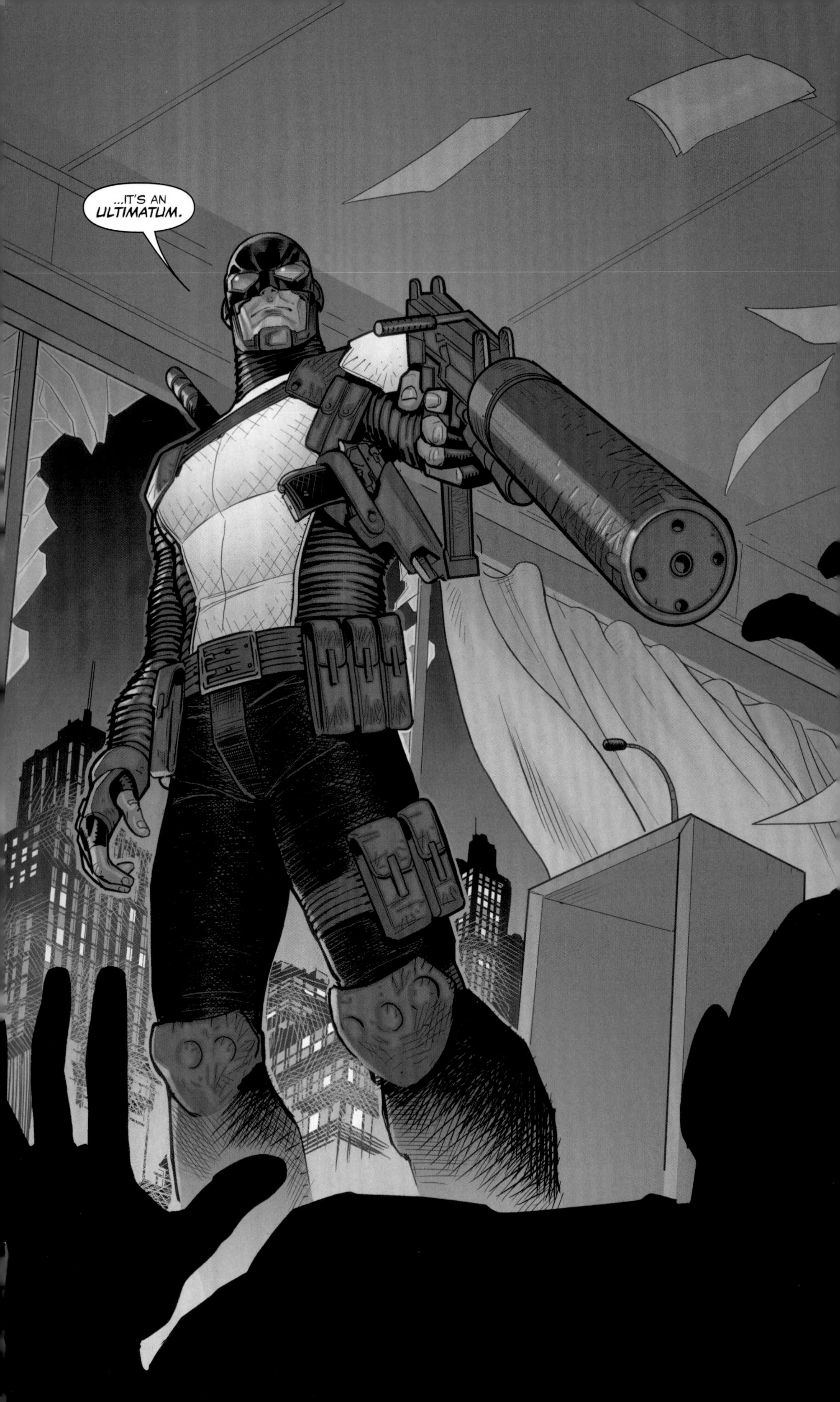
...IT'S AN ULTIMATUM.

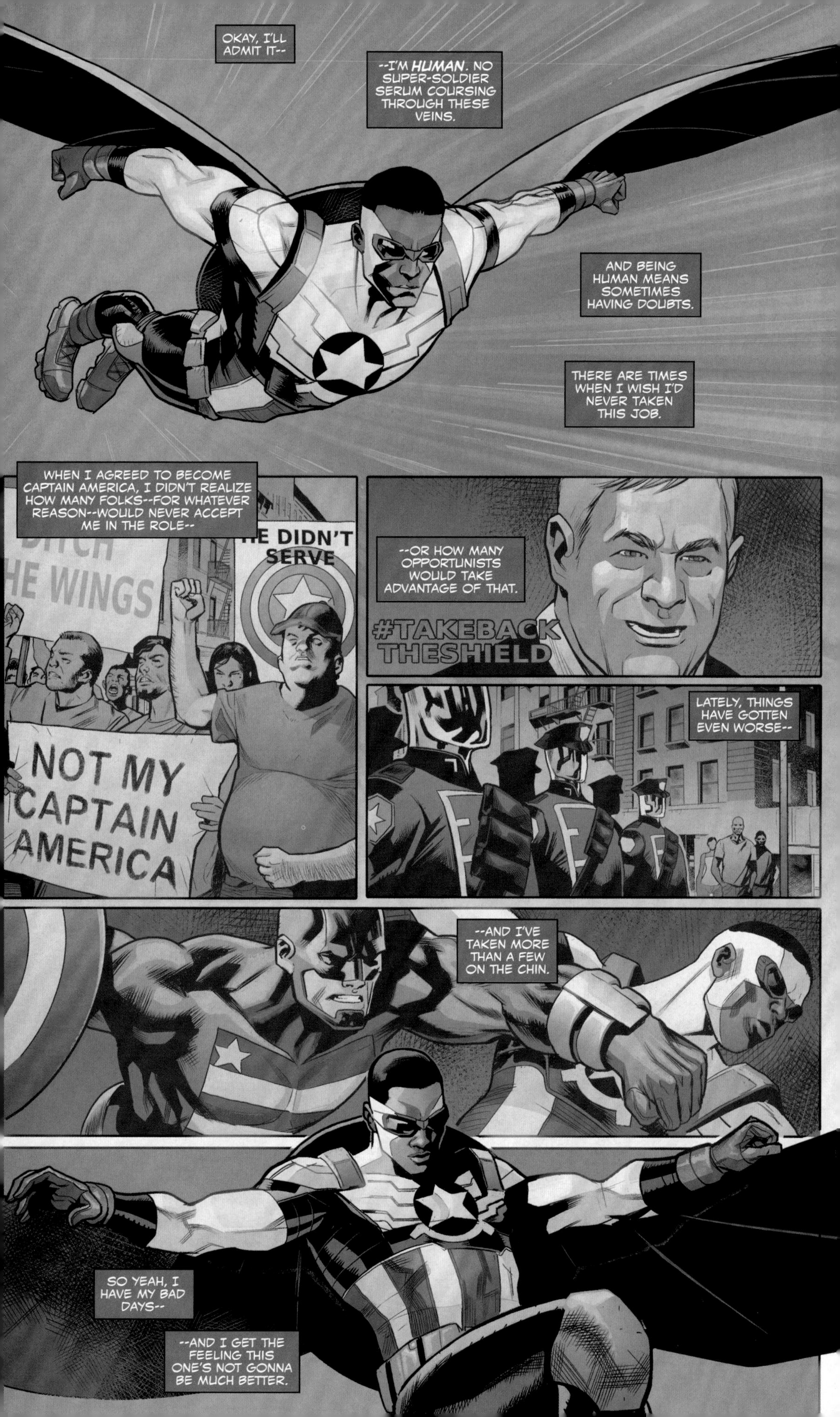
OKAY, I'LL ADMIT IT--
--I'M HUMAN. NO SUPER-SOLDIER SERUM COURSING THROUGH THESE VEINS.
AND BEING HUMAN MEANS SOMETIMES HAVING DOUBTS.
THERE ARE TIMES WHEN I WISH I'D NEVER TAKEN THIS JOB.
WHEN I AGREED TO BECOME CAPTAIN AMERICA, I DIDN'T REALIZE HOW MANY FOLKS--FOR WHATEVER REASON--WOULD NEVER ACCEPT ME IN THE ROLE--
HE WINGS
HE DIDN'T SERVE
NOT MY CAPTAIN AMERICA
--OR HOW MANY OPPORTUNISTS WOULD TAKE ADVANTAGE OF THAT.
#TAKEBACK THESHIELD
LATELY, THINGS HAVE GOTTEN EVEN WORSE--
--AND I'VE TAKEN MORE THAN A FEW ON THE CHIN.
SO YEAH, I HAVE MY BAD DAYS--
--AND I GET THE FEELING THIS ONE'S NOT GONNA BE MUCH BETTER.

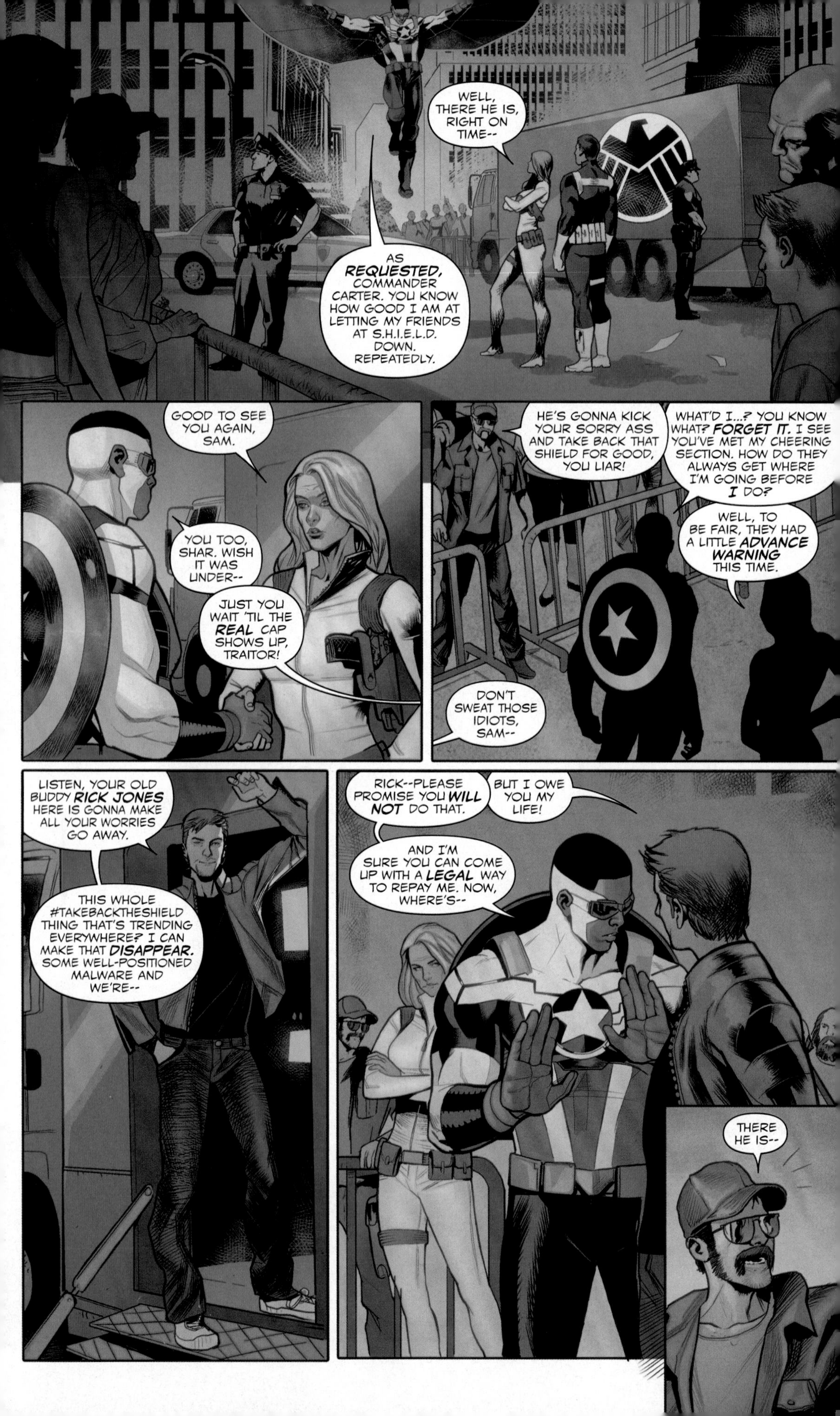
WELL, THERE HE IS, RIGHT ON TIME--
AS REQUESTED, COMMANDER CARTER. YOU KNOW HOW GOOD I AM AT LETTING MY FRIENDS AT S.H.I.E.L.D. DOWN. REPEATEDLY.
GOOD TO SEE YOU AGAIN, SAM.
YOU TOO, SHAR. WISH IT WAS UNDER--
JUST YOU WAIT 'TIL THE REAL CAP SHOWS UP, TRAITOR!
HE'S GONNA KICK YOUR SORRY ASS AND TAKE BACK THAT SHIELD FOR GOOD, YOU LIAR!
WHAT'D I...? YOU KNOW WHAT? FORGET IT. I SEE YOU'VE MET MY CHEERING SECTION. HOW DO THEY ALWAYS GET WHERE I'M GOING BEFORE I DO?
WELL, TO BE FAIR, THEY HAD A LITTLE ADVANCE WARNING THIS TIME.
DON'T SWEAT THOSE IDIOTS, SAM--
LISTEN, YOUR OLD BUDDY RICK JONES HERE IS GONNA MAKE ALL YOUR WORRIES GO AWAY.
THIS WHOLE #TAKEBACKTHESHIELD THING THAT'S TRENDING EVERYWHERE? I CAN MAKE THAT DISAPPEAR. SOME WELL-POSITIONED MALWARE AND WE'RE--
RICK--PLEASE PROMISE YOU WILL NOT DO THAT.
BUT I OWE YOU MY LIFE!
AND I'M SURE YOU CAN COME UP WITH A LEGAL WAY TO REPAY ME. NOW, WHERE'S--
THERE HE IS--

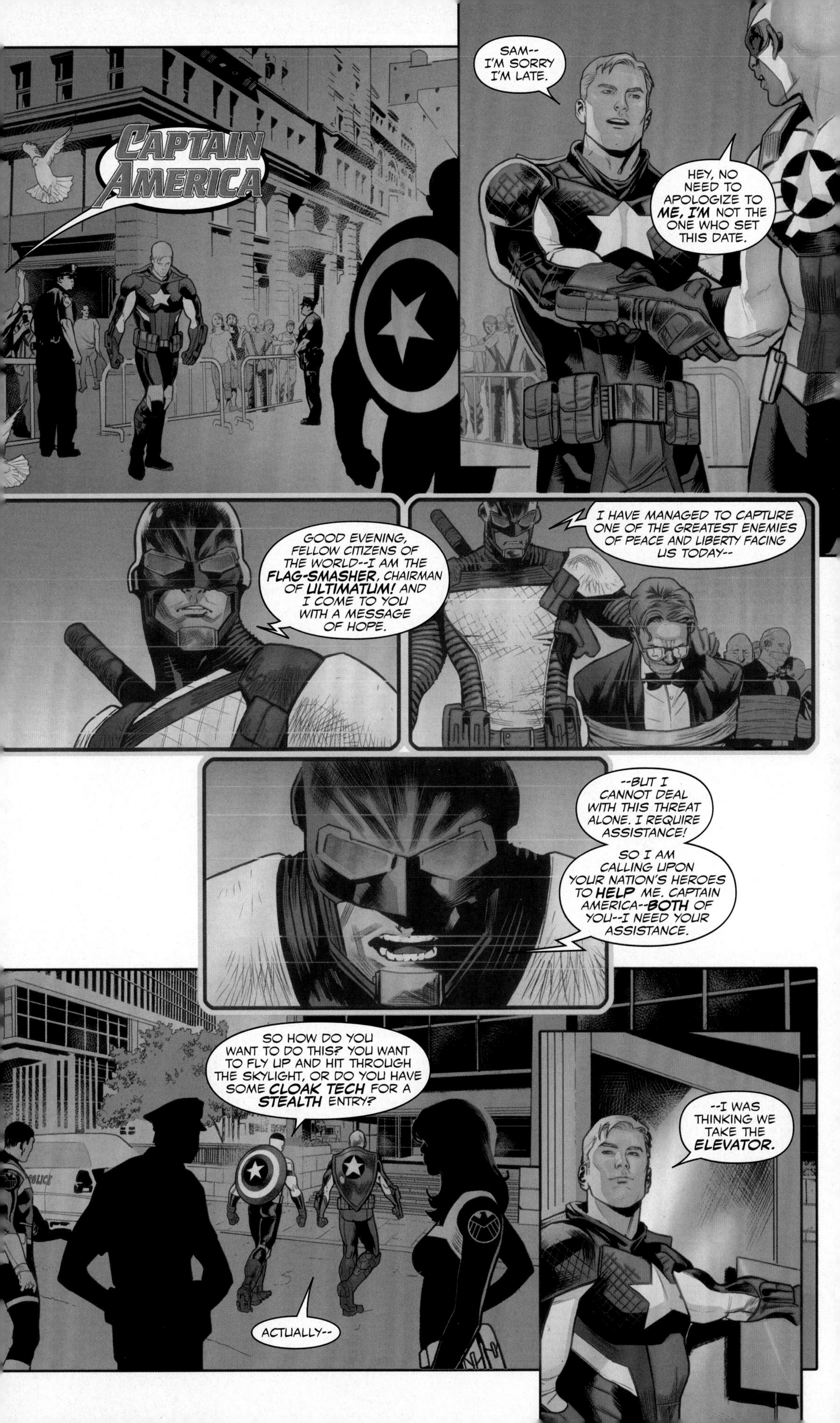
CAPTAIN AMERICA
SAM-- I'M SORRY I'M LATE.
HEY, NO NEED TO APOLOGIZE TO ME, I'M NOT THE ONE WHO SET THIS DATE.
GOOD EVENING, FELLOW CITIZENS OF THE WORLD--I AM THE FLAG-SMASHER, CHAIRMAN OF ULTIMATUM! AND I COME TO YOU WITH A MESSAGE OF HOPE.
I HAVE MANAGED TO CAPTURE ONE OF THE GREATEST ENEMIES OF PEACE AND LIBERTY FACING US TODAY--
--BUT I CANNOT DEAL WITH THIS THREAT ALONE. I REQUIRE ASSISTANCE!
SO I AM CALLING UPON YOUR NATION'S HEROES TO HELP ME. CAPTAIN AMERICA--BOTH OF YOU--I NEED YOUR ASSISTANCE.
SO HOW DO YOU WANT TO DO THIS? YOU WANT TO FLY UP AND HIT THROUGH THE SKYLIGHT, OR DO YOU HAVE SOME CLOAK TECH FOR A STEALTH ENTRY?
ACTUALLY--
--I WAS THINKING WE TAKE THE ELEVATOR.

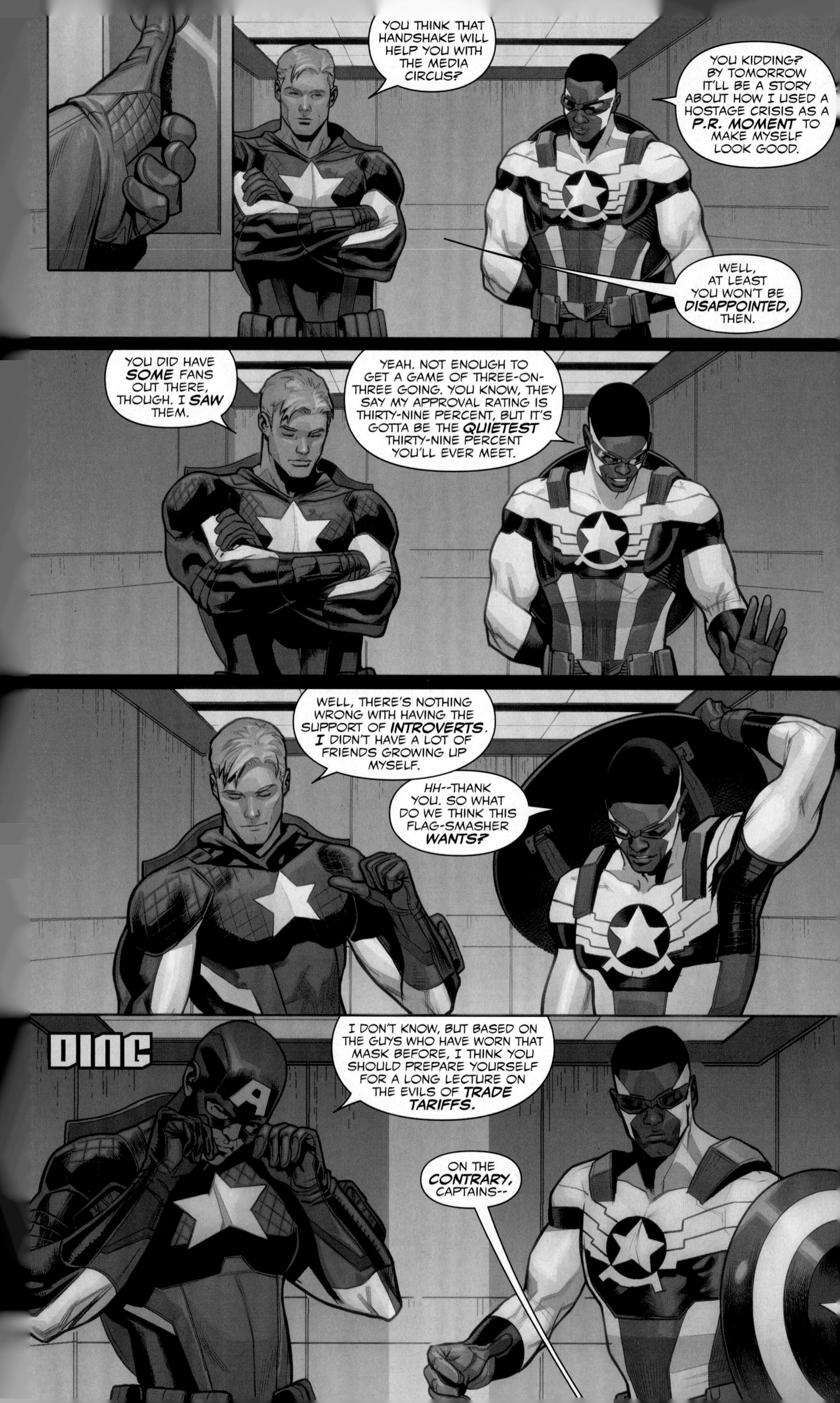
YOU THINK THAT HANDSHAKE WILL HELP YOU WITH THE MEDIA CIRCUS?
YOU KIDDING? BY TOMORROW IT'LL BE A STORY ABOUT HOW I USED A HOSTAGE CRISIS AS A P.R. MOMENT TO MAKE MYSELF LOOK GOOD.
WELL, AT LEAST YOU WON'T BE DISAPPOINTED, THEN.
YOU DID HAVE SOME FANS OUT THERE, THOUGH. I SAW THEM.
YEAH. NOT ENOUGH TO GET A GAME OF THREE-ON-THREE GOING. YOU KNOW, THEY SAY MY APPROVAL RATING IS THIRTY-NINE PERCENT, BUT IT'S GOTTA BE THE QUIETEST THIRTY-NINE PERCENT YOU'LL EVER MEET.
WELL, THERE'S NOTHING WRONG WITH HAVING THE SUPPORT OF INTROVERTS. I DIDN'T HAVE A LOT OF FRIENDS GROWING UP MYSELF.
HH--THANK YOU. SO WHAT DO WE THINK THIS FLAG-SMASHER WANTS?
DING
I DON'T KNOW, BUT BASED ON THE GUYS WHO HAVE WORN THAT MASK BEFORE, I THINK YOU SHOULD PREPARE YOURSELF FOR A LONG LECTURE ON THE EVILS OF TRADE TARIFFS.
ON THE CONTRARY, CAPTAINS--

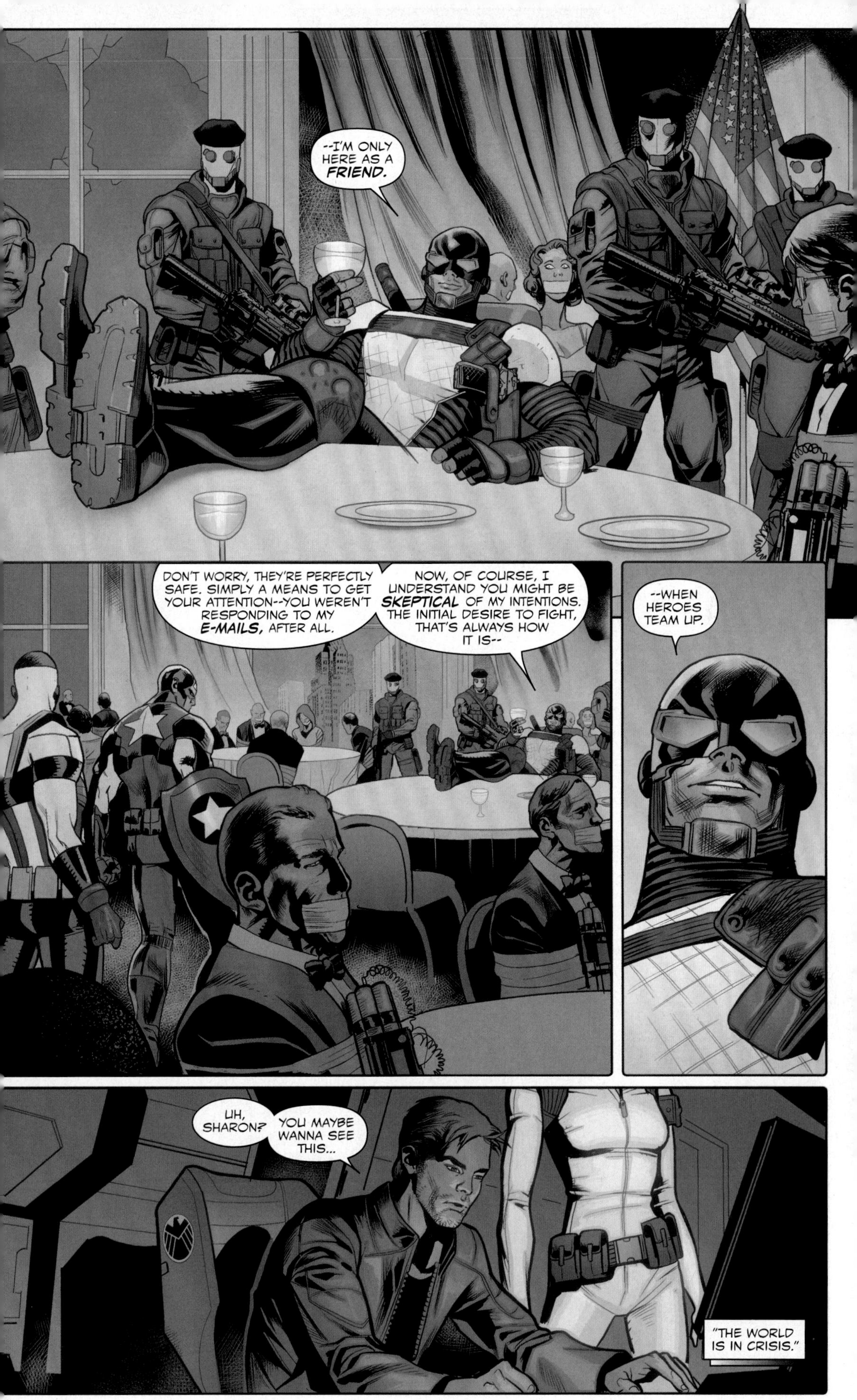
--I'M ONLY HERE AS A FRIEND.
DON'T WORRY, THEY'RE PERFECTLY SAFE. SIMPLY A MEANS TO GET YOUR ATTENTION--YOU WEREN'T RESPONDING TO MY E-MAILS, AFTER ALL.
NOW, OF COURSE, I UNDERSTAND YOU MIGHT BE SKEPTICAL OF MY INTENTIONS. THE INITIAL DESIRE TO FIGHT, THAT'S ALWAYS HOW IT IS--
--WHEN HEROES TEAM UP.
UH, SHARON?
YOU MAYBE WANNA SEE THIS...
"THE WORLD IS IN CRISIS."

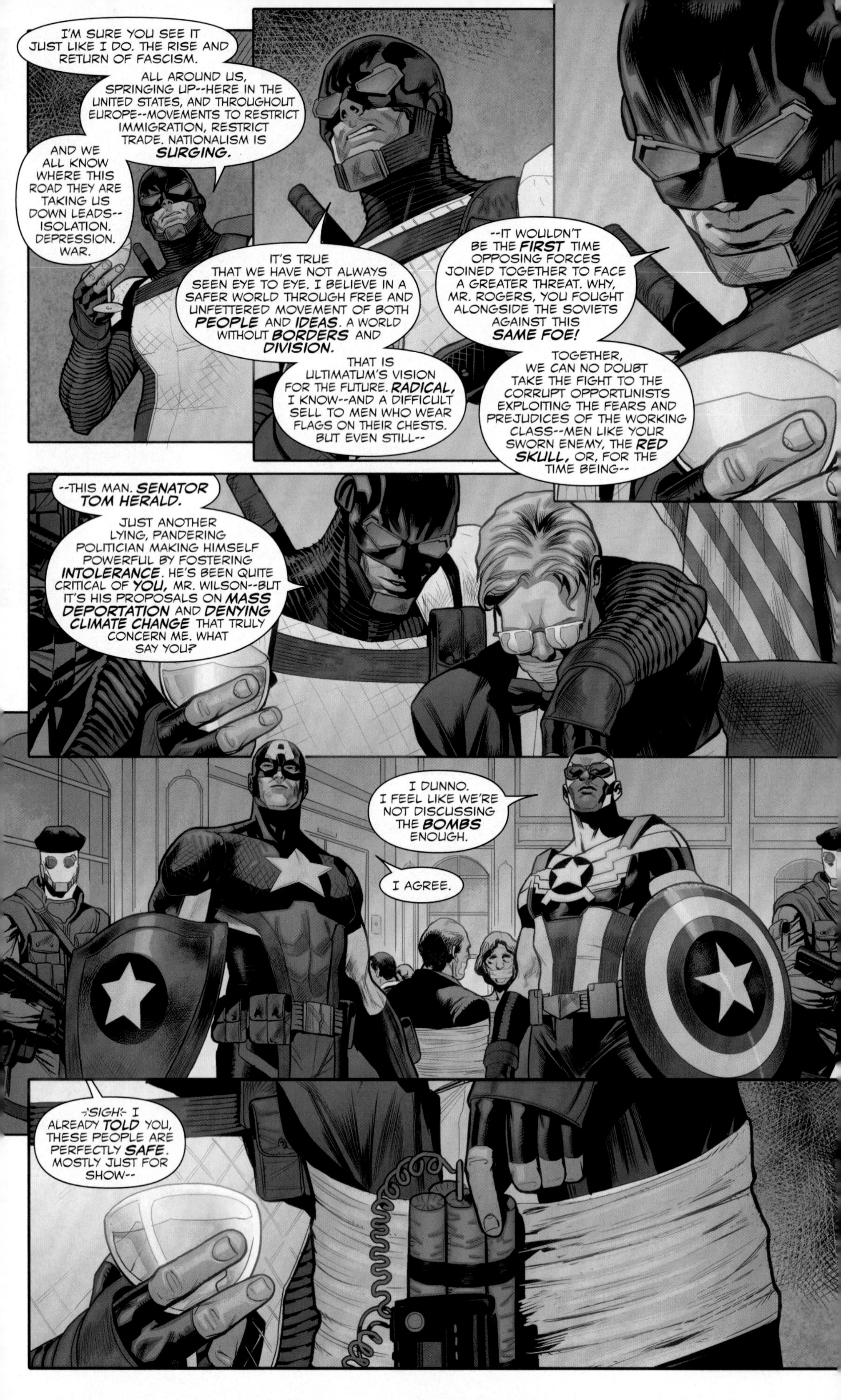
I'M SURE YOU SEE IT JUST LIKE I DO. THE RISE AND RETURN OF FASCISM.
ALL AROUND US, SPRINGING UP--HERE IN THE UNITED STATES, AND THROUGHOUT EUROPE--MOVEMENTS TO RESTRICT IMMIGRATION, RESTRICT TRADE. NATIONALISM IS SURGING.
AND WE ALL KNOW WHERE THIS ROAD THEY ARE TAKING US DOWN LEADS--ISOLATION. DEPRESSION. WAR.
IT'S TRUE THAT WE HAVE NOT ALWAYS SEEN EYE TO EYE. I BELIEVE IN A SAFER WORLD THROUGH FREE AND UNFETTERED MOVEMENT OF BOTH PEOPLE AND IDEAS. A WORLD WITHOUT BORDERS AND DIVISION.
THAT IS ULTIMATUM'S VISION FOR THE FUTURE. RADICAL, I KNOW--AND A DIFFICULT SELL TO MEN WHO WEAR FLAGS ON THEIR CHESTS. BUT EVEN STILL--
--IT WOULDN'T BE THE FIRST TIME OPPOSING FORCES JOINED TOGETHER TO FACE A GREATER THREAT. WHY, MR. ROGERS, YOU FOUGHT ALONGSIDE THE SOVIETS AGAINST THIS SAME FOE!
TOGETHER, WE CAN NO DOUBT TAKE THE FIGHT TO THE CORRUPT OPPORTUNISTS EXPLOITING THE FEARS AND PREJUDICES OF THE WORKING CLASS--MEN LIKE YOUR SWORN ENEMY, THE RED SKULL, OR, FOR THE TIME BEING--
--THIS MAN. SENATOR TOM HERALD.
JUST ANOTHER LYING, PANDERING POLITICIAN MAKING HIMSELF POWERFUL BY FOSTERING INTOLERANCE. HE'S BEEN QUITE CRITICAL OF YOU, MR. WILSON--BUT IT'S HIS PROPOSALS ON MASS DEPORTATION AND DENYING CLIMATE CHANGE THAT TRULY CONCERN ME. WHAT SAY YOU?
I DUNNO. I FEEL LIKE WE'RE NOT DISCUSSING THE BOMBS ENOUGH.
I AGREE.
SIGH I ALREADY TOLD YOU, THESE PEOPLE ARE PERFECTLY SAFE. MOSTLY JUST FOR SHOW--

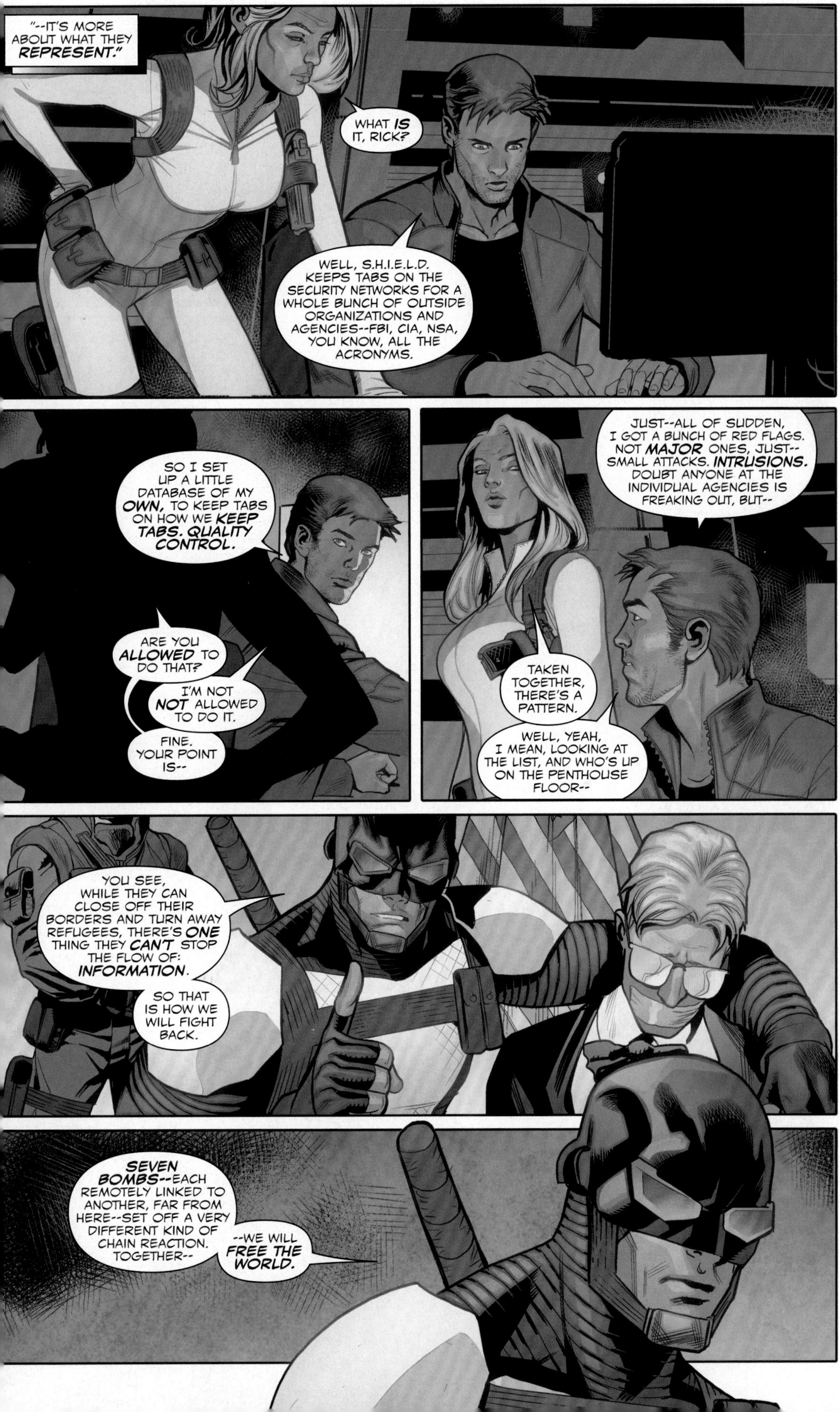
"--IT'S MORE ABOUT WHAT THEY *REPRESENT.*"
WHAT *IS* IT, RICK?
WELL, S.H.I.E.L.D. KEEPS TABS ON THE SECURITY NETWORKS FOR A WHOLE BUNCH OF OUTSIDE ORGANIZATIONS AND AGENCIES--FBI, CIA, NSA, YOU KNOW, ALL THE ACRONYMS.
SO I SET UP A LITTLE DATABASE OF MY *OWN,* TO KEEP TABS ON HOW WE *KEEP TABS. QUALITY CONTROL.*
ARE YOU *ALLOWED* TO DO THAT?
I'M NOT *NOT* ALLOWED TO DO IT.
FINE. YOUR POINT IS--
JUST--ALL OF SUDDEN, I GOT A BUNCH OF RED FLAGS. NOT *MAJOR* ONES, JUST--SMALL ATTACKS. *INTRUSIONS.* DOUBT ANYONE AT THE INDIVIDUAL AGENCIES IS FREAKING OUT, BUT--
TAKEN TOGETHER, THERE'S A PATTERN.
WELL, YEAH, I MEAN, LOOKING AT THE LIST, AND WHO'S UP ON THE PENTHOUSE FLOOR--
YOU SEE, WHILE THEY CAN CLOSE OFF THEIR BORDERS AND TURN AWAY REFUGEES, THERE'S *ONE* THING THEY *CAN'T* STOP THE FLOW OF: *INFORMATION*.
SO THAT IS HOW WE WILL FIGHT BACK.
SEVEN BOMBS--EACH REMOTELY LINKED TO ANOTHER, FAR FROM HERE--SET OFF A VERY DIFFERENT KIND OF CHAIN REACTION. TOGETHER--
--WE WILL *FREE THE WORLD.*

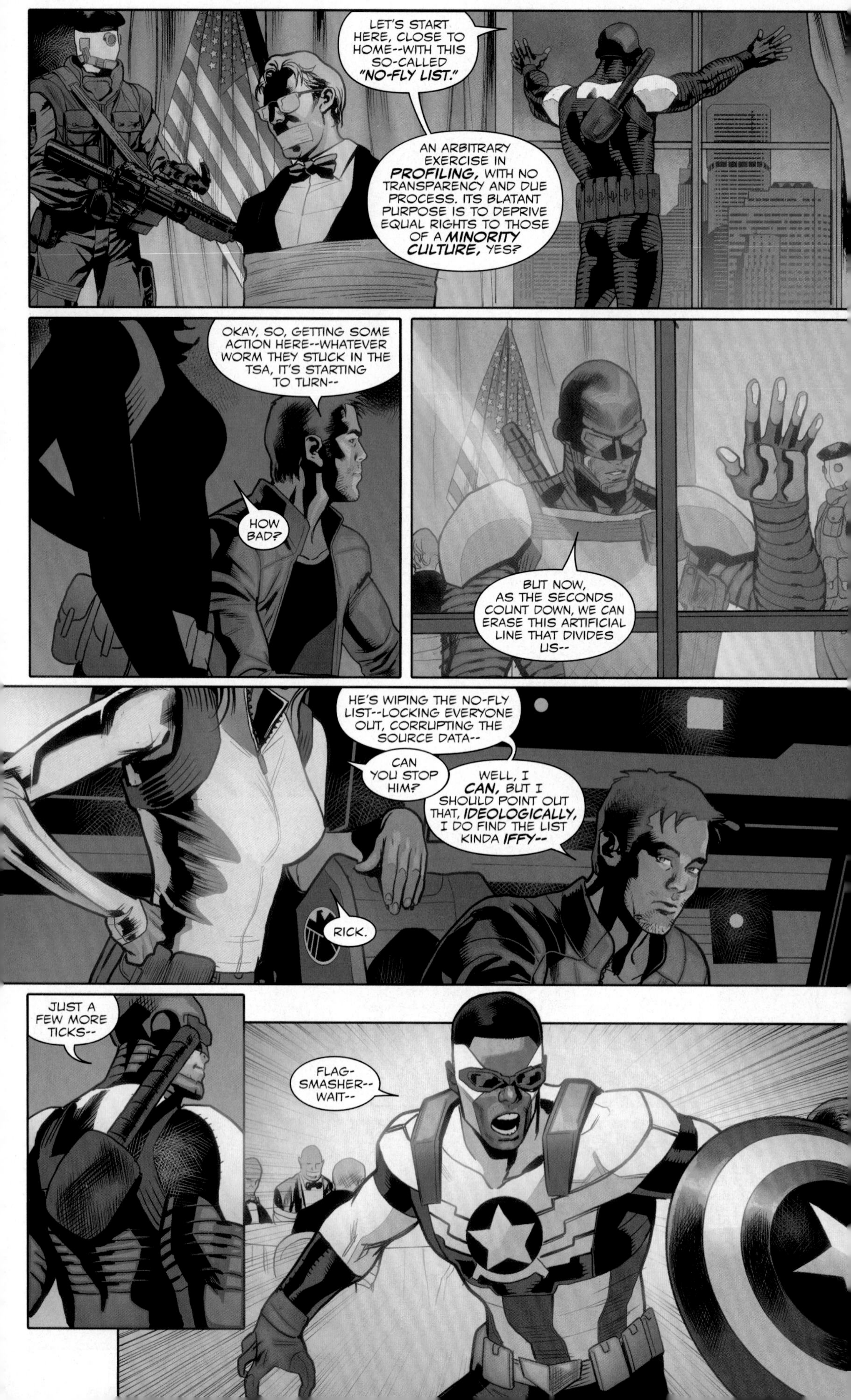
LET'S START HERE, CLOSE TO HOME--WITH THIS SO-CALLED "NO-FLY LIST."
AN ARBITRARY EXERCISE IN PROFILING, WITH NO TRANSPARENCY AND DUE PROCESS. ITS BLATANT PURPOSE IS TO DEPRIVE EQUAL RIGHTS TO THOSE OF A MINORITY CULTURE, YES?
OKAY, SO, GETTING SOME ACTION HERE--WHATEVER WORM THEY STUCK IN THE TSA, IT'S STARTING TO TURN--
HOW BAD?
BUT NOW, AS THE SECONDS COUNT DOWN, WE CAN ERASE THIS ARTIFICIAL LINE THAT DIVIDES US--
HE'S WIPING THE NO-FLY LIST--LOCKING EVERYONE OUT, CORRUPTING THE SOURCE DATA--
CAN YOU STOP HIM?
WELL, I CAN, BUT I SHOULD POINT OUT THAT, IDEOLOGICALLY, I DO FIND THE LIST KINDA IFFY--
RICK.
JUST A FEW MORE TICKS--
FLAG-SMASHER--WAIT--

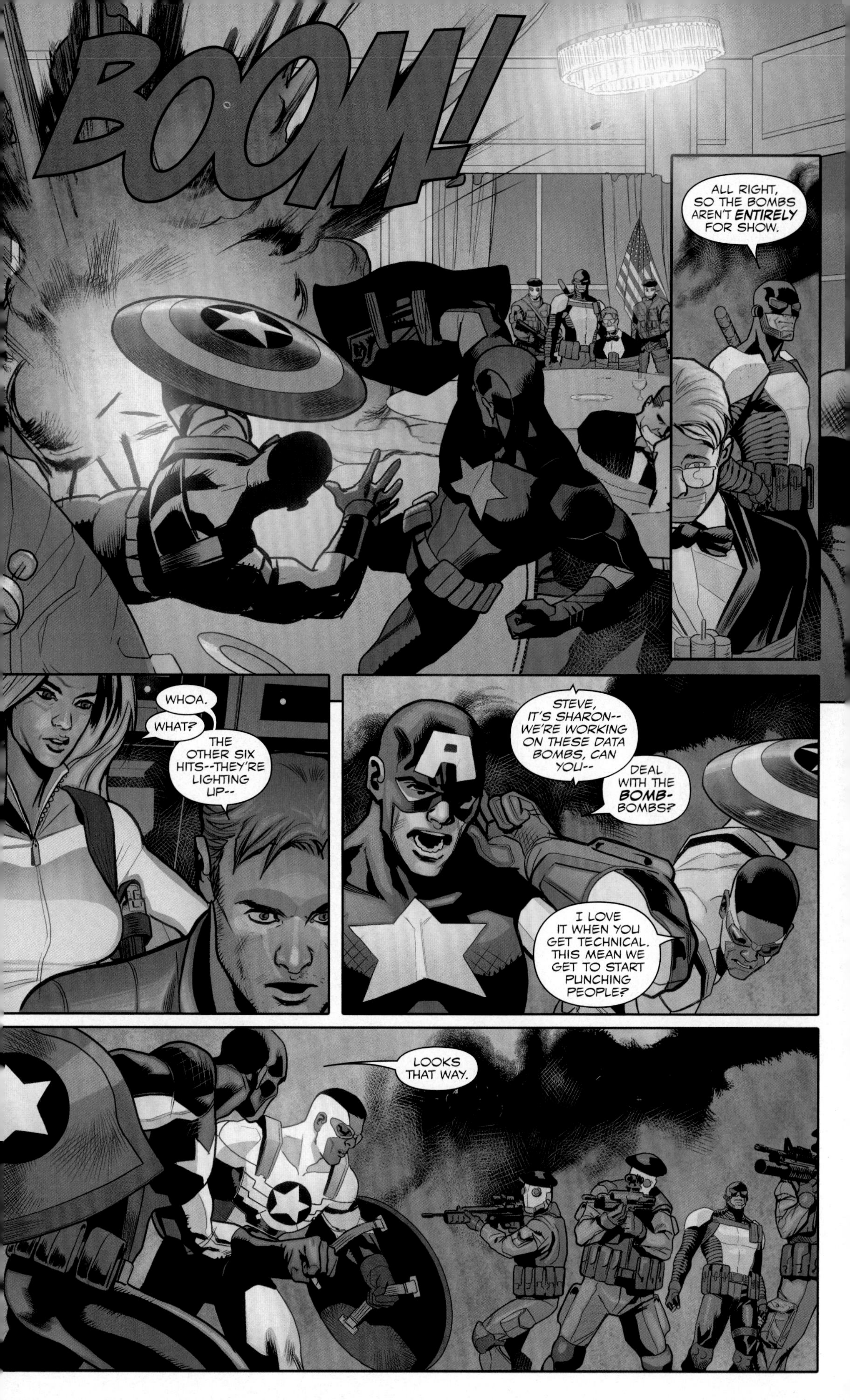
BOOM!
ALL RIGHT, SO THE BOMBS AREN'T ENTIRELY FOR SHOW.
WHOA.
WHAT?
THE OTHER SIX HITS--THEY'RE LIGHTING UP--
STEVE, IT'S SHARON-- WE'RE WORKING ON THESE DATA BOMBS, CAN YOU--
DEAL WITH THE BOMB-BOMBS?
I LOVE IT WHEN YOU GET TECHNICAL. THIS MEAN WE GET TO START PUNCHING PEOPLE?
LOOKS THAT WAY.

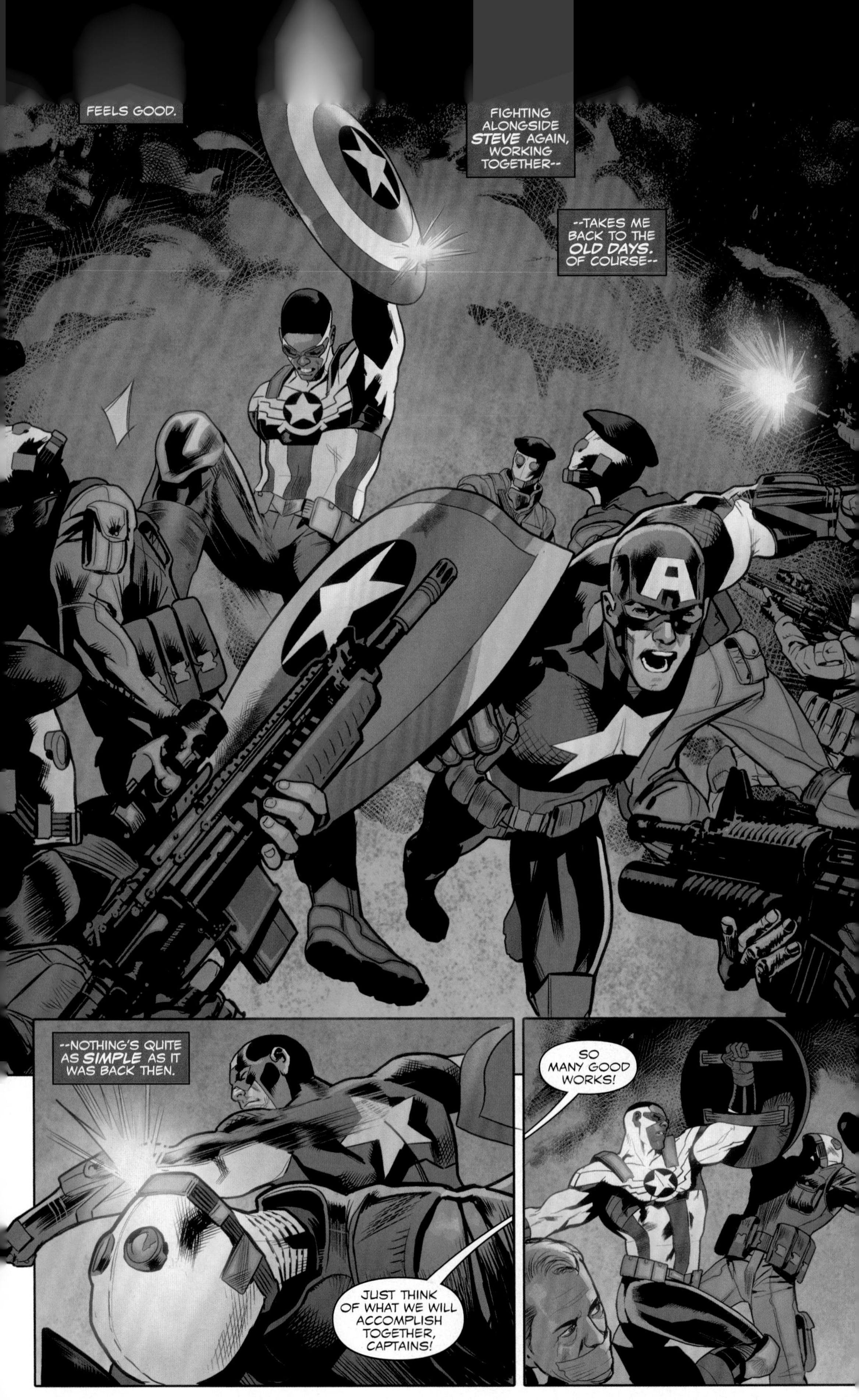
FEELS GOOD.
FIGHTING ALONGSIDE STEVE AGAIN, WORKING TOGETHER--
--TAKES ME BACK TO THE OLD DAYS. OF COURSE--
--NOTHING'S QUITE AS SIMPLE AS IT WAS BACK THEN.
JUST THINK OF WHAT WE WILL ACCOMPLISH TOGETHER, CAPTAINS!
SO MANY GOOD WORKS!

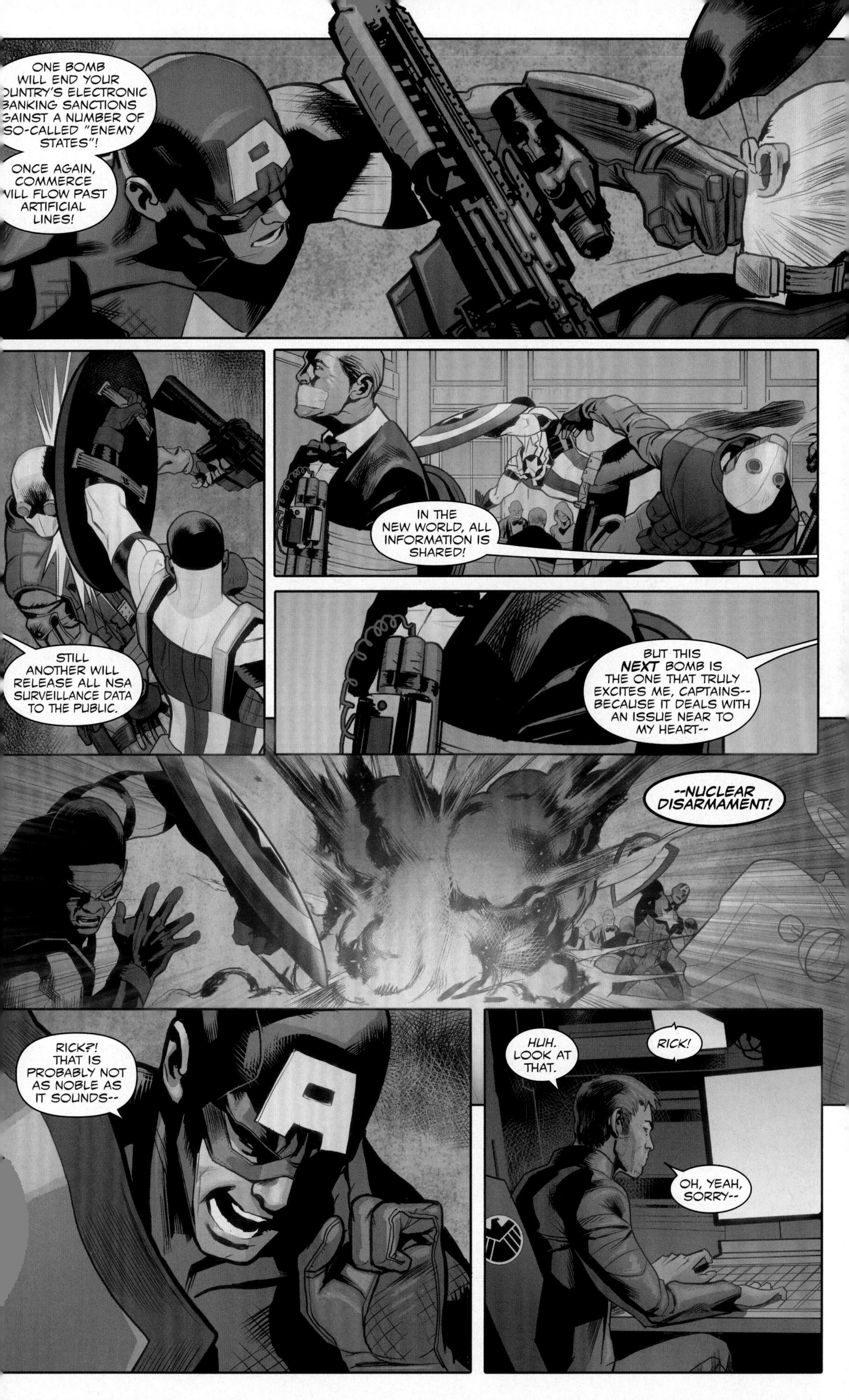
ONE BOMB WILL END YOUR COUNTRY'S ELECTRONIC BANKING SANCTIONS AGAINST A NUMBER OF SO-CALLED "ENEMY STATES"!
ONCE AGAIN, COMMERCE WILL FLOW PAST ARTIFICIAL LINES!
IN THE NEW WORLD, ALL INFORMATION IS SHARED!
STILL ANOTHER WILL RELEASE ALL NSA SURVEILLANCE DATA TO THE PUBLIC.
BUT THIS **NEXT** BOMB IS THE ONE THAT TRULY EXCITES ME, CAPTAINS-- BECAUSE IT DEALS WITH AN ISSUE NEAR TO MY HEART--
--NUCLEAR DISARMAMENT!
RICK?! THAT IS PROBABLY NOT AS NOBLE AS IT SOUNDS--
HUH. LOOK AT THAT.
RICK!
OH, YEAH, SORRY--

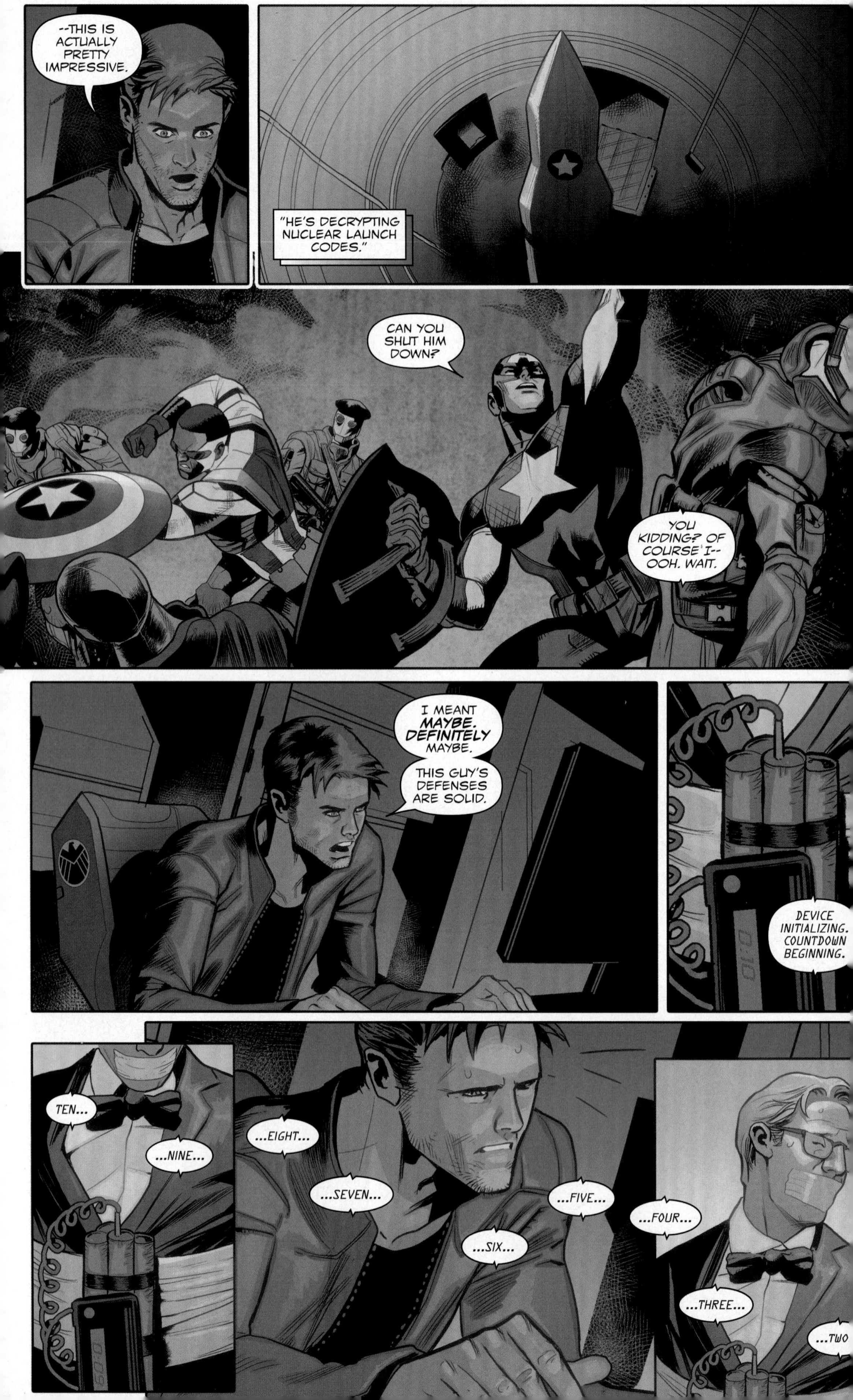
--THIS IS ACTUALLY PRETTY IMPRESSIVE.
"HE'S DECRYPTING NUCLEAR LAUNCH CODES."
CAN YOU SHUT HIM DOWN?
YOU KIDDING? OF COURSE I-- OOH. WAIT.
I MEANT MAYBE. DEFINITELY MAYBE.
THIS GUY'S DEFENSES ARE SOLID.
DEVICE INITIALIZING. COUNTDOWN BEGINNING.
TEN...
...NINE...
...EIGHT...
...SEVEN...
...SIX...
...FIVE...
...FOUR...
...THREE...
...TWO

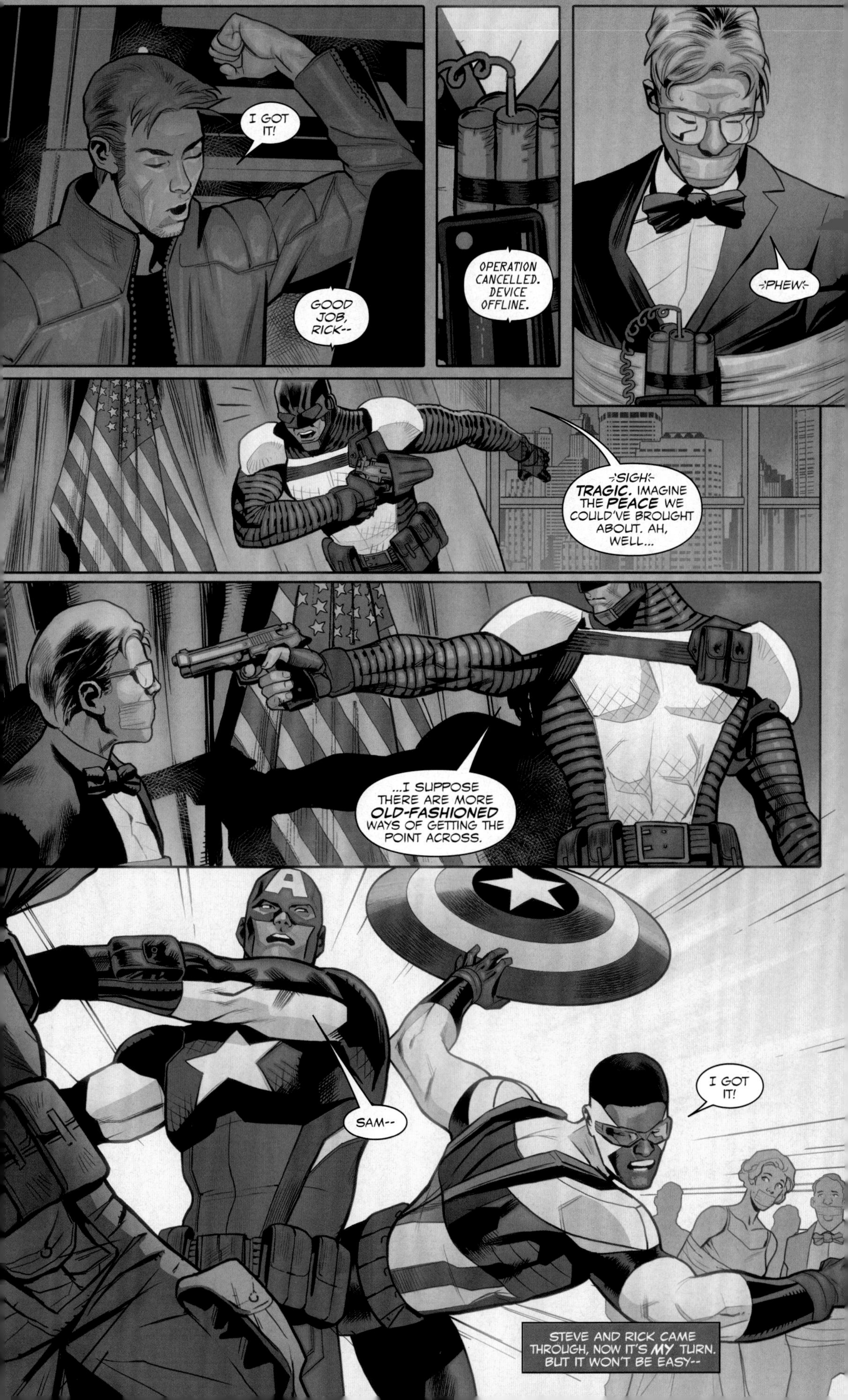
I GOT IT!
GOOD JOB, RICK--
OPERATION CANCELLED. DEVICE OFFLINE.
-PHEW-
-SIGH- TRAGIC. IMAGINE THE PEACE WE COULD'VE BROUGHT ABOUT. AH, WELL...
...I SUPPOSE THERE ARE MORE OLD-FASHIONED WAYS OF GETTING THE POINT ACROSS.
SAM--
I GOT IT!
STEVE AND RICK CAME THROUGH, NOW IT'S MY TURN. BUT IT WON'T BE EASY--

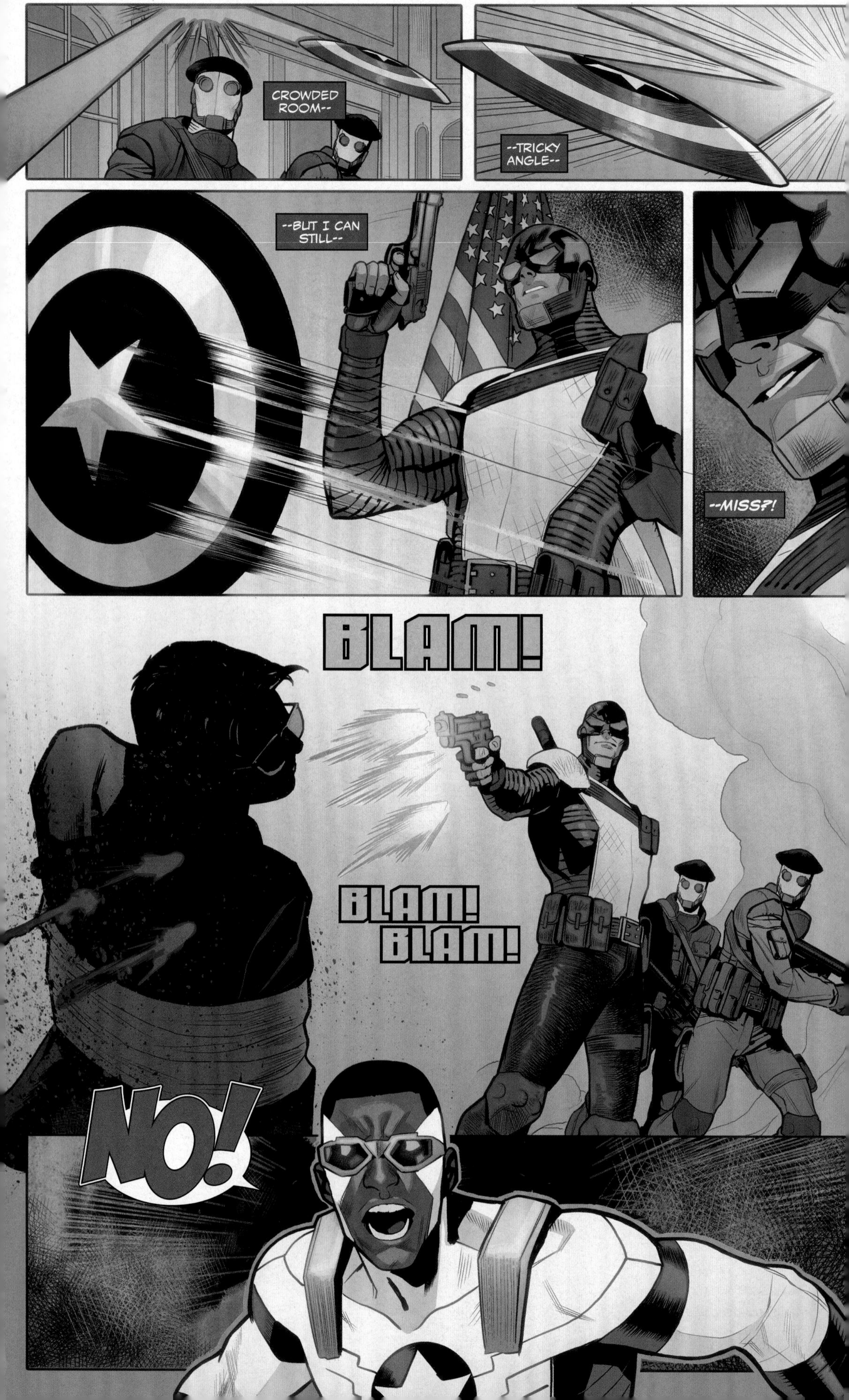
CROWDED ROOM--
--TRICKY ANGLE--
--BUT I CAN STILL--
--MISS?!
BLAM!
BLAM! BLAM!
NO!

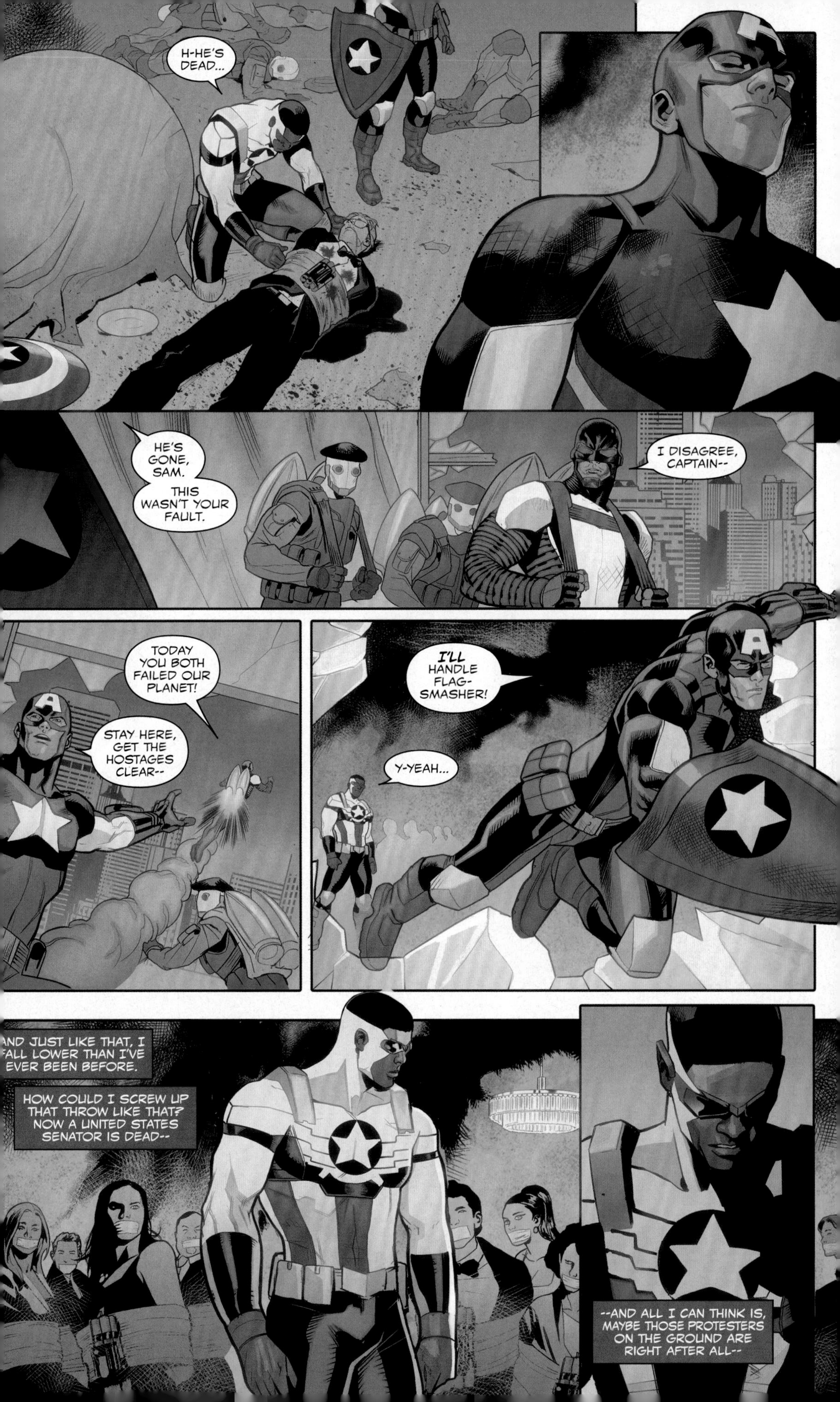

H-HE'S DEAD...
HE'S GONE, SAM.
THIS WASN'T YOUR FAULT.
I DISAGREE, CAPTAIN--
TODAY YOU BOTH FAILED OUR PLANET!
STAY HERE, GET THE HOSTAGES CLEAR--
I'LL HANDLE FLAG-SMASHER!
Y-YEAH...
AND JUST LIKE THAT, I FALL LOWER THAN I'VE EVER BEEN BEFORE.
HOW COULD I SCREW UP THAT THROW LIKE THAT? NOW A UNITED STATES SENATOR IS DEAD--
--AND ALL I CAN THINK IS, MAYBE THOSE PROTESTERS ON THE GROUND ARE RIGHT AFTER ALL--

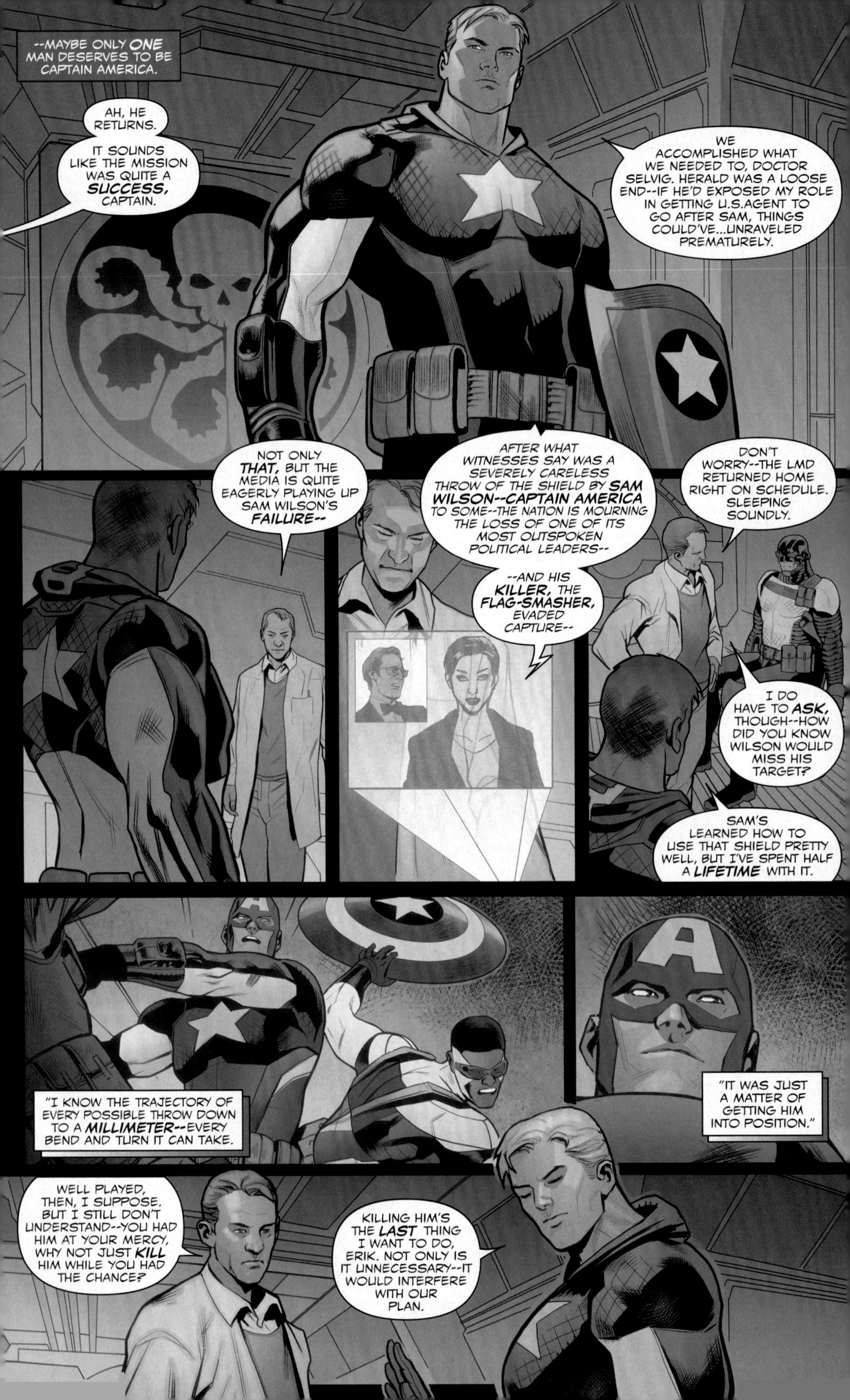

--MAYBE ONLY ONE MAN DESERVES TO BE CAPTAIN AMERICA.
AH, HE RETURNS.
IT SOUNDS LIKE THE MISSION WAS QUITE A SUCCESS, CAPTAIN.
WE ACCOMPLISHED WHAT WE NEEDED TO, DOCTOR SELVIG. HERALD WAS A LOOSE END--IF HE'D EXPOSED MY ROLE IN GETTING U.S.AGENT TO GO AFTER SAM, THINGS COULD'VE...UNRAVELED PREMATURELY.
NOT ONLY THAT, BUT THE MEDIA IS QUITE EAGERLY PLAYING UP SAM WILSON'S FAILURE--
AFTER WHAT WITNESSES SAY WAS A SEVERELY CARELESS THROW OF THE SHIELD BY SAM WILSON--CAPTAIN AMERICA TO SOME--THE NATION IS MOURNING THE LOSS OF ONE OF ITS MOST OUTSPOKEN POLITICAL LEADERS--
--AND HIS KILLER, THE FLAG-SMASHER, EVADED CAPTURE--
DON'T WORRY--THE LMD RETURNED HOME RIGHT ON SCHEDULE. SLEEPING SOUNDLY.
I DO HAVE TO ASK, THOUGH--HOW DID YOU KNOW WILSON WOULD MISS HIS TARGET?
SAM'S LEARNED HOW TO USE THAT SHIELD PRETTY WELL, BUT I'VE SPENT HALF A LIFETIME WITH IT.
"I KNOW THE TRAJECTORY OF EVERY POSSIBLE THROW DOWN TO A MILLIMETER--EVERY BEND AND TURN IT CAN TAKE.
"IT WAS JUST A MATTER OF GETTING HIM INTO POSITION."
WELL PLAYED, THEN, I SUPPOSE. BUT I STILL DON'T UNDERSTAND--YOU HAD HIM AT YOUR MERCY, WHY NOT JUST KILL HIM WHILE YOU HAD THE CHANCE?
KILLING HIM'S THE LAST THING I WANT TO DO, ERIK. NOT ONLY IS IT UNNECESSARY--IT WOULD INTERFERE WITH OUR PLAN.

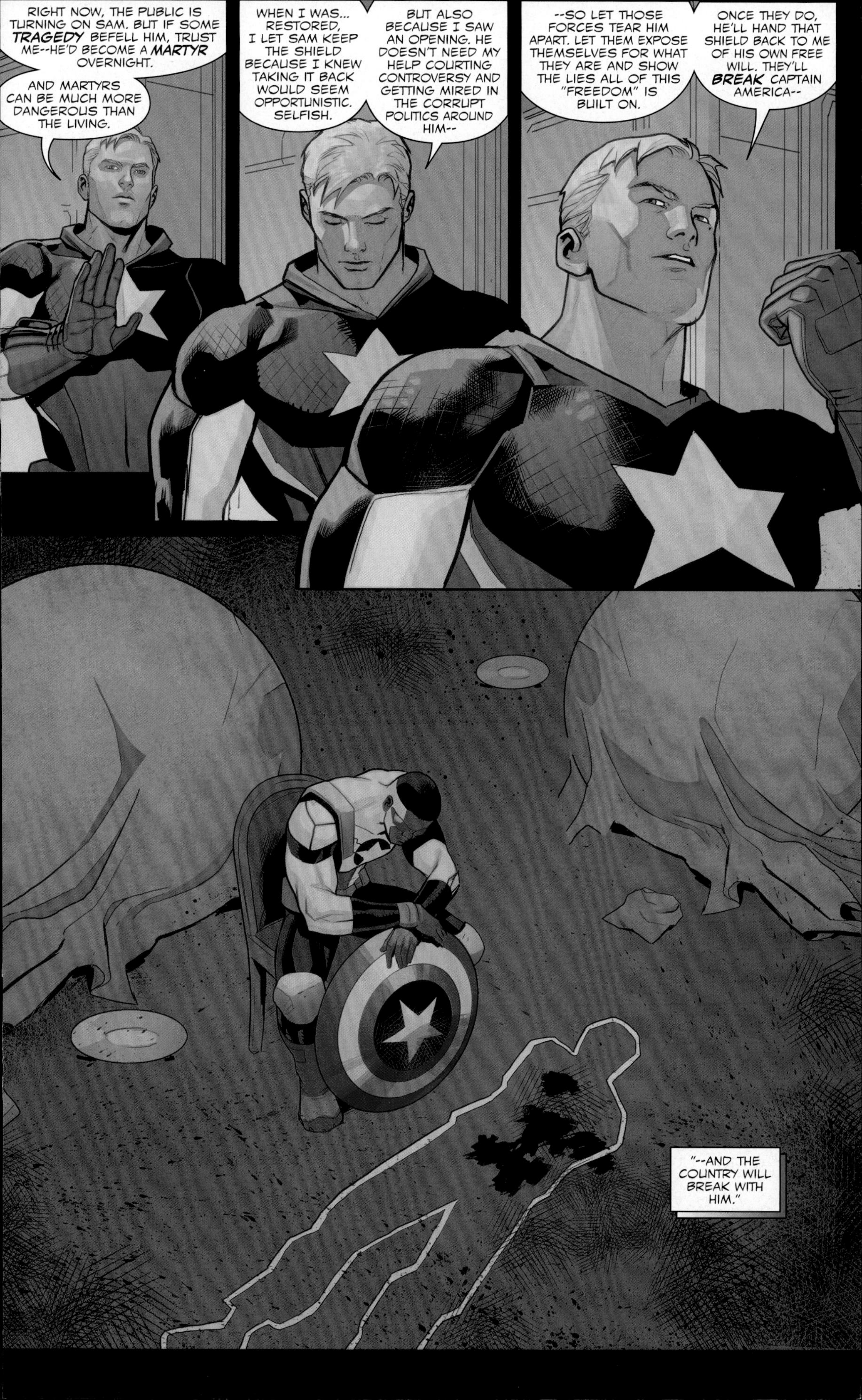
RIGHT NOW, THE PUBLIC IS TURNING ON SAM. BUT IF SOME TRAGEDY BEFELL HIM, TRUST ME--HE'D BECOME A MARTYR OVERNIGHT.
AND MARTYRS CAN BE MUCH MORE DANGEROUS THAN THE LIVING.
WHEN I WAS... RESTORED, I LET SAM KEEP THE SHIELD BECAUSE I KNEW TAKING IT BACK WOULD SEEM OPPORTUNISTIC. SELFISH.
BUT ALSO BECAUSE I SAW AN OPENING. HE DOESN'T NEED MY HELP COURTING CONTROVERSY AND GETTING MIRED IN THE CORRUPT POLITICS AROUND HIM--
--SO LET THOSE FORCES TEAR HIM APART. LET THEM EXPOSE THEMSELVES FOR WHAT THEY ARE AND SHOW THE LIES ALL OF THIS "FREEDOM" IS BUILT ON.
ONCE THEY DO, HE'LL HAND THAT SHIELD BACK TO ME OF HIS OWN FREE WILL. THEY'LL BREAK CAPTAIN AMERICA--
"--AND THE COUNTRY WILL BREAK WITH HIM."

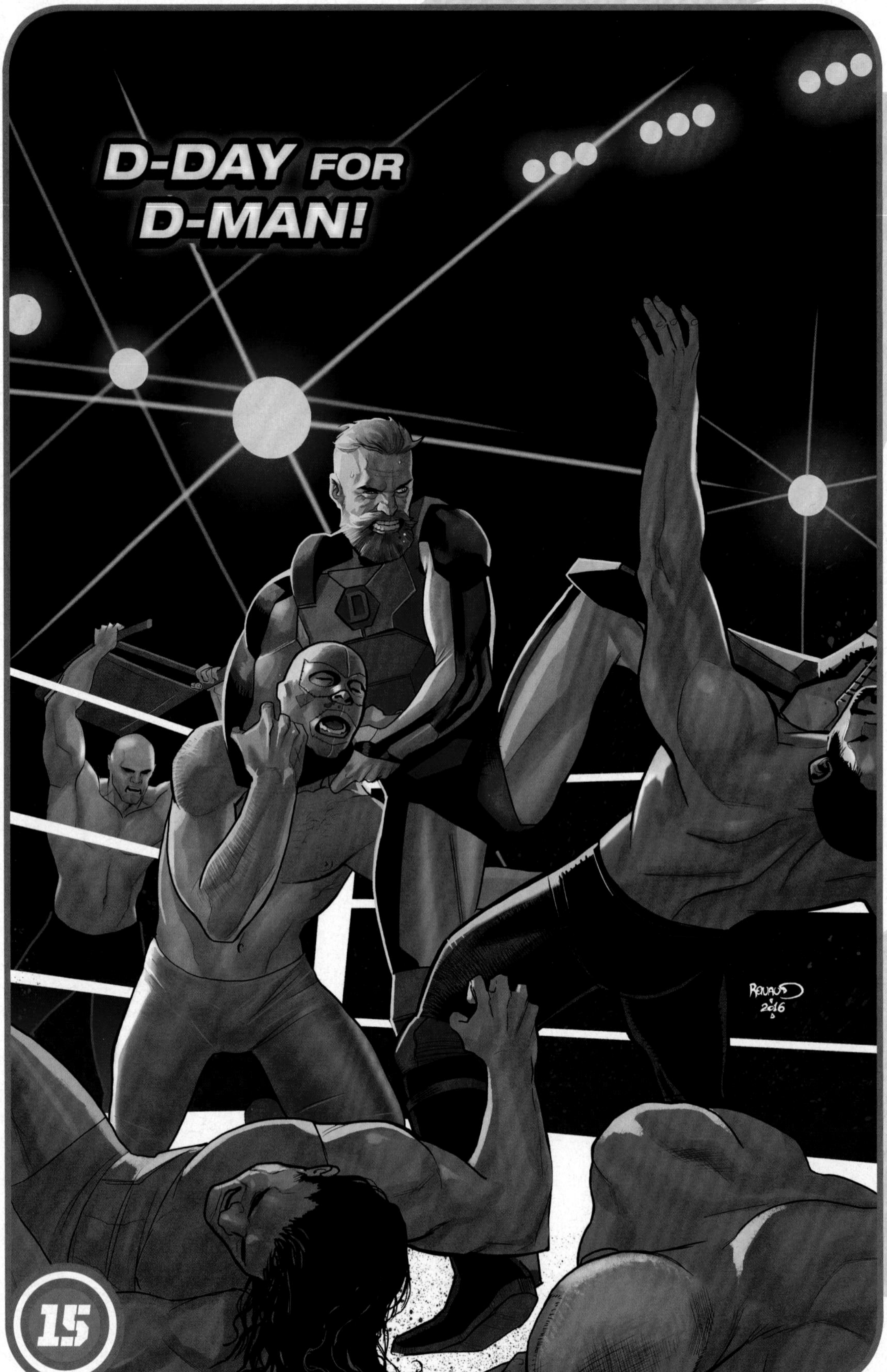
D-DAY FOR D-MAN!
15

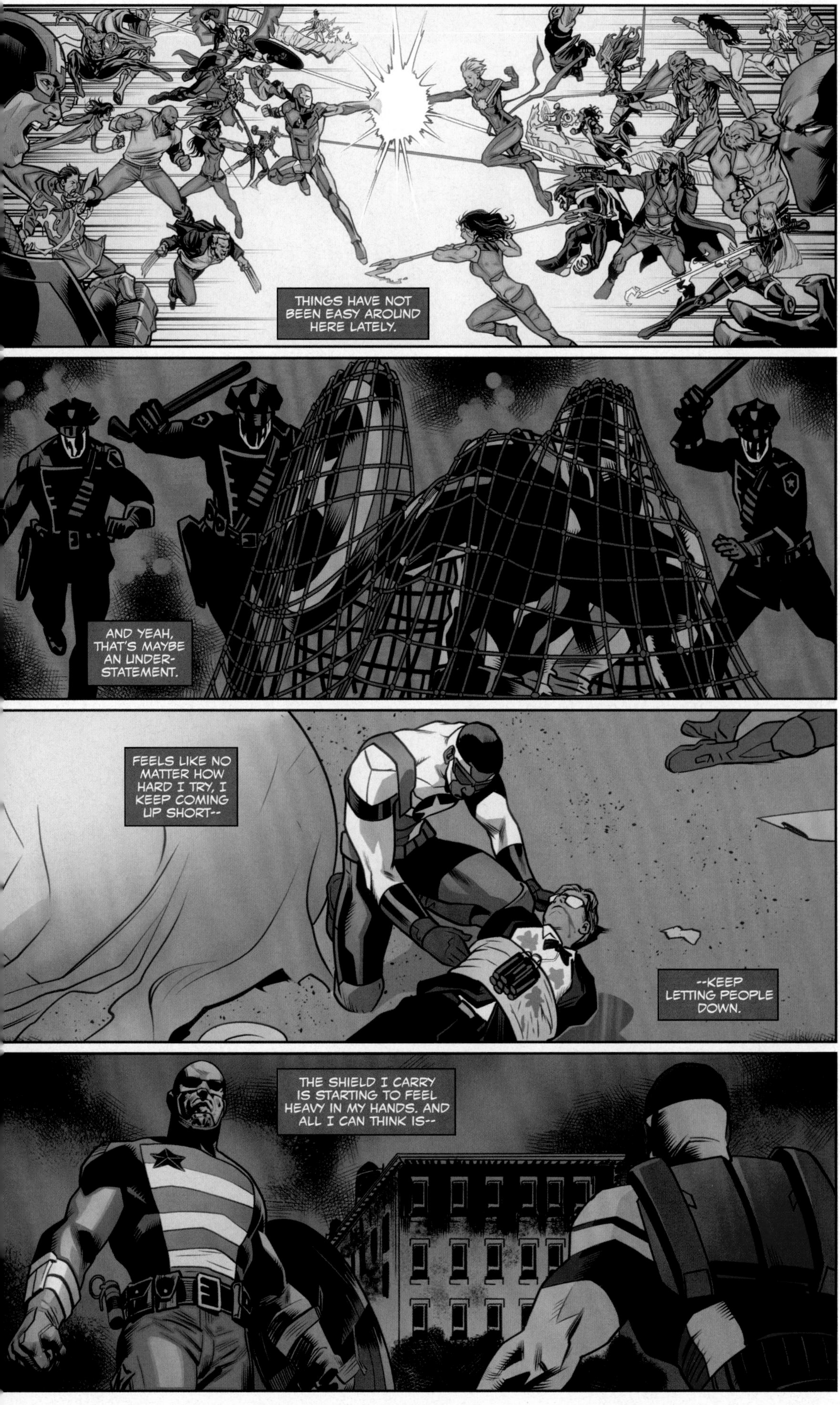
THINGS HAVE NOT BEEN EASY AROUND HERE LATELY.
AND YEAH, THAT'S MAYBE AN UNDER-STATEMENT.
FEELS LIKE NO MATTER HOW HARD I TRY, I KEEP COMING UP SHORT--
--KEEP LETTING PEOPLE DOWN.
THE SHIELD I CARRY IS STARTING TO FEEL HEAVY IN MY HANDS. AND ALL I CAN THINK IS--

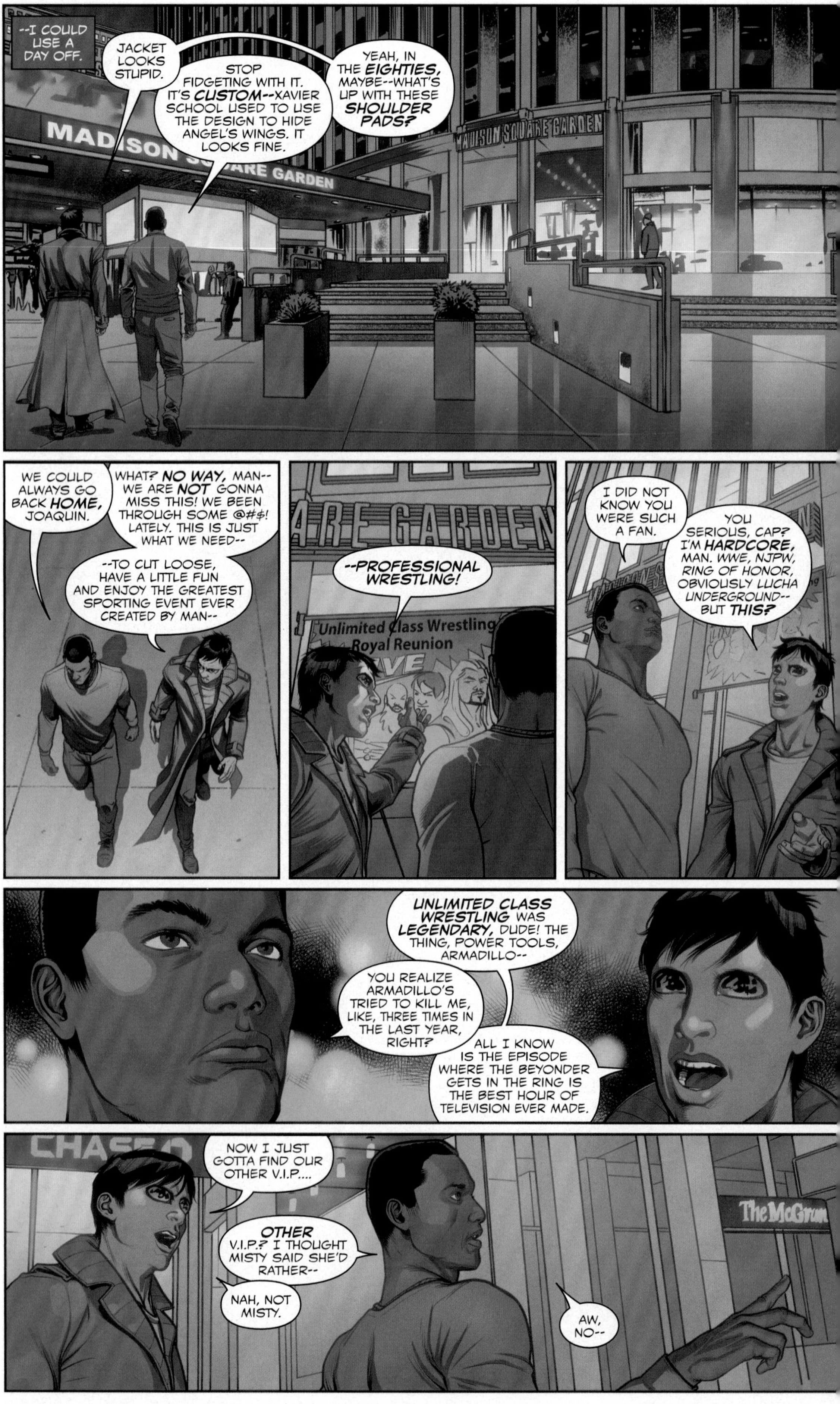
--I COULD USE A DAY OFF.
JACKET LOOKS STUPID.
STOP FIDGETING WITH IT. IT'S **CUSTOM**--XAVIER SCHOOL USED TO USE THE DESIGN TO HIDE ANGEL'S WINGS. IT LOOKS FINE.
YEAH, IN THE **EIGHTIES,** MAYBE--WHAT'S UP WITH THESE **SHOULDER PADS?**
MADISON SQUARE GARDEN
MADISON SQUARE GARDEN
WE COULD ALWAYS GO BACK **HOME,** JOAQUIN.
WHAT? **NO WAY,** MAN--WE ARE **NOT** GONNA MISS THIS! WE BEEN THROUGH SOME @#$! LATELY. THIS IS JUST WHAT WE NEED--
--TO CUT LOOSE, HAVE A LITTLE FUN AND ENJOY THE GREATEST SPORTING EVENT EVER CREATED BY MAN--
--**PROFESSIONAL WRESTLING!**
Unlimited Class Wrestling
Royal Reunion
I DID NOT KNOW YOU WERE SUCH A FAN.
YOU SERIOUS, CAP? I'M **HARDCORE,** MAN. WWE, NJPW, RING OF HONOR, OBVIOUSLY LUCHA UNDERGROUND--BUT **THIS?**
UNLIMITED CLASS WRESTLING WAS **LEGENDARY,** DUDE! THE THING, POWER TOOLS, ARMADILLO--
YOU REALIZE ARMADILLO'S TRIED TO KILL ME, LIKE, THREE TIMES IN THE LAST YEAR, RIGHT?
ALL I KNOW IS THE EPISODE WHERE THE BEYONDER GETS IN THE RING IS THE BEST HOUR OF TELEVISION EVER MADE.
NOW I JUST GOTTA FIND OUR OTHER V.I.P....
OTHER V.I.P.? I THOUGHT MISTY SAID SHE'D RATHER--
NAH, NOT MISTY.
AW, NO--

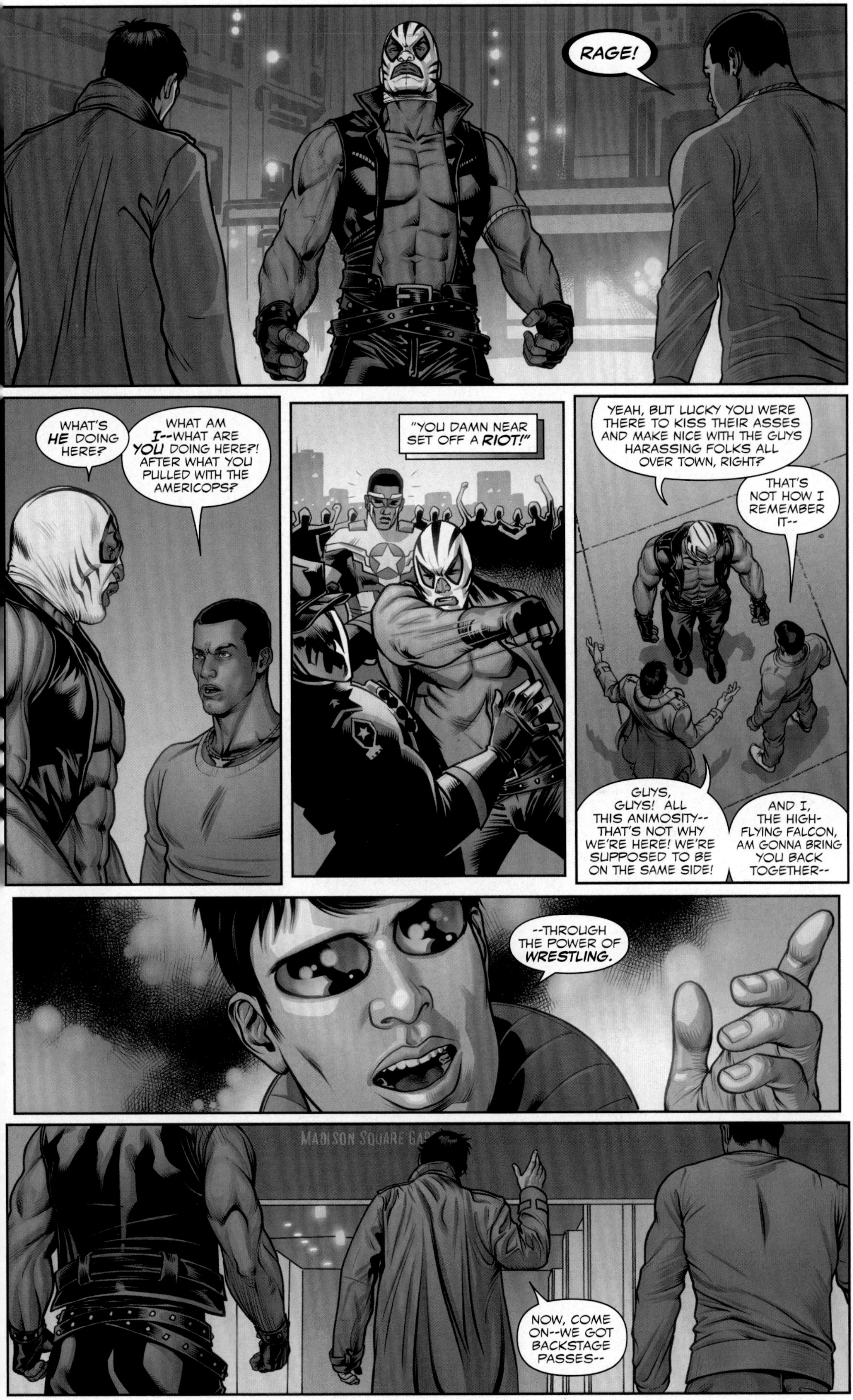

RAGE!
WHAT'S HE DOING HERE?
WHAT AM I--WHAT ARE YOU DOING HERE?! AFTER WHAT YOU PULLED WITH THE AMERICOPS?
"YOU DAMN NEAR SET OFF A RIOT!"
YEAH, BUT LUCKY YOU WERE THERE TO KISS THEIR ASSES AND MAKE NICE WITH THE GUYS HARASSING FOLKS ALL OVER TOWN, RIGHT?
THAT'S NOT HOW I REMEMBER IT--
GUYS, GUYS! ALL THIS ANIMOSITY-- THAT'S NOT WHY WE'RE HERE! WE'RE SUPPOSED TO BE ON THE SAME SIDE!
AND I, THE HIGH-FLYING FALCON, AM GONNA BRING YOU BACK TOGETHER--
--THROUGH THE POWER OF WRESTLING.
NOW, COME ON--WE GOT BACKSTAGE PASSES--

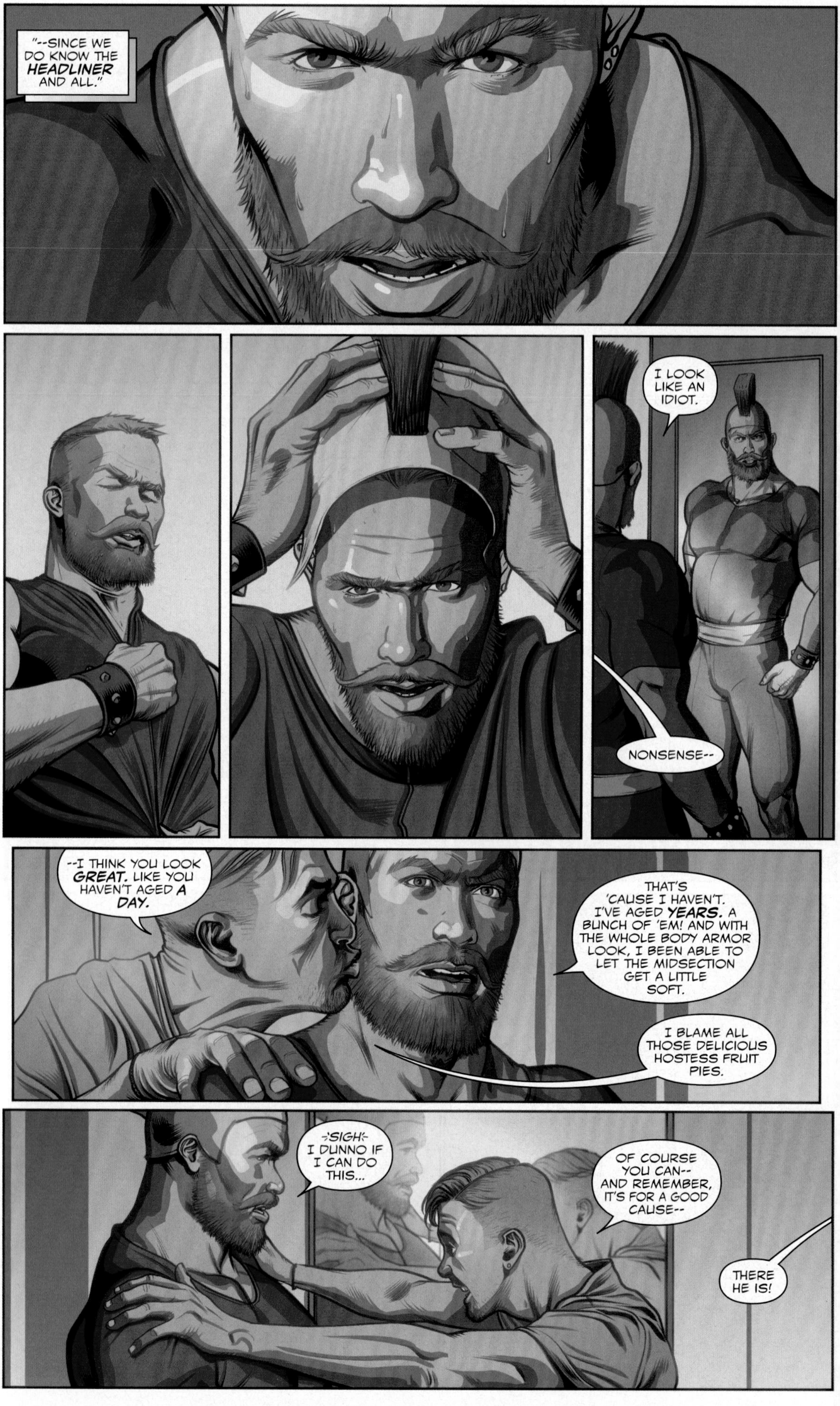
"--SINCE WE DO KNOW THE **HEADLINER** AND ALL."
I LOOK LIKE AN IDIOT.
NONSENSE--
--I THINK YOU LOOK **GREAT.** LIKE YOU HAVEN'T AGED **A DAY.**
THAT'S 'CAUSE I HAVEN'T. I'VE AGED **YEARS.** A BUNCH OF 'EM! AND WITH THE WHOLE BODY ARMOR LOOK, I BEEN ABLE TO LET THE MIDSECTION GET A LITTLE SOFT.
I BLAME ALL THOSE DELICIOUS HOSTESS FRUIT PIES.
-SIGH- I DUNNO IF I CAN DO THIS...
OF COURSE YOU CAN--AND REMEMBER, IT'S FOR A GOOD CAUSE--
THERE HE IS!

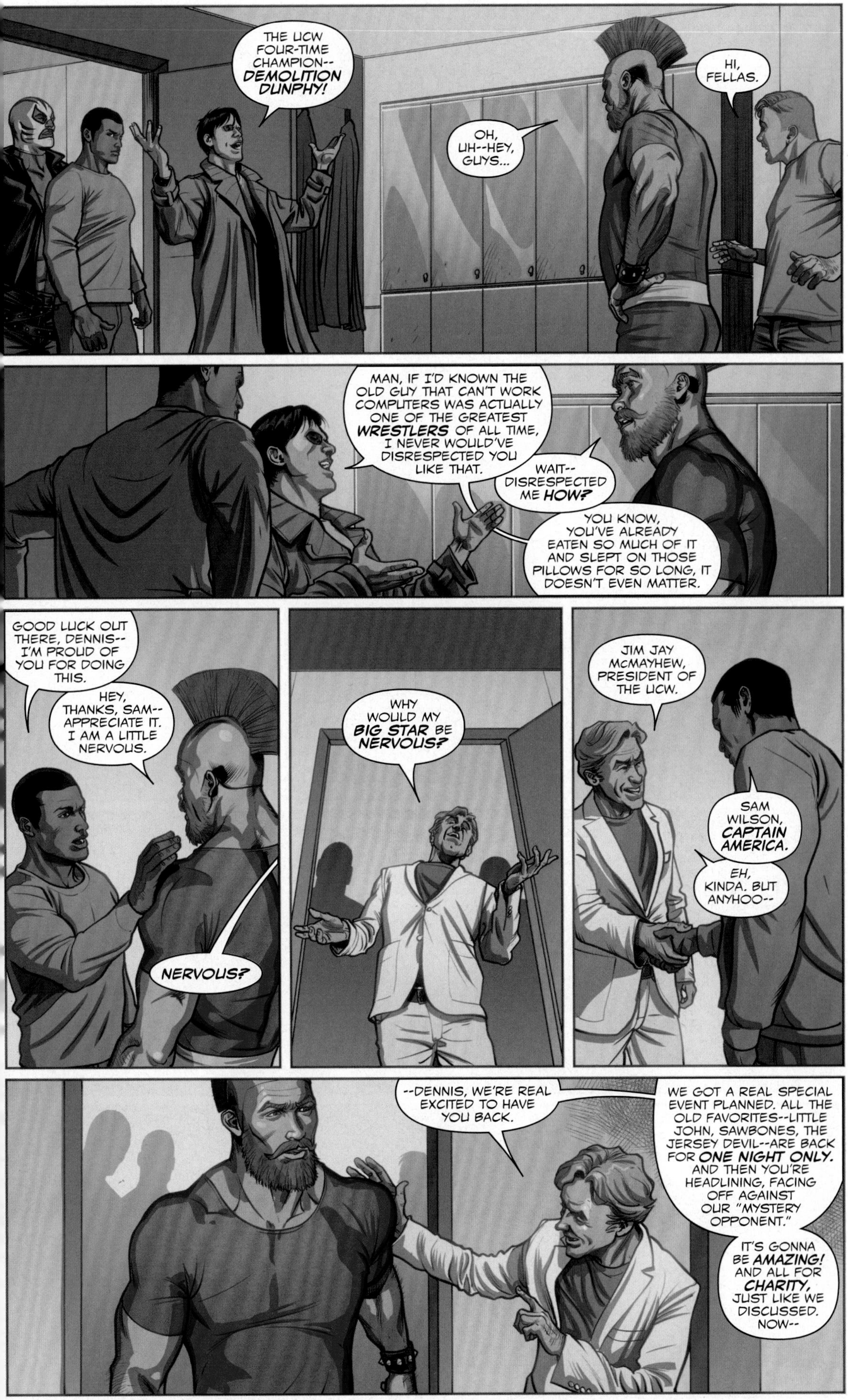
THE UCW FOUR-TIME CHAMPION-- DEMOLITION DUNPHY!
OH, UH--HEY, GUYS...
HI, FELLAS.
MAN, IF I'D KNOWN THE OLD GUY THAT CAN'T WORK COMPUTERS WAS ACTUALLY ONE OF THE GREATEST WRESTLERS OF ALL TIME, I NEVER WOULD'VE DISRESPECTED YOU LIKE THAT.
WAIT-- DISRESPECTED ME HOW?
YOU KNOW, YOU'VE ALREADY EATEN SO MUCH OF IT AND SLEPT ON THOSE PILLOWS FOR SO LONG, IT DOESN'T EVEN MATTER.
GOOD LUCK OUT THERE, DENNIS-- I'M PROUD OF YOU FOR DOING THIS.
HEY, THANKS, SAM-- APPRECIATE IT. I AM A LITTLE NERVOUS.
NERVOUS?
WHY WOULD MY BIG STAR BE NERVOUS?
JIM JAY MCMAYHEW, PRESIDENT OF THE UCW.
SAM WILSON, CAPTAIN AMERICA.
EH, KINDA. BUT ANYHOO--
--DENNIS, WE'RE REAL EXCITED TO HAVE YOU BACK.
WE GOT A REAL SPECIAL EVENT PLANNED. ALL THE OLD FAVORITES--LITTLE JOHN, SAWBONES, THE JERSEY DEVIL--ARE BACK FOR ONE NIGHT ONLY. AND THEN YOU'RE HEADLINING, FACING OFF AGAINST OUR "MYSTERY OPPONENT."
IT'S GONNA BE AMAZING! AND ALL FOR CHARITY, JUST LIKE WE DISCUSSED. NOW--

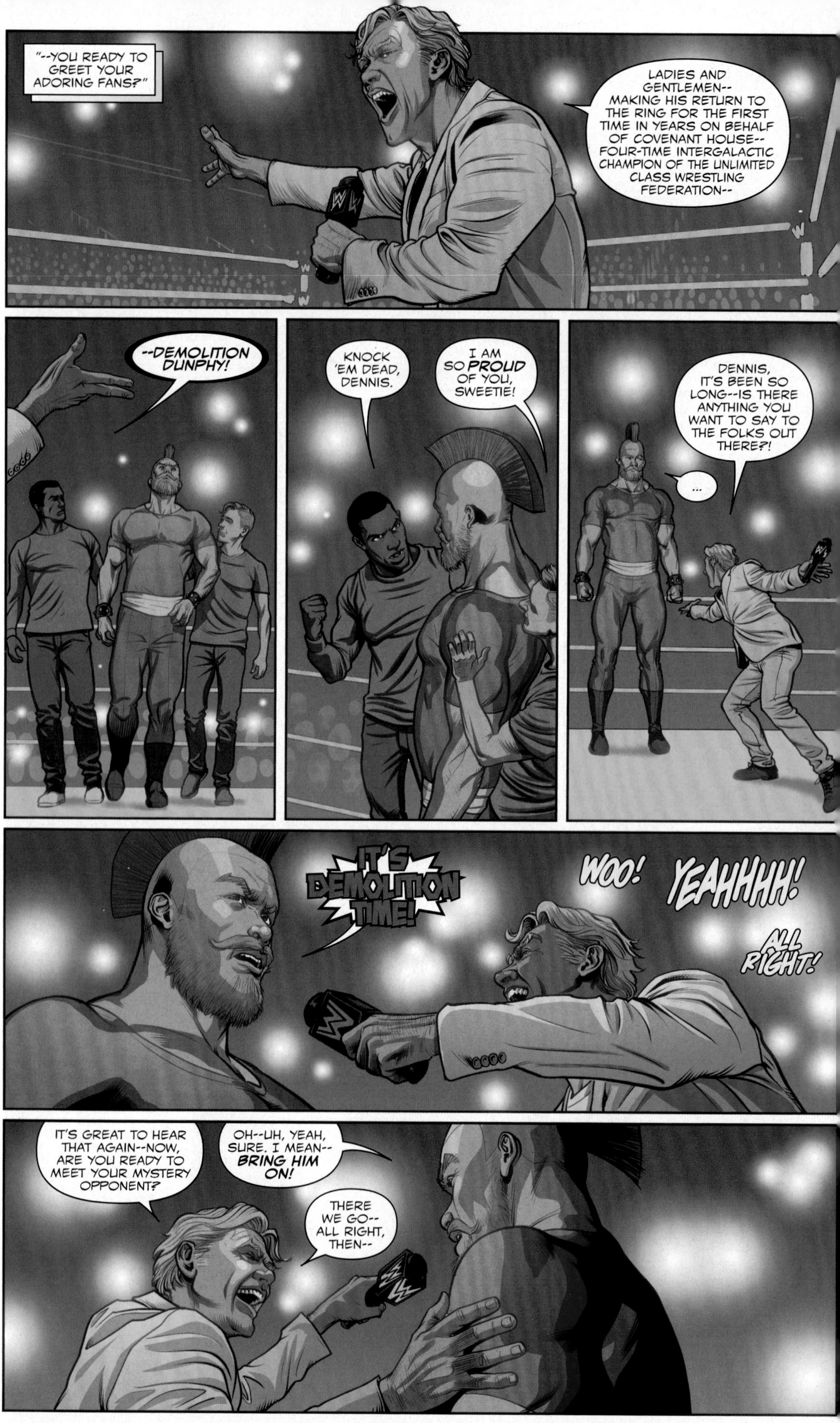
"--YOU READY TO GREET YOUR ADORING FANS?"
LADIES AND GENTLEMEN-- MAKING HIS RETURN TO THE RING FOR THE FIRST TIME IN YEARS ON BEHALF OF COVENANT HOUSE-- FOUR-TIME INTERGALACTIC CHAMPION OF THE UNLIMITED CLASS WRESTLING FEDERATION--
--DEMOLITION DUNPHY!
KNOCK 'EM DEAD, DENNIS.
I AM SO PROUD OF YOU, SWEETIE!
DENNIS, IT'S BEEN SO LONG--IS THERE ANYTHING YOU WANT TO SAY TO THE FOLKS OUT THERE?!
...
IT'S DEMOLITION TIME!
WOO!
YEAHHHH!
ALL RIGHT!
IT'S GREAT TO HEAR THAT AGAIN--NOW, ARE YOU READY TO MEET YOUR MYSTERY OPPONENT?
OH--UH, YEAH, SURE. I MEAN-- BRING HIM ON!
THERE WE GO-- ALL RIGHT, THEN--

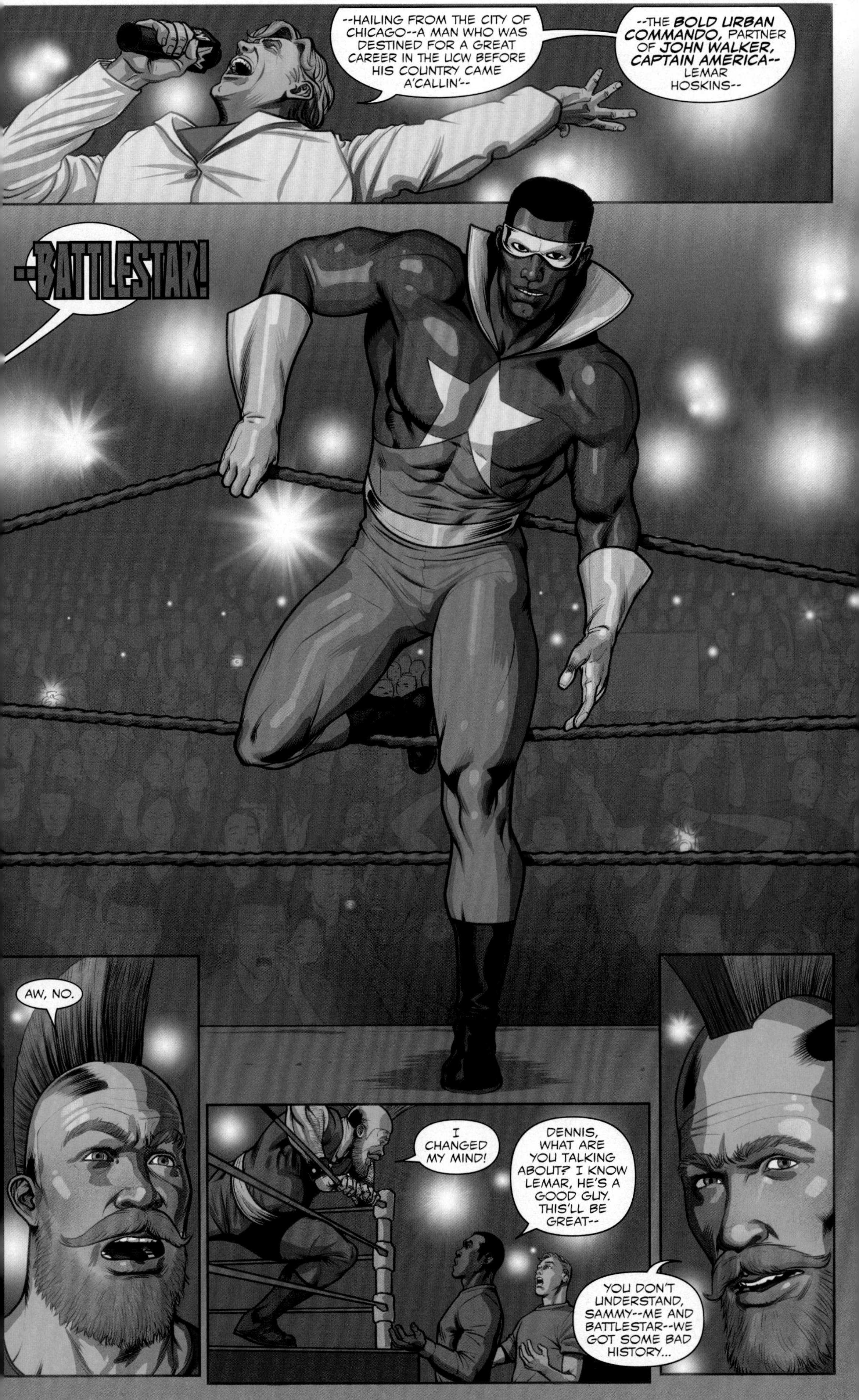
--HAILING FROM THE CITY OF CHICAGO--A MAN WHO WAS DESTINED FOR A GREAT CAREER IN THE UCW BEFORE HIS COUNTRY CAME A'CALLIN'--
--THE BOLD URBAN COMMANDO, PARTNER OF JOHN WALKER, CAPTAIN AMERICA-- LEMAR HOSKINS--
--BATTLESTAR!
AW, NO.
I CHANGED MY MIND!
DENNIS, WHAT ARE YOU TALKING ABOUT? I KNOW LEMAR, HE'S A GOOD GUY. THIS'LL BE GREAT--
YOU DON'T UNDERSTAND, SAMMY--ME AND BATTLESTAR--WE GOT SOME BAD HISTORY...

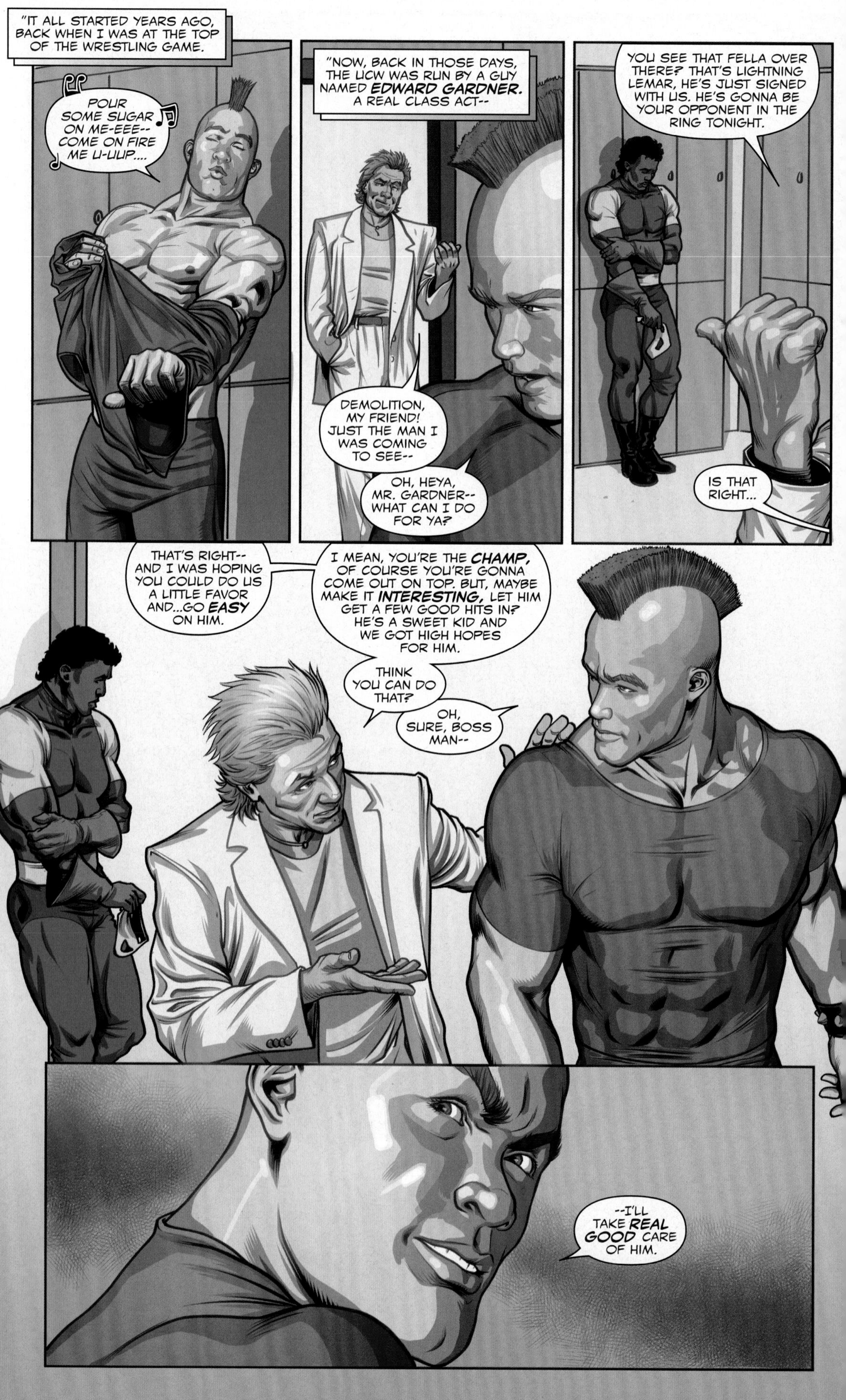
"IT ALL STARTED YEARS AGO, BACK WHEN I WAS AT THE TOP OF THE WRESTLING GAME.
POUR SOME SUGAR ON ME-EEE-- COME ON FIRE ME U-UUP....
"NOW, BACK IN THOSE DAYS, THE UCW WAS RUN BY A GUY NAMED EDWARD GARDNER. A REAL CLASS ACT--
DEMOLITION, MY FRIEND! JUST THE MAN I WAS COMING TO SEE--
OH, HEYA, MR. GARDNER-- WHAT CAN I DO FOR YA?
YOU SEE THAT FELLA OVER THERE? THAT'S LIGHTNING LEMAR, HE'S JUST SIGNED WITH US. HE'S GONNA BE YOUR OPPONENT IN THE RING TONIGHT.
IS THAT RIGHT...
THAT'S RIGHT-- AND I WAS HOPING YOU COULD DO US A LITTLE FAVOR AND...GO EASY ON HIM.
I MEAN, YOU'RE THE CHAMP, OF COURSE YOU'RE GONNA COME OUT ON TOP. BUT, MAYBE MAKE IT INTERESTING, LET HIM GET A FEW GOOD HITS IN? HE'S A SWEET KID AND WE GOT HIGH HOPES FOR HIM.
THINK YOU CAN DO THAT?
OH, SURE, BOSS MAN--
--I'LL TAKE REAL GOOD CARE OF HIM.

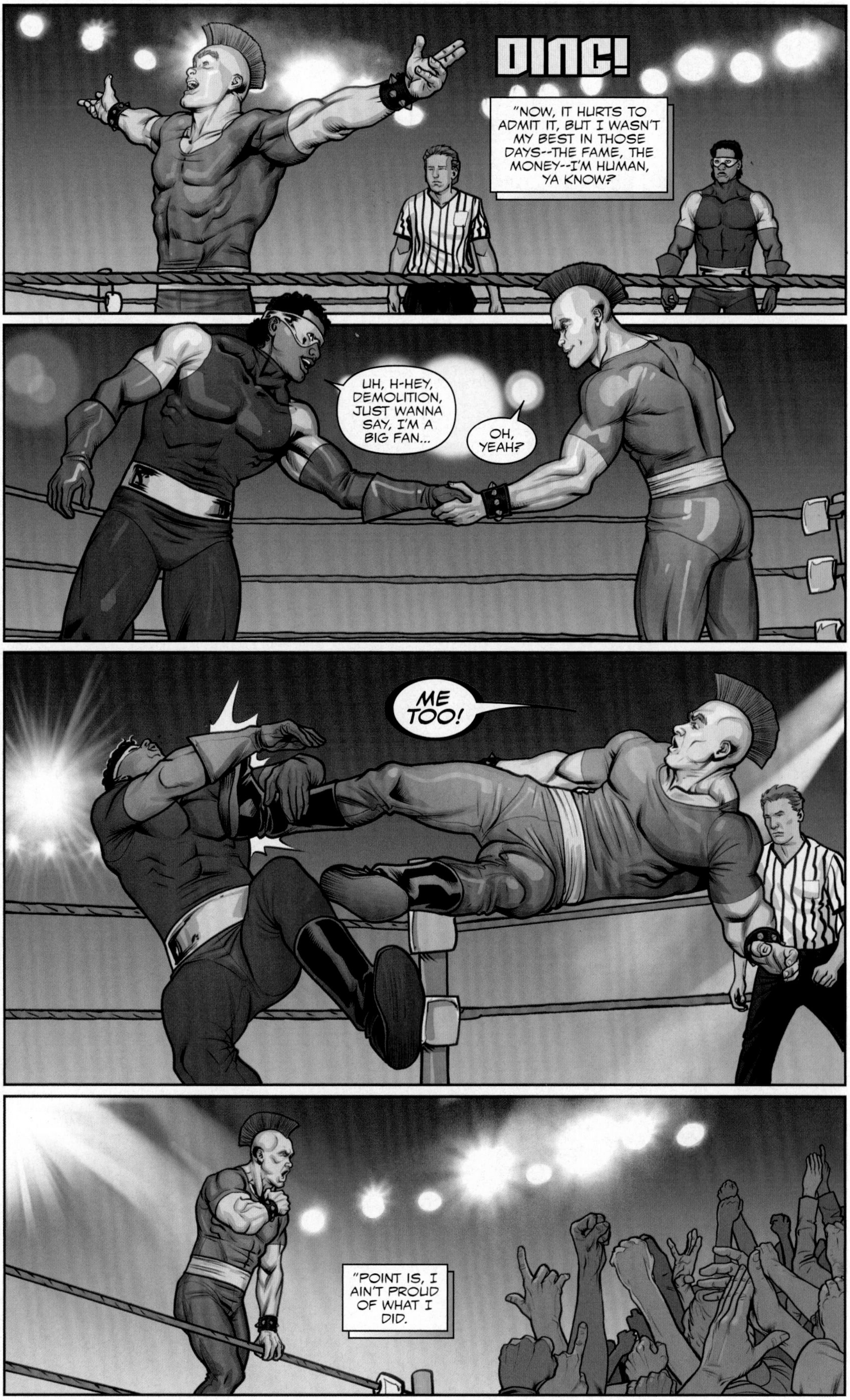
DING!
"NOW, IT HURTS TO ADMIT IT, BUT I WASN'T MY BEST IN THOSE DAYS--THE FAME, THE MONEY--I'M HUMAN, YA KNOW?
UH, H-HEY, DEMOLITION, JUST WANNA SAY, I'M A BIG FAN...
OH, YEAH?
ME TOO!
"POINT IS, I AIN'T PROUD OF WHAT I DID.

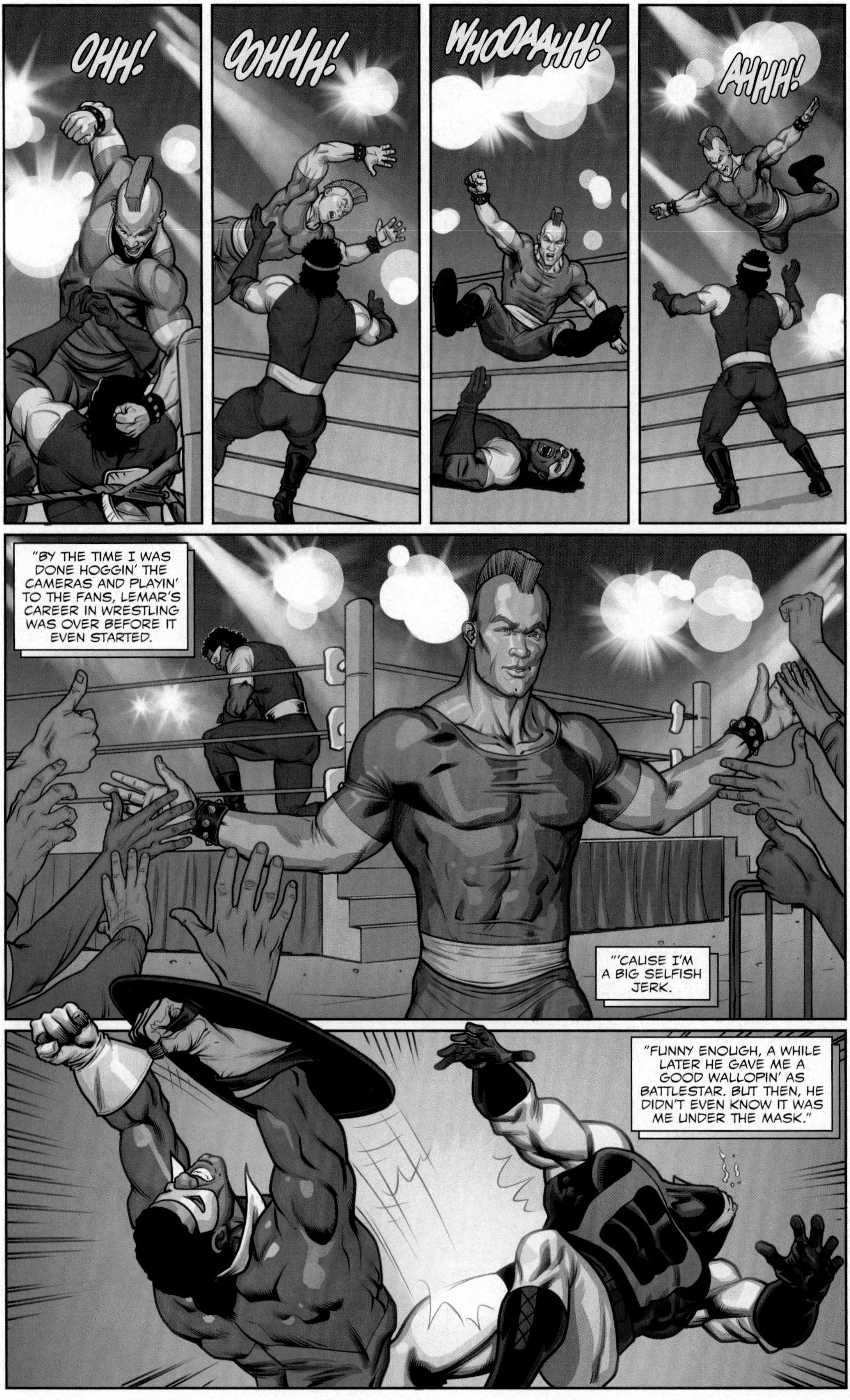
OHH!
OOHHH!
WHOOAAHH!
AHHH!
"BY THE TIME I WAS DONE HOGGIN' THE CAMERAS AND PLAYIN' TO THE FANS, LEMAR'S CAREER IN WRESTLING WAS OVER BEFORE IT EVEN STARTED.
"'CAUSE I'M A BIG SELFISH JERK.
"FUNNY ENOUGH, A WHILE LATER HE GAVE ME A GOOD WALLOPIN' AS BATTLESTAR. BUT THEN, HE DIDN'T EVEN KNOW IT WAS ME UNDER THE MASK."

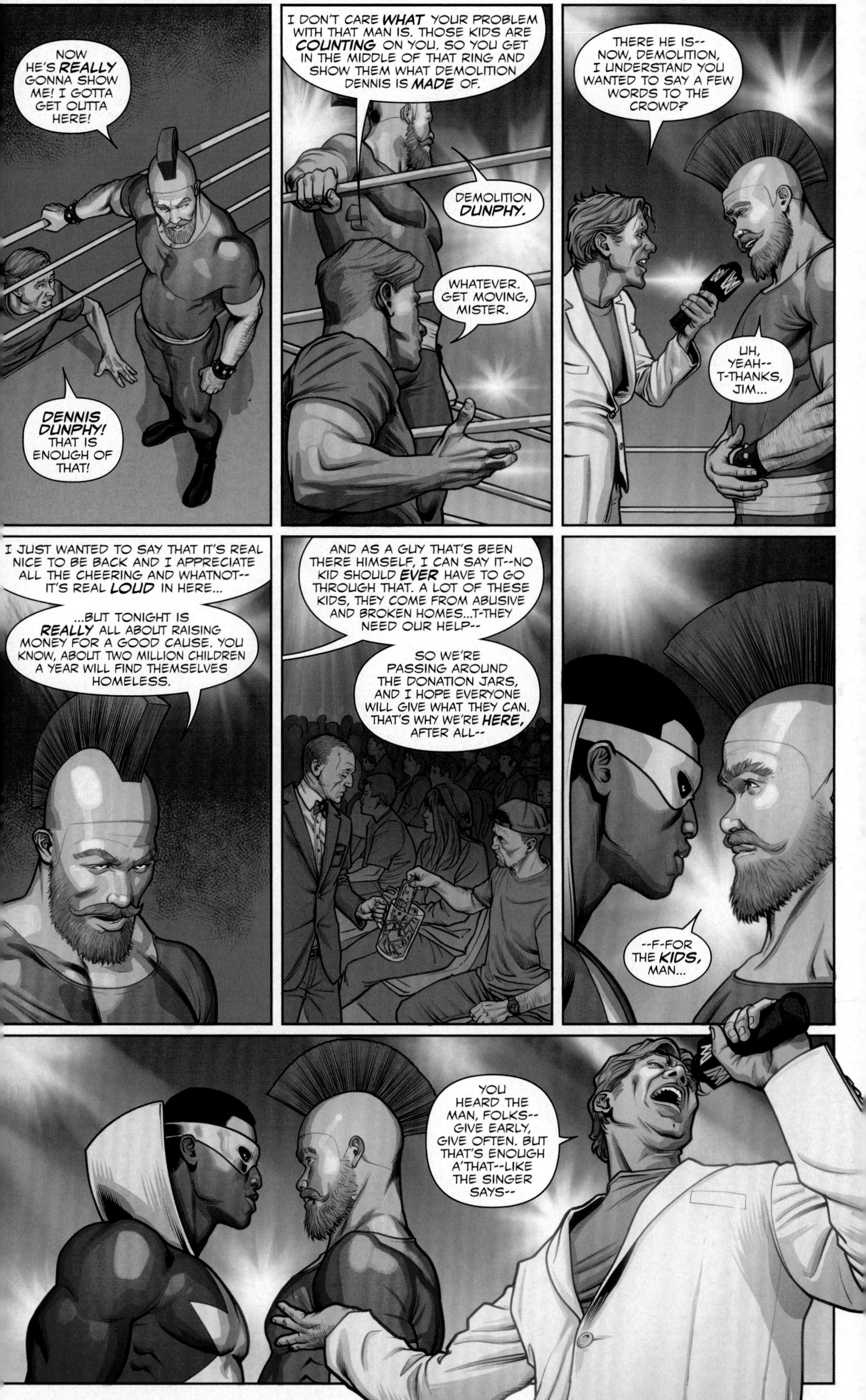

NOW HE'S REALLY GONNA SHOW ME! I GOTTA GET OUTTA HERE!
DENNIS DUNPHY! THAT IS ENOUGH OF THAT!
I DON'T CARE WHAT YOUR PROBLEM WITH THAT MAN IS. THOSE KIDS ARE COUNTING ON YOU. SO YOU GET IN THE MIDDLE OF THAT RING AND SHOW THEM WHAT DEMOLITION DENNIS IS MADE OF.
DEMOLITION DUNPHY.
WHATEVER. GET MOVING, MISTER.
THERE HE IS--NOW, DEMOLITION, I UNDERSTAND YOU WANTED TO SAY A FEW WORDS TO THE CROWD?
UH, YEAH--T-THANKS, JIM...
I JUST WANTED TO SAY THAT IT'S REAL NICE TO BE BACK AND I APPRECIATE ALL THE CHEERING AND WHATNOT--IT'S REAL LOUD IN HERE...
...BUT TONIGHT IS REALLY ALL ABOUT RAISING MONEY FOR A GOOD CAUSE. YOU KNOW, ABOUT TWO MILLION CHILDREN A YEAR WILL FIND THEMSELVES HOMELESS.
AND AS A GUY THAT'S BEEN THERE HIMSELF, I CAN SAY IT--NO KID SHOULD EVER HAVE TO GO THROUGH THAT. A LOT OF THESE KIDS, THEY COME FROM ABUSIVE AND BROKEN HOMES...T-THEY NEED OUR HELP--
SO WE'RE PASSING AROUND THE DONATION JARS, AND I HOPE EVERYONE WILL GIVE WHAT THEY CAN. THAT'S WHY WE'RE HERE, AFTER ALL--
--F-FOR THE KIDS, MAN...
YOU HEARD THE MAN, FOLKS--GIVE EARLY, GIVE OFTEN. BUT THAT'S ENOUGH A'THAT--LIKE THE SINGER SAYS--

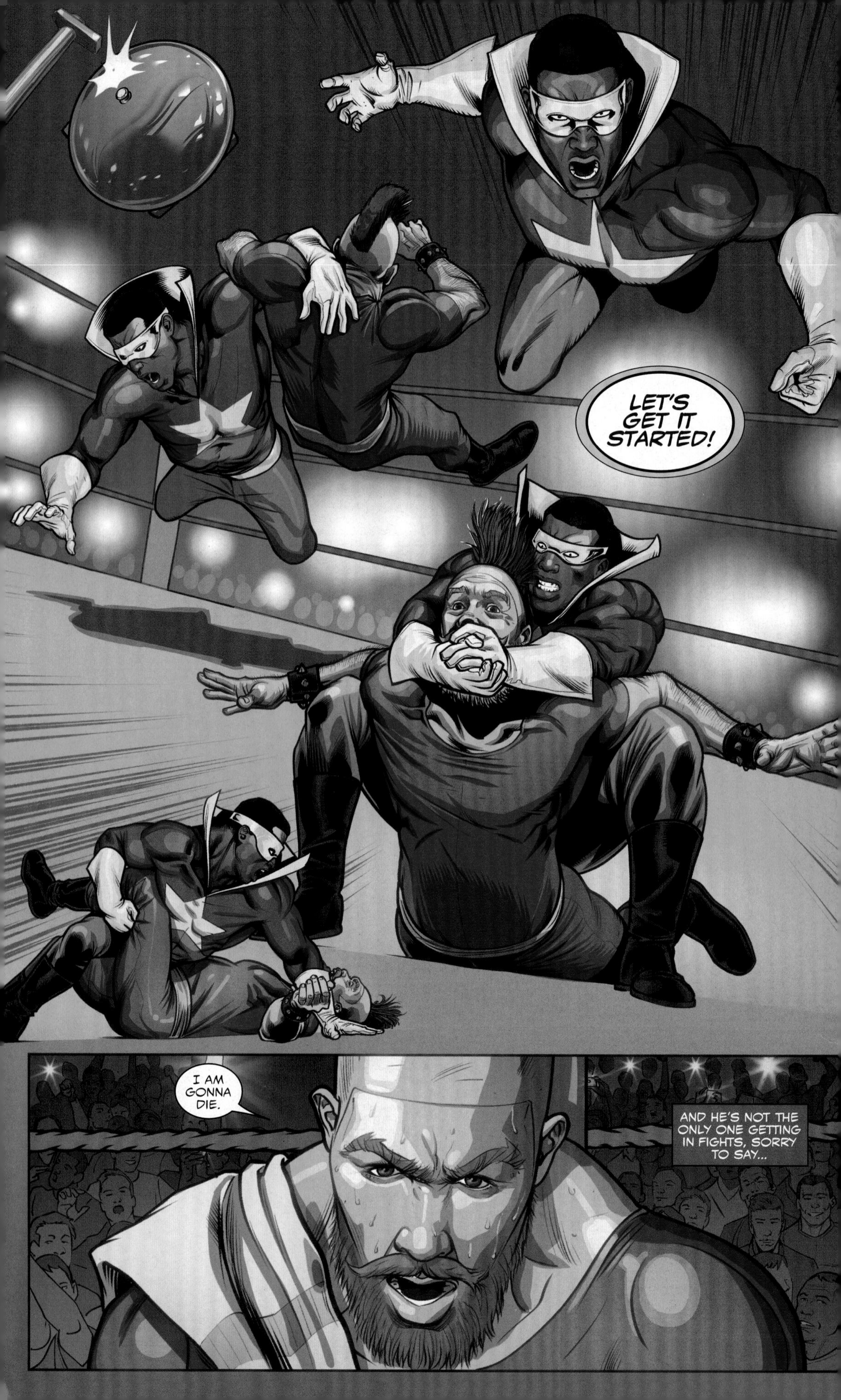
LET'S GET IT STARTED!
I AM GONNA DIE.
AND HE'S NOT THE ONLY ONE GETTING IN FIGHTS, SORRY TO SAY...

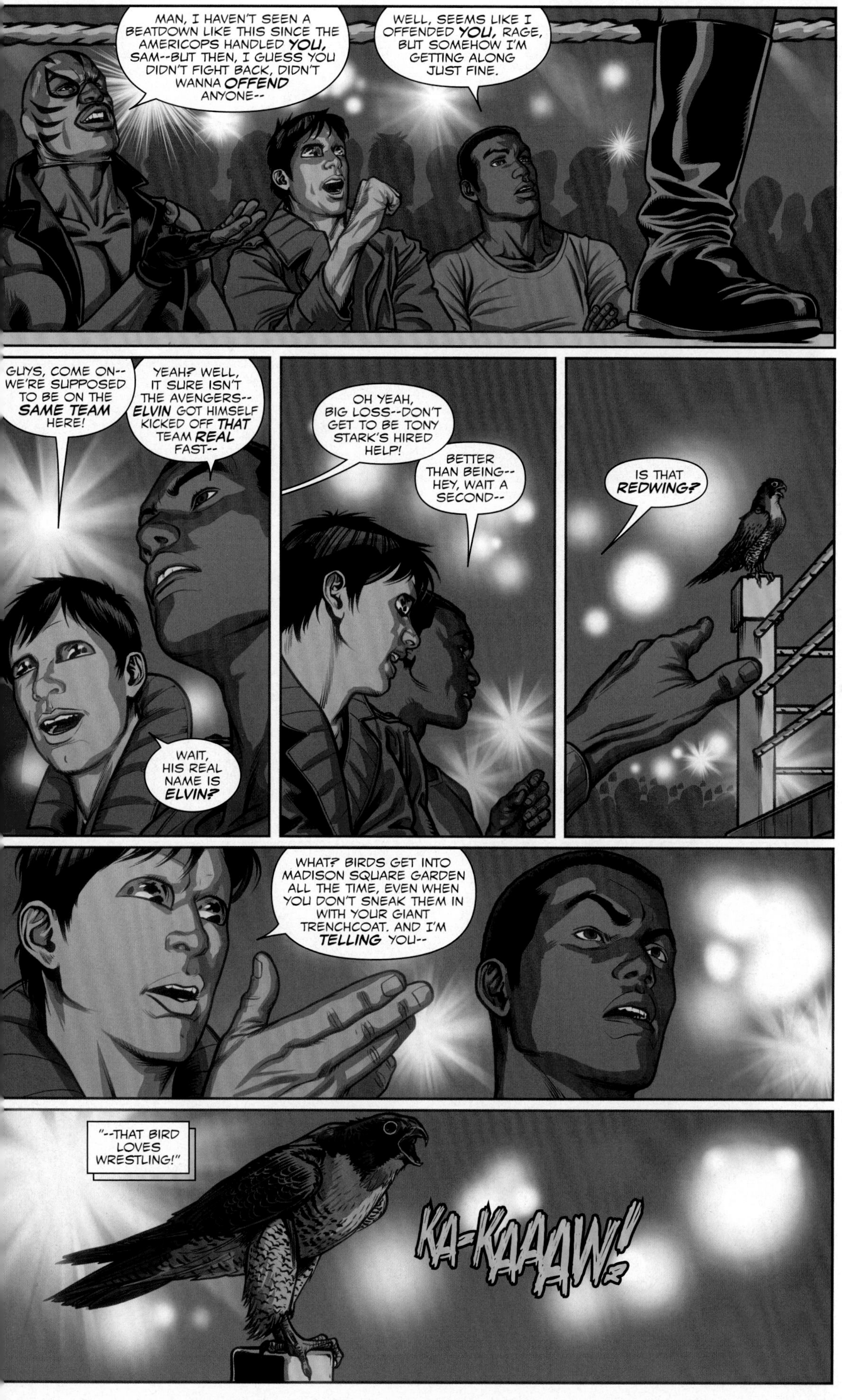
MAN, I HAVEN'T SEEN A BEATDOWN LIKE THIS SINCE THE AMERICOPS HANDLED YOU, SAM--BUT THEN, I GUESS YOU DIDN'T FIGHT BACK, DIDN'T WANNA OFFEND ANYONE--
WELL, SEEMS LIKE I OFFENDED YOU, RAGE, BUT SOMEHOW I'M GETTING ALONG JUST FINE.
GUYS, COME ON--WE'RE SUPPOSED TO BE ON THE SAME TEAM HERE!
YEAH? WELL, IT SURE ISN'T THE AVENGERS--ELVIN GOT HIMSELF KICKED OFF THAT TEAM REAL FAST--
WAIT, HIS REAL NAME IS ELVIN?
OH YEAH, BIG LOSS--DON'T GET TO BE TONY STARK'S HIRED HELP!
BETTER THAN BEING--HEY, WAIT A SECOND--
IS THAT REDWING?
WHAT? BIRDS GET INTO MADISON SQUARE GARDEN ALL THE TIME, EVEN WHEN YOU DON'T SNEAK THEM IN WITH YOUR GIANT TRENCHCOAT. AND I'M TELLING YOU--
"--THAT BIRD LOVES WRESTLING!"
KA-KAAAW!

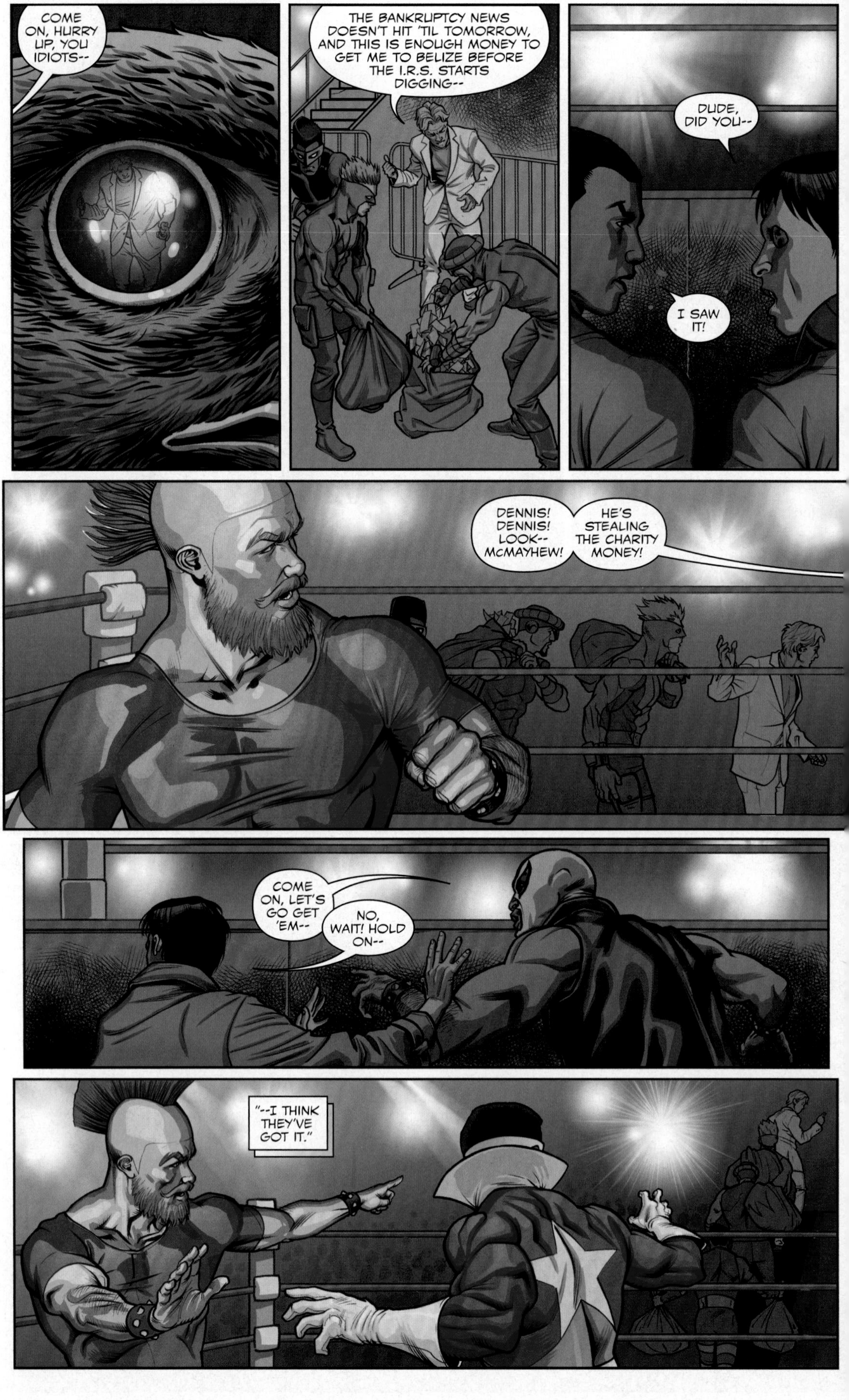
COME ON, HURRY UP, YOU IDIOTS--
THE BANKRUPTCY NEWS DOESN'T HIT 'TIL TOMORROW, AND THIS IS ENOUGH MONEY TO GET ME TO BELIZE BEFORE THE I.R.S. STARTS DIGGING--
DUDE, DID YOU--
I SAW IT!
DENNIS! DENNIS! LOOK-- McMAYHEW!
HE'S STEALING THE CHARITY MONEY!
COME ON, LET'S GO GET 'EM--
NO, WAIT! HOLD ON--
"--I THINK THEY'VE GOT IT."

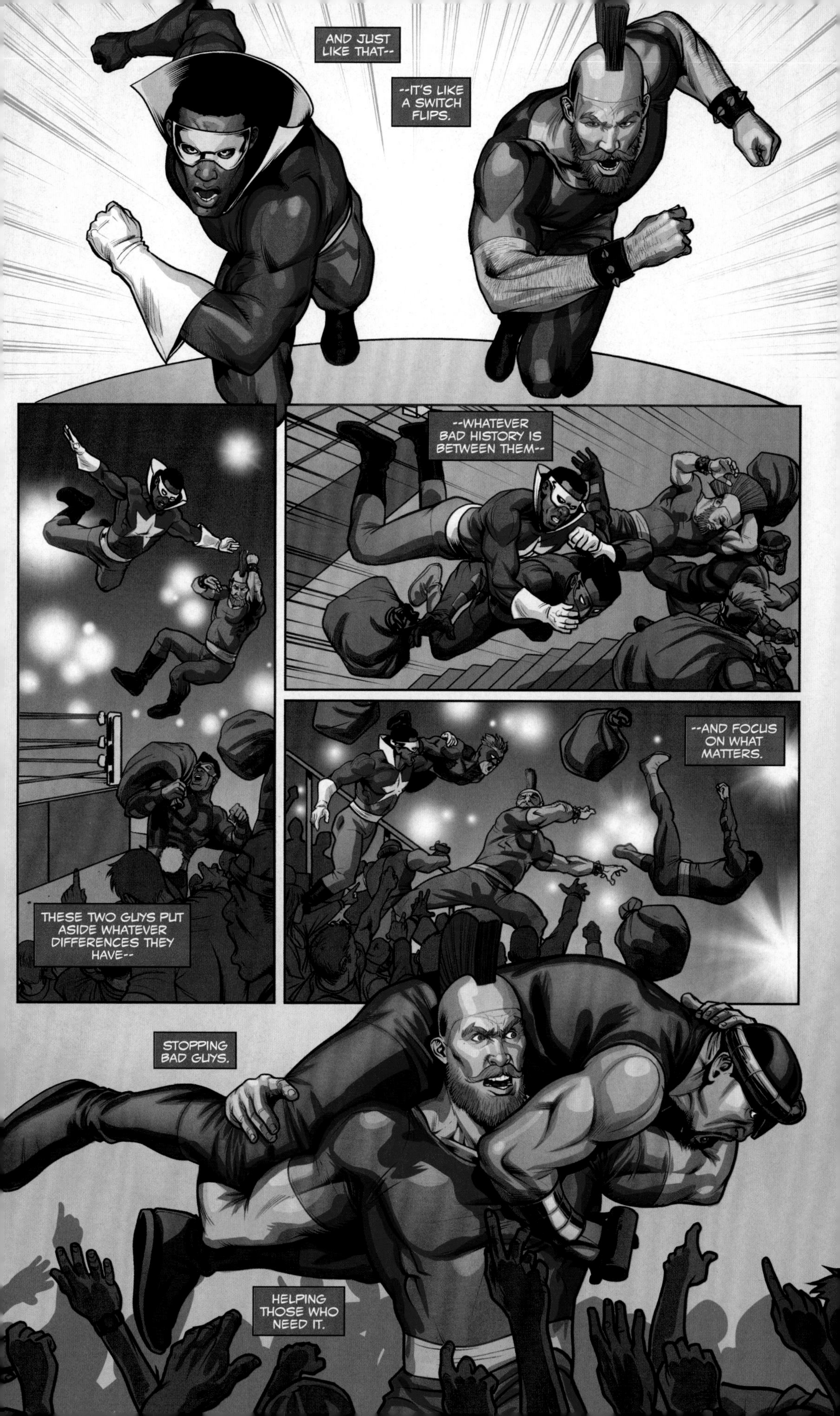
AND JUST LIKE THAT--
--IT'S LIKE A SWITCH FLIPS.
THESE TWO GUYS PUT ASIDE WHATEVER DIFFERENCES THEY HAVE--
--WHATEVER BAD HISTORY IS BETWEEN THEM--
--AND FOCUS ON WHAT MATTERS.
STOPPING BAD GUYS.
HELPING THOSE WHO NEED IT.

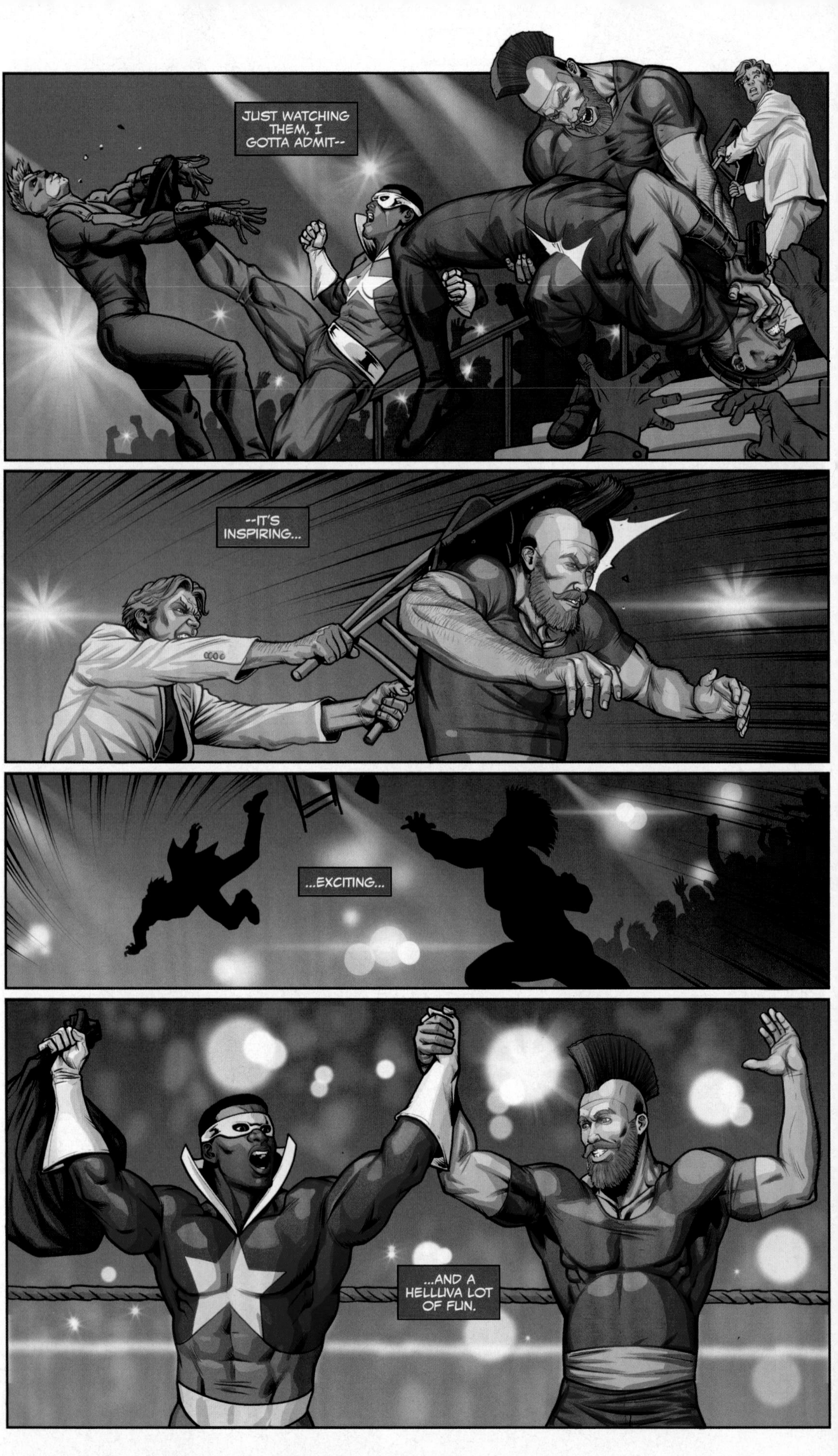
JUST WATCHING THEM, I GOTTA ADMIT--
--IT'S INSPIRING...
...EXCITING...
...AND A HELLUVA LOT OF FUN.

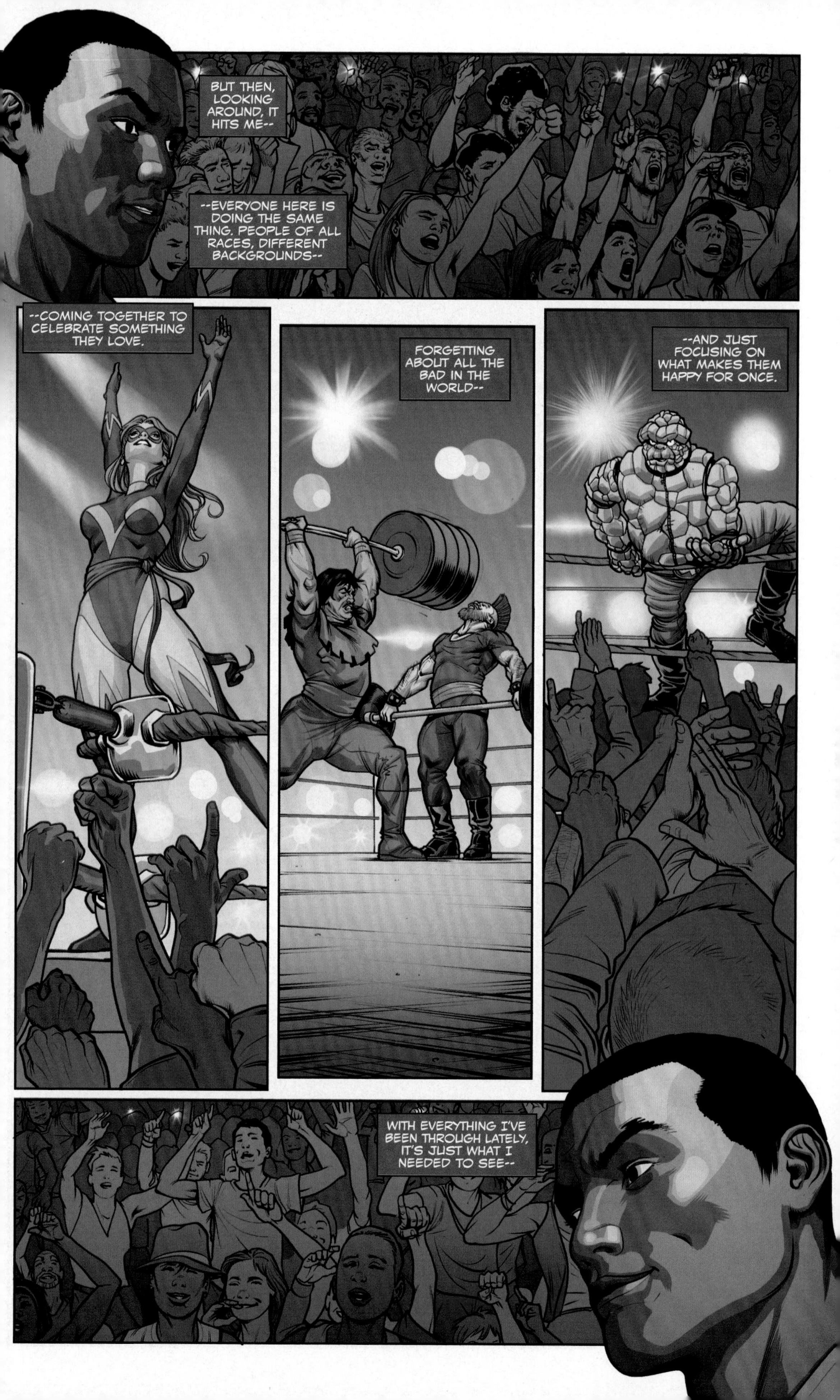
BUT THEN, LOOKING AROUND, IT HITS ME--
--EVERYONE HERE IS DOING THE SAME THING. PEOPLE OF ALL RACES, DIFFERENT BACKGROUNDS--
--COMING TOGETHER TO CELEBRATE SOMETHING THEY LOVE.
FORGETTING ABOUT ALL THE BAD IN THE WORLD--
--AND JUST FOCUSING ON WHAT MAKES THEM HAPPY FOR ONCE.
WITH EVERYTHING I'VE BEEN THROUGH LATELY, IT'S JUST WHAT I NEEDED TO SEE--

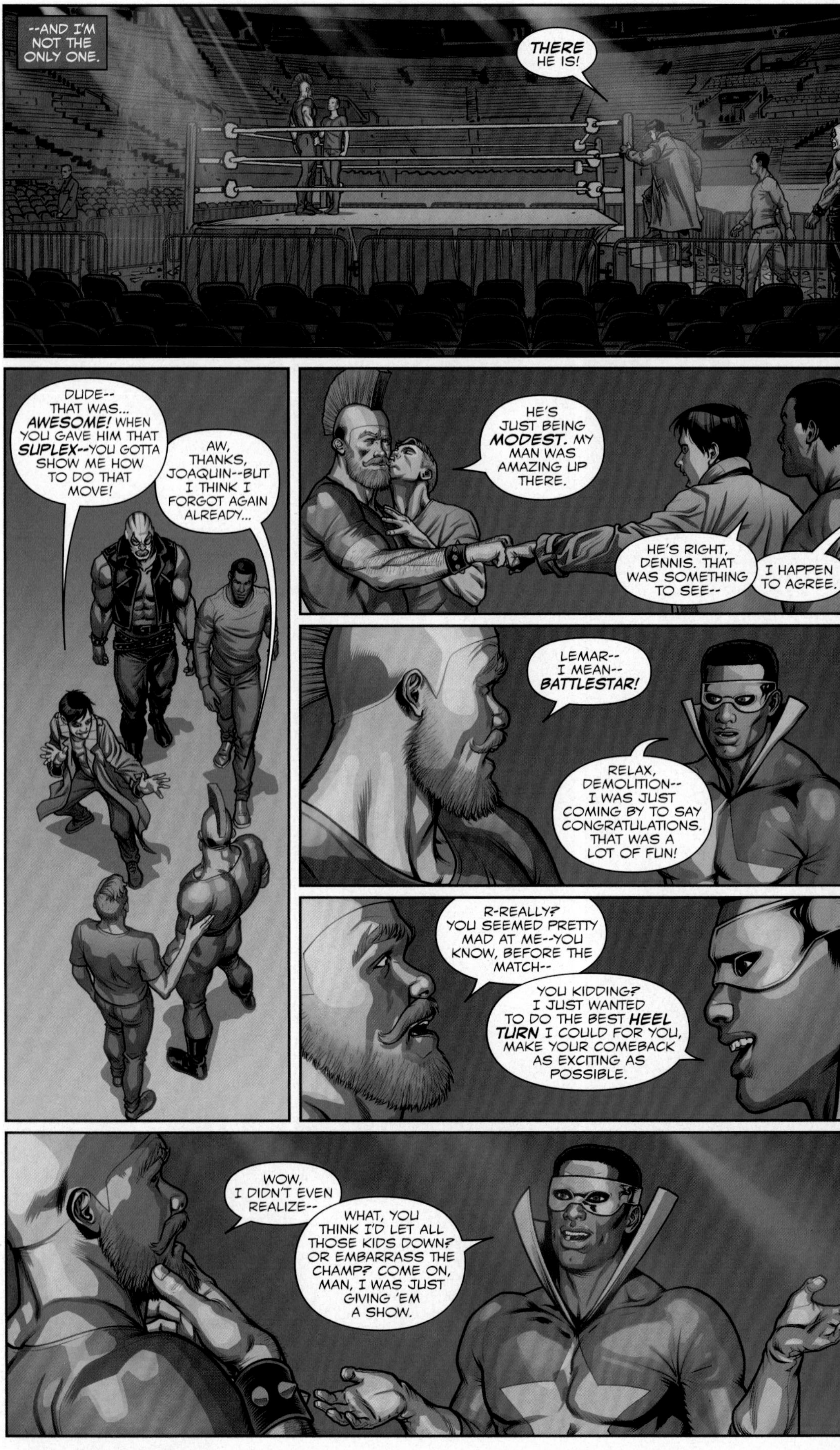

--AND I'M NOT THE ONLY ONE.
THERE HE IS!
DUDE-- THAT WAS... AWESOME! WHEN YOU GAVE HIM THAT SUPLEX--YOU GOTTA SHOW ME HOW TO DO THAT MOVE!
AW, THANKS, JOAQUIN--BUT I THINK I FORGOT AGAIN ALREADY...
HE'S JUST BEING MODEST. MY MAN WAS AMAZING UP THERE.
HE'S RIGHT, DENNIS. THAT WAS SOMETHING TO SEE--
I HAPPEN TO AGREE.
LEMAR-- I MEAN-- BATTLESTAR!
RELAX, DEMOLITION-- I WAS JUST COMING BY TO SAY CONGRATULATIONS. THAT WAS A LOT OF FUN!
R-REALLY? YOU SEEMED PRETTY MAD AT ME--YOU KNOW, BEFORE THE MATCH--
YOU KIDDING? I JUST WANTED TO DO THE BEST HEEL TURN I COULD FOR YOU, MAKE YOUR COMEBACK AS EXCITING AS POSSIBLE.
WOW, I DIDN'T EVEN REALIZE--
WHAT, YOU THINK I'D LET ALL THOSE KIDS DOWN? OR EMBARRASS THE CHAMP? COME ON, MAN, I WAS JUST GIVING 'EM A SHOW.

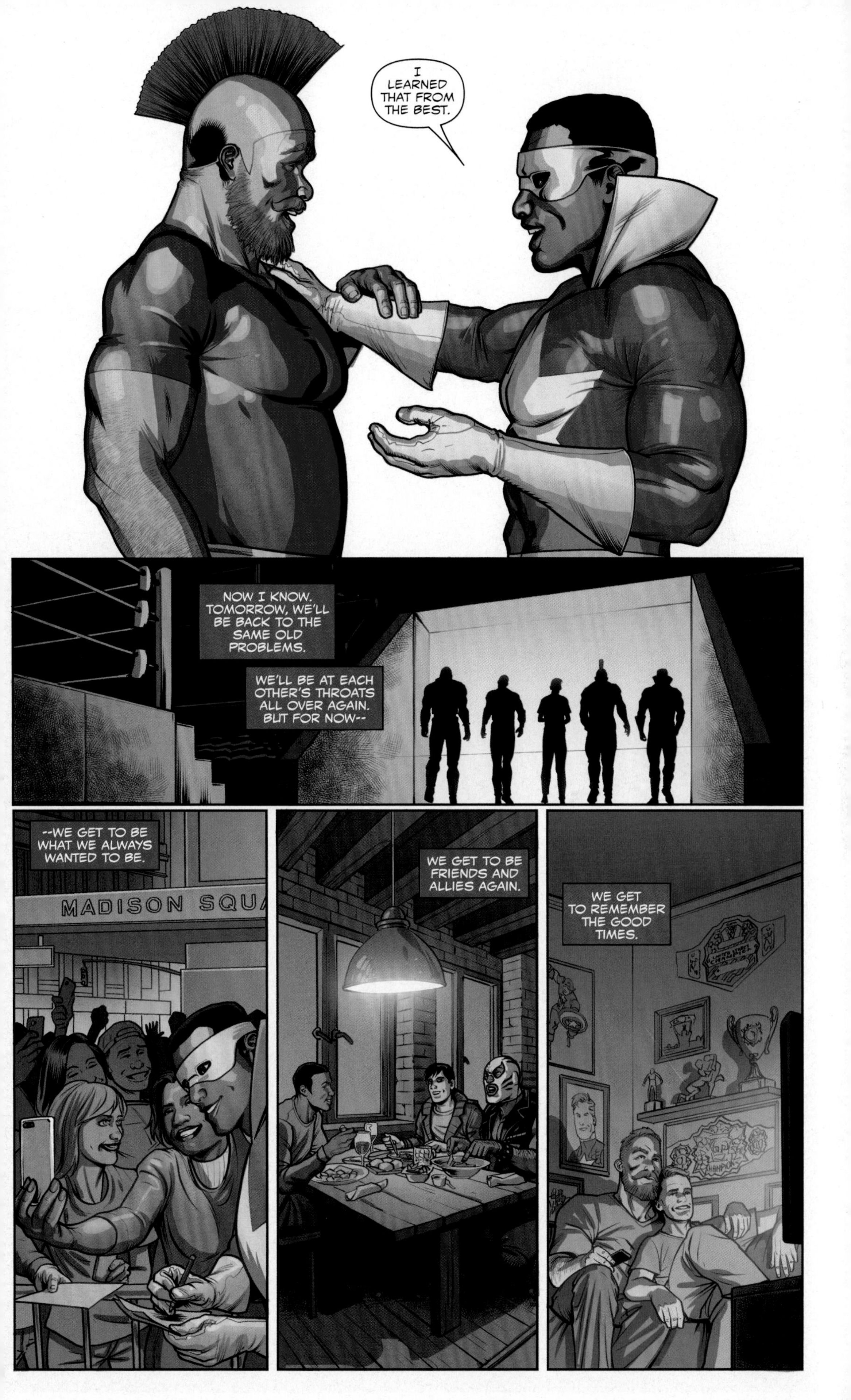

I LEARNED THAT FROM THE BEST.
NOW I KNOW. TOMORROW, WE'LL BE BACK TO THE SAME OLD PROBLEMS.
WE'LL BE AT EACH OTHER'S THROATS ALL OVER AGAIN. BUT FOR NOW--
--WE GET TO BE WHAT WE ALWAYS WANTED TO BE.
MADISON SQUA
WE GET TO BE FRIENDS AND ALLIES AGAIN.
WE GET TO REMEMBER THE GOOD TIMES.

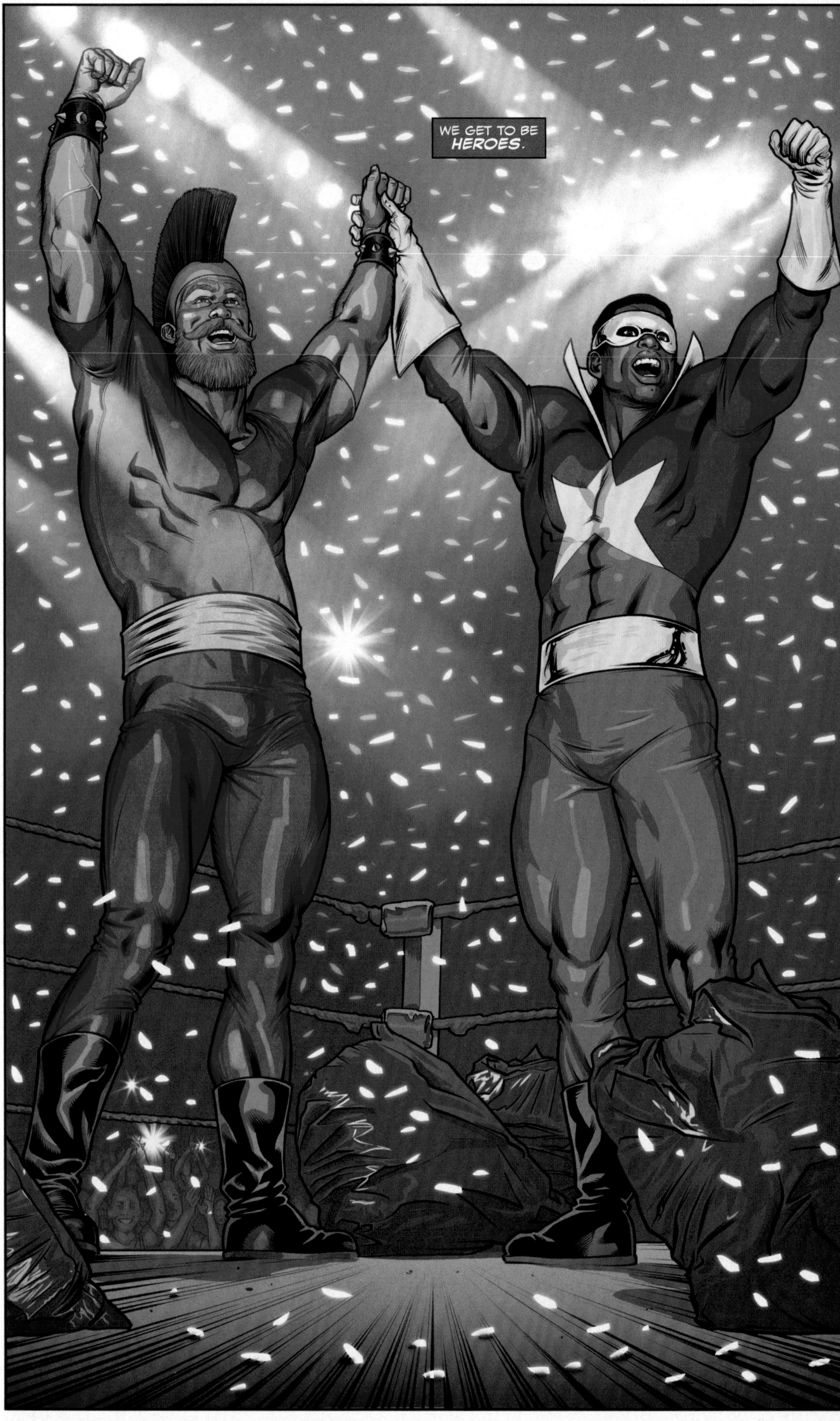
WE GET TO BE *HEROES*.

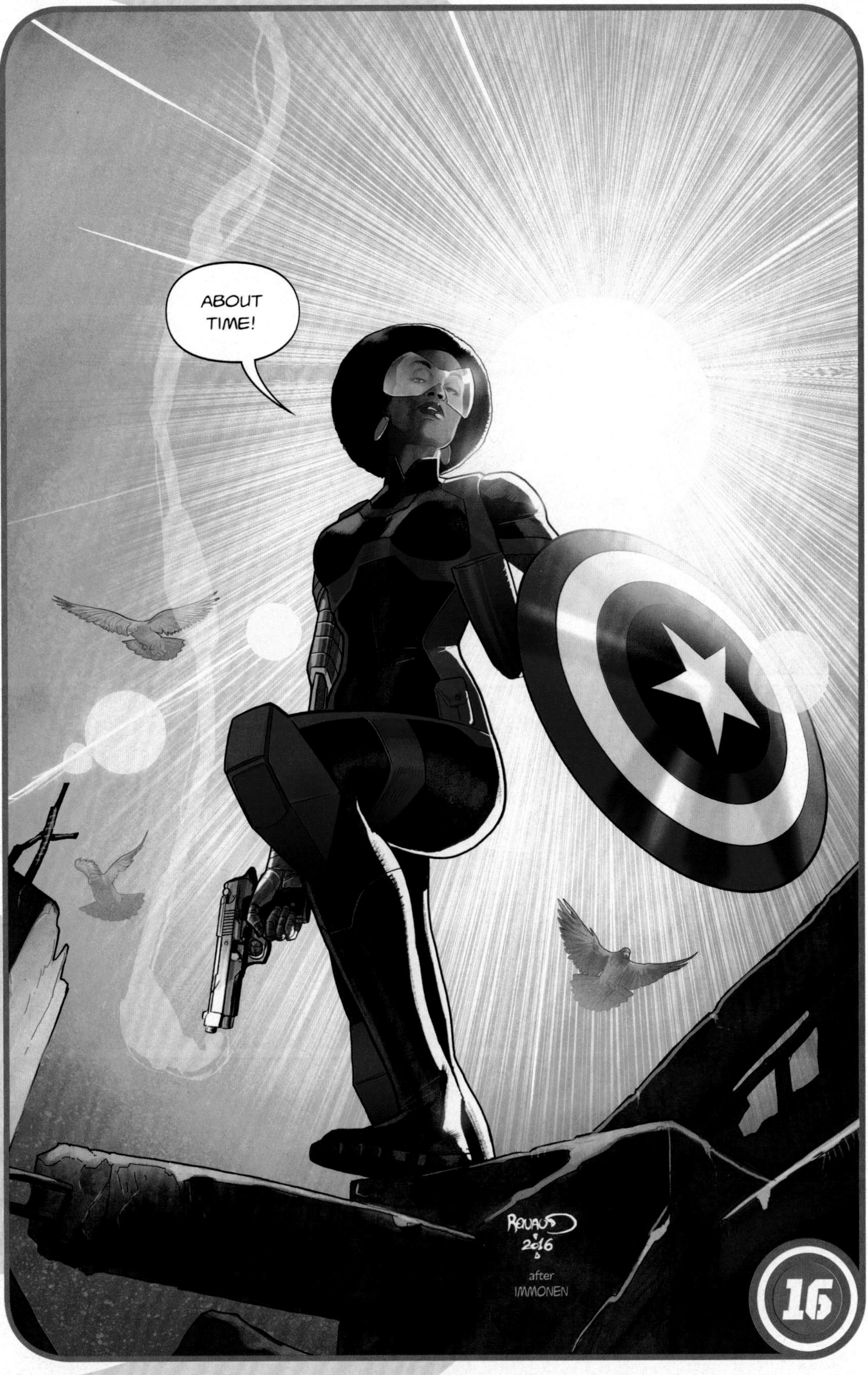
ABOUT TIME!
RENAUD 2016
after IMMONEN
16

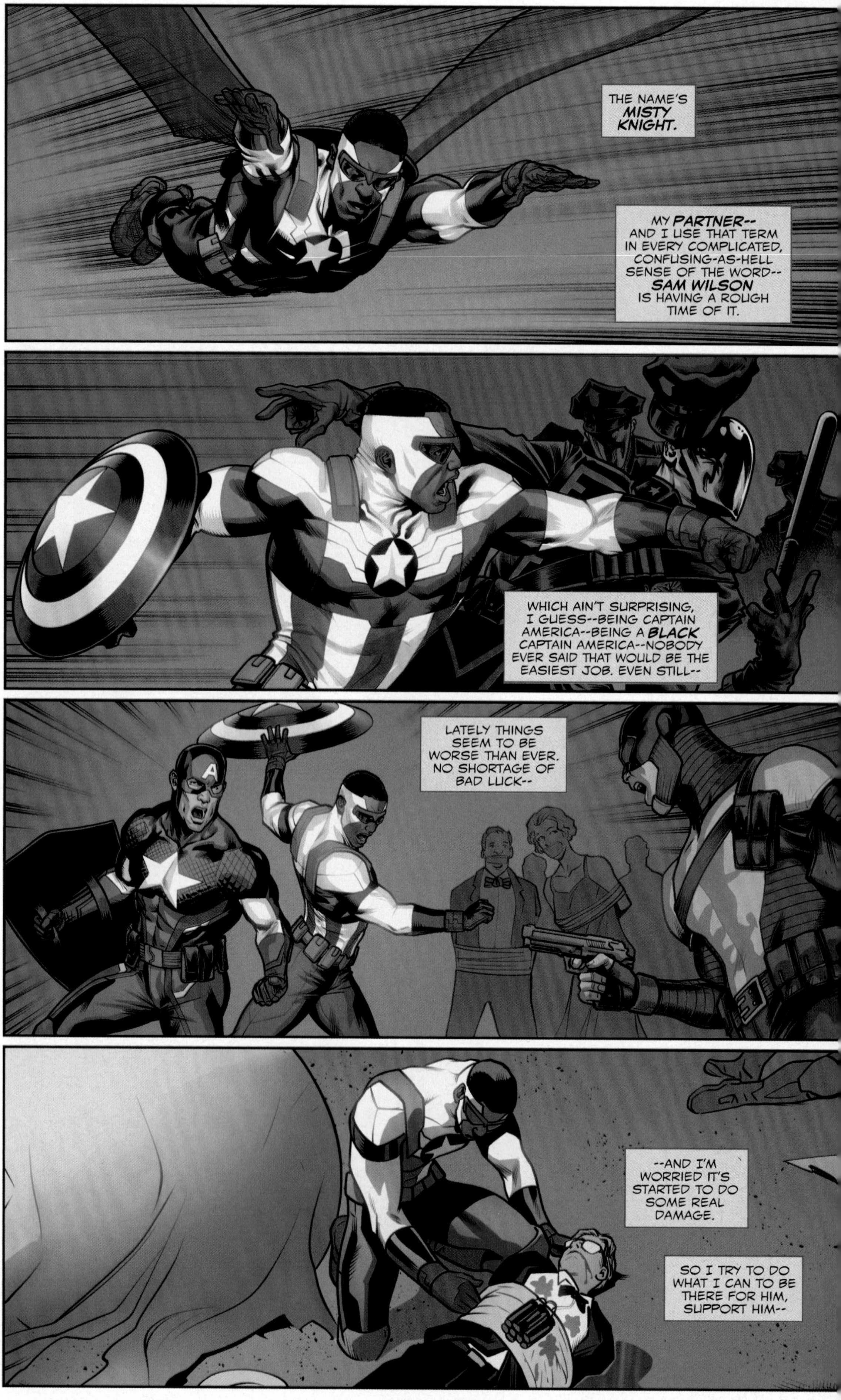
THE NAME'S MISTY KNIGHT.
MY PARTNER-- AND I USE THAT TERM IN EVERY COMPLICATED, CONFUSING-AS-HELL SENSE OF THE WORD-- SAM WILSON IS HAVING A ROUGH TIME OF IT.
WHICH AIN'T SURPRISING, I GUESS--BEING CAPTAIN AMERICA--BEING A BLACK CAPTAIN AMERICA--NOBODY EVER SAID THAT WOULD BE THE EASIEST JOB. EVEN STILL--
LATELY THINGS SEEM TO BE WORSE THAN EVER. NO SHORTAGE OF BAD LUCK--
--AND I'M WORRIED IT'S STARTED TO DO SOME REAL DAMAGE.
SO I TRY TO DO WHAT I CAN TO BE THERE FOR HIM, SUPPORT HIM--

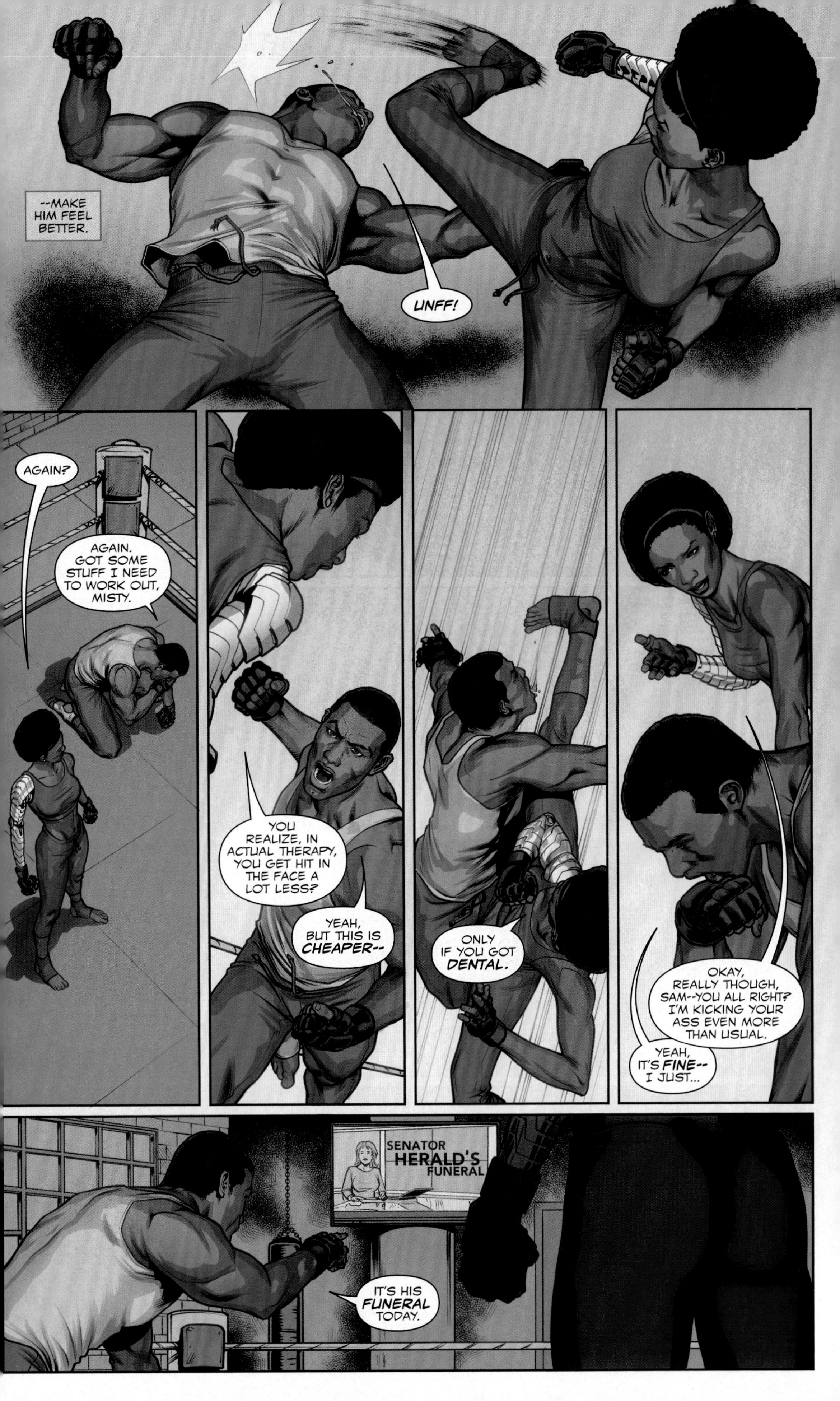
--MAKE HIM FEEL BETTER.
UNFF!
AGAIN?
AGAIN. GOT SOME STUFF I NEED TO WORK OUT, MISTY.
YOU REALIZE, IN ACTUAL THERAPY, YOU GET HIT IN THE FACE A LOT LESS?
YEAH, BUT THIS IS CHEAPER--
ONLY IF YOU GOT DENTAL.
OKAY, REALLY THOUGH, SAM--YOU ALL RIGHT? I'M KICKING YOUR ASS EVEN MORE THAN USUAL.
YEAH, IT'S FINE-- I JUST...
SENATOR HERALD'S FUNERAL
IT'S HIS FUNERAL TODAY.

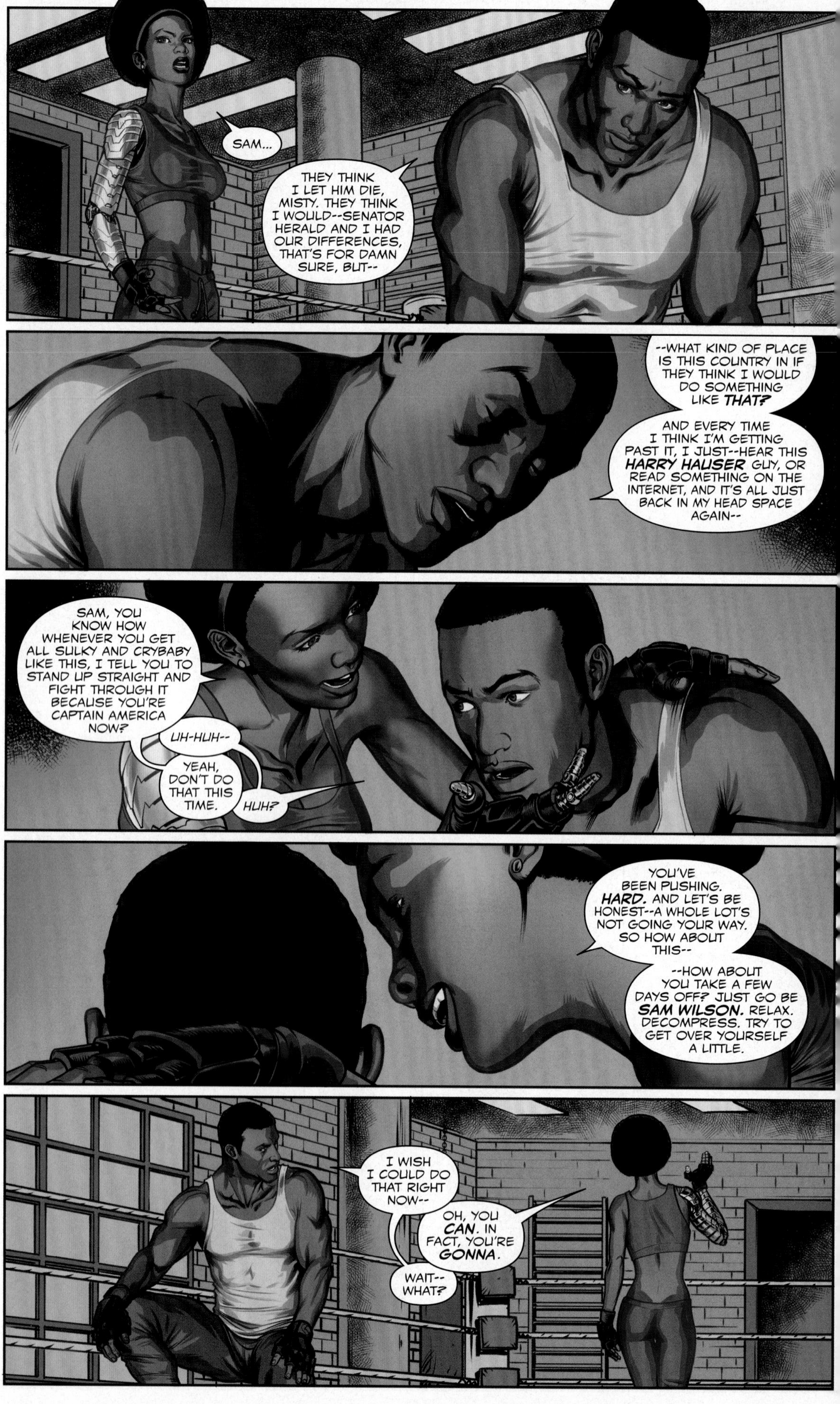
SAM...
THEY THINK I LET HIM DIE, MISTY. THEY THINK I WOULD--SENATOR HERALD AND I HAD OUR DIFFERENCES, THAT'S FOR DAMN SURE, BUT--
--WHAT KIND OF PLACE IS THIS COUNTRY IN IF THEY THINK I WOULD DO SOMETHING LIKE THAT?
AND EVERY TIME I THINK I'M GETTING PAST IT, I JUST--HEAR THIS HARRY HAUSER GUY, OR READ SOMETHING ON THE INTERNET, AND IT'S ALL JUST BACK IN MY HEAD SPACE AGAIN--
SAM, YOU KNOW HOW WHENEVER YOU GET ALL SULKY AND CRYBABY LIKE THIS, I TELL YOU TO STAND UP STRAIGHT AND FIGHT THROUGH IT BECAUSE YOU'RE CAPTAIN AMERICA NOW?
UH-HUH--
YEAH, DON'T DO THAT THIS TIME.
HUH?
YOU'VE BEEN PUSHING. HARD. AND LET'S BE HONEST--A WHOLE LOT'S NOT GOING YOUR WAY. SO HOW ABOUT THIS--
--HOW ABOUT YOU TAKE A FEW DAYS OFF? JUST GO BE SAM WILSON. RELAX. DECOMPRESS. TRY TO GET OVER YOURSELF A LITTLE.
I WISH I COULD DO THAT RIGHT NOW--
OH, YOU CAN. IN FACT, YOU'RE GONNA.
WAIT-- WHAT?

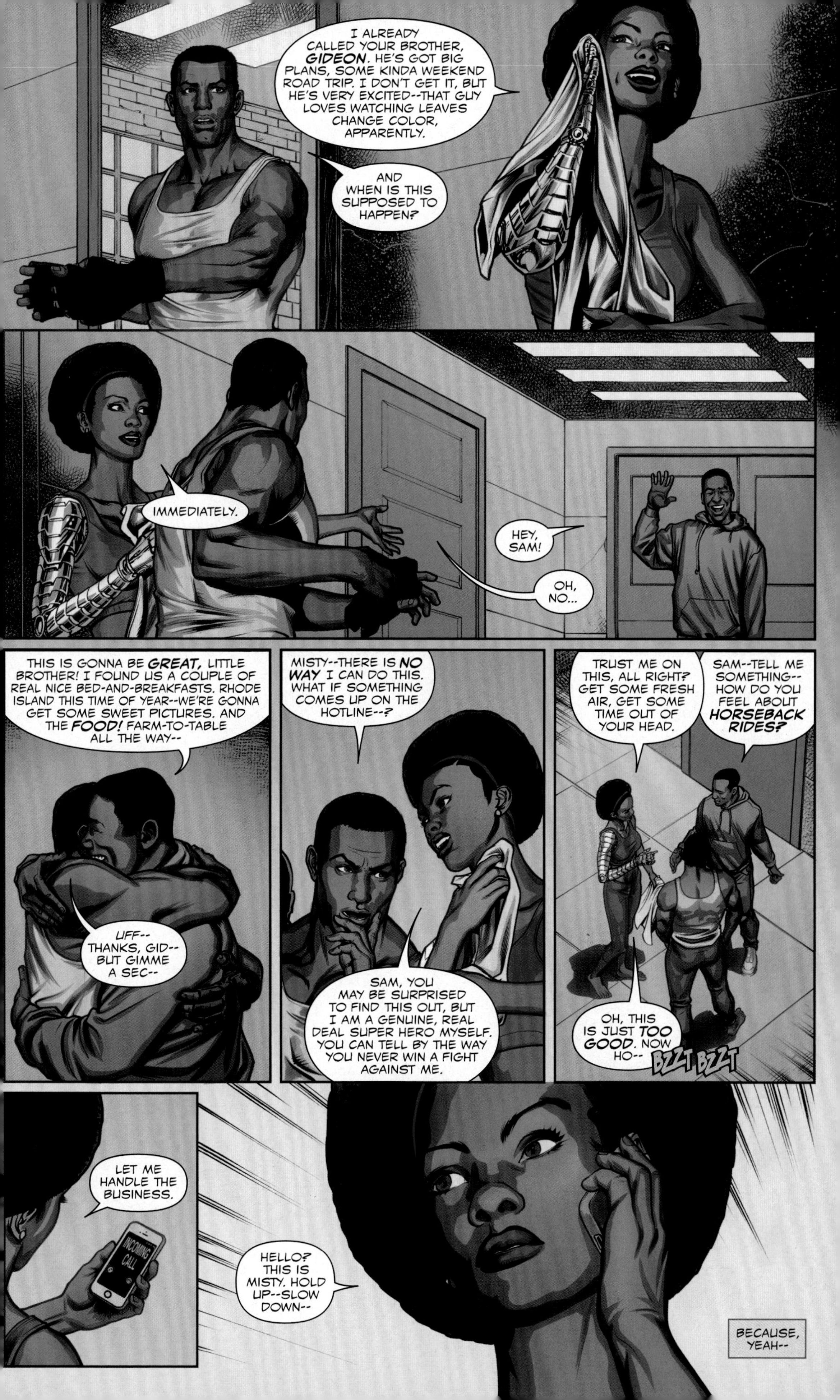
I ALREADY CALLED YOUR BROTHER, GIDEON. HE'S GOT BIG PLANS, SOME KINDA WEEKEND ROAD TRIP. I DON'T GET IT, BUT HE'S VERY EXCITED--THAT GUY LOVES WATCHING LEAVES CHANGE COLOR, APPARENTLY.
AND WHEN IS THIS SUPPOSED TO HAPPEN?
IMMEDIATELY.
HEY, SAM!
OH, NO...
THIS IS GONNA BE GREAT, LITTLE BROTHER! I FOUND US A COUPLE OF REAL NICE BED-AND-BREAKFASTS. RHODE ISLAND THIS TIME OF YEAR--WE'RE GONNA GET SOME SWEET PICTURES. AND THE FOOD! FARM-TO-TABLE ALL THE WAY--
UFF--THANKS, GID--BUT GIMME A SEC--
MISTY--THERE IS NO WAY I CAN DO THIS. WHAT IF SOMETHING COMES UP ON THE HOTLINE--?
SAM, YOU MAY BE SURPRISED TO FIND THIS OUT, BUT I AM A GENUINE, REAL DEAL SUPER HERO MYSELF. YOU CAN TELL BY THE WAY YOU NEVER WIN A FIGHT AGAINST ME.
TRUST ME ON THIS, ALL RIGHT? GET SOME FRESH AIR, GET SOME TIME OUT OF YOUR HEAD.
SAM--TELL ME SOMETHING--HOW DO YOU FEEL ABOUT HORSEBACK RIDES?
OH, THIS IS JUST TOO GOOD. NOW HO--
BZZT BZZT
LET ME HANDLE THE BUSINESS.
INCOMING CALL
HELLO? THIS IS MISTY. HOLD UP--SLOW DOWN--
BECAUSE, YEAH--

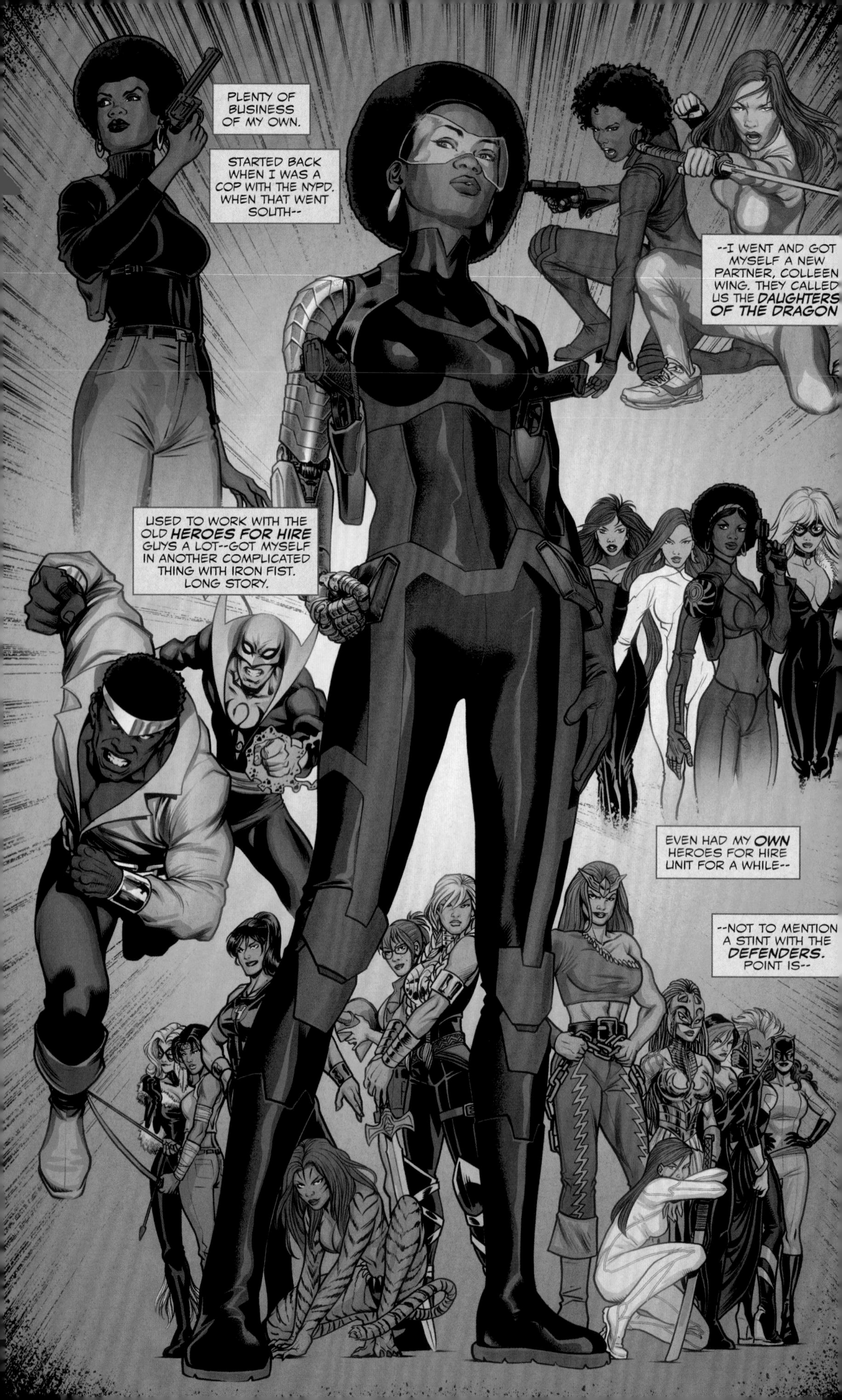
PLENTY OF BUSINESS OF MY OWN.
STARTED BACK WHEN I WAS A COP WITH THE NYPD. WHEN THAT WENT SOUTH--
--I WENT AND GOT MYSELF A NEW PARTNER, COLLEEN WING. THEY CALLED US THE DAUGHTERS OF THE DRAGON
USED TO WORK WITH THE OLD HEROES FOR HIRE GUYS A LOT--GOT MYSELF IN ANOTHER COMPLICATED THING WITH IRON FIST. LONG STORY.
EVEN HAD MY OWN HEROES FOR HIRE UNIT FOR A WHILE--
--NOT TO MENTION A STINT WITH THE DEFENDERS. POINT IS--

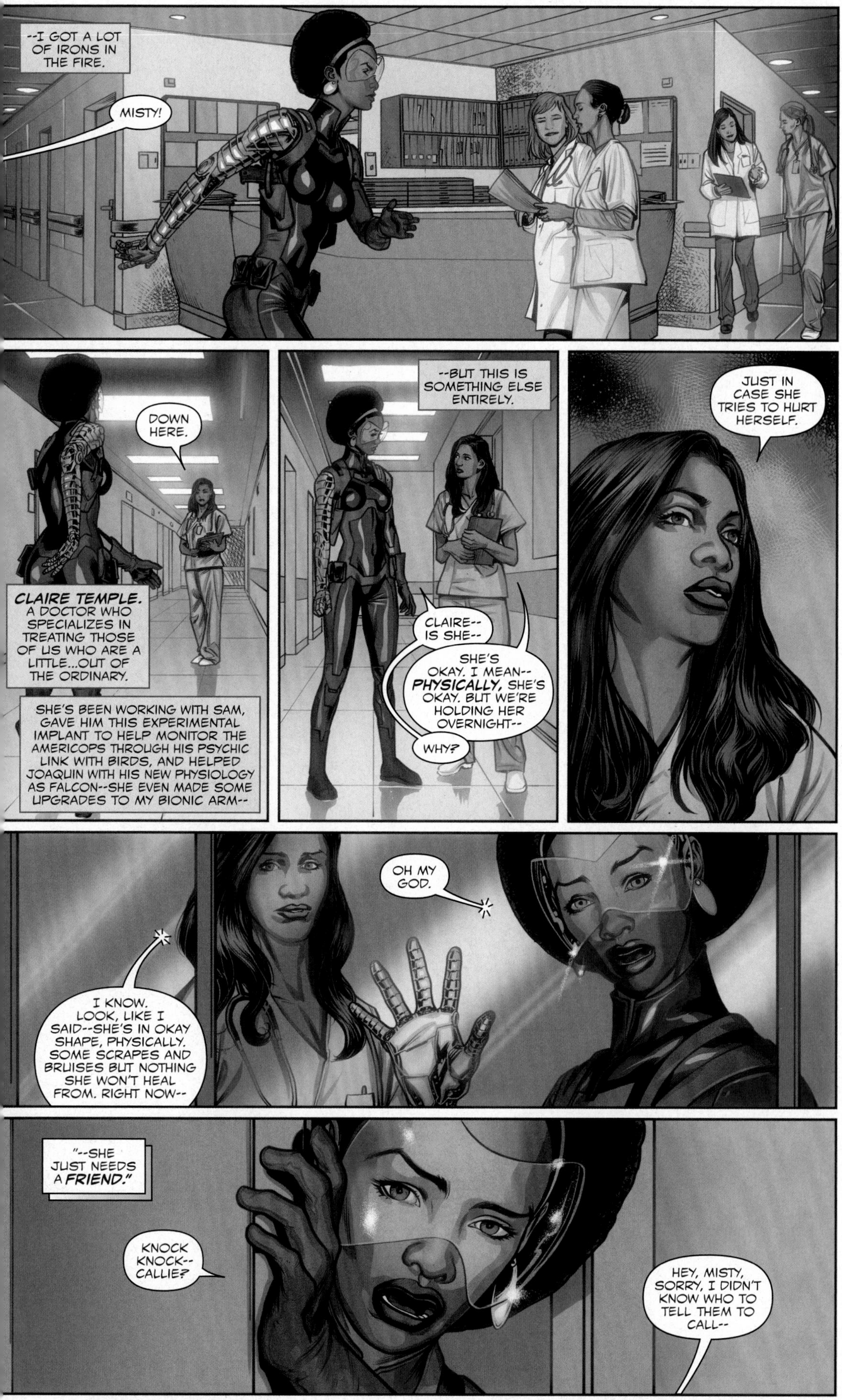
--I GOT A LOT OF IRONS IN THE FIRE.
MISTY!
DOWN HERE.
CLAIRE TEMPLE. A DOCTOR WHO SPECIALIZES IN TREATING THOSE OF US WHO ARE A LITTLE...OUT OF THE ORDINARY.
SHE'S BEEN WORKING WITH SAM, GAVE HIM THIS EXPERIMENTAL IMPLANT TO HELP MONITOR THE AMERICOPS THROUGH HIS PSYCHIC LINK WITH BIRDS, AND HELPED JOAQUIN WITH HIS NEW PHYSIOLOGY AS FALCON--SHE EVEN MADE SOME UPGRADES TO MY BIONIC ARM--
--BUT THIS IS SOMETHING ELSE ENTIRELY.
CLAIRE-- IS SHE--
SHE'S OKAY. I MEAN-- PHYSICALLY, SHE'S OKAY. BUT WE'RE HOLDING HER OVERNIGHT--
WHY?
JUST IN CASE SHE TRIES TO HURT HERSELF.
OH MY GOD.
I KNOW. LOOK, LIKE I SAID--SHE'S IN OKAY SHAPE, PHYSICALLY. SOME SCRAPES AND BRUISES BUT NOTHING SHE WON'T HEAL FROM. RIGHT NOW--
"--SHE JUST NEEDS A FRIEND."
KNOCK KNOCK-- CALLIE?
HEY, MISTY, SORRY, I DIDN'T KNOW WHO TO TELL THEM TO CALL--

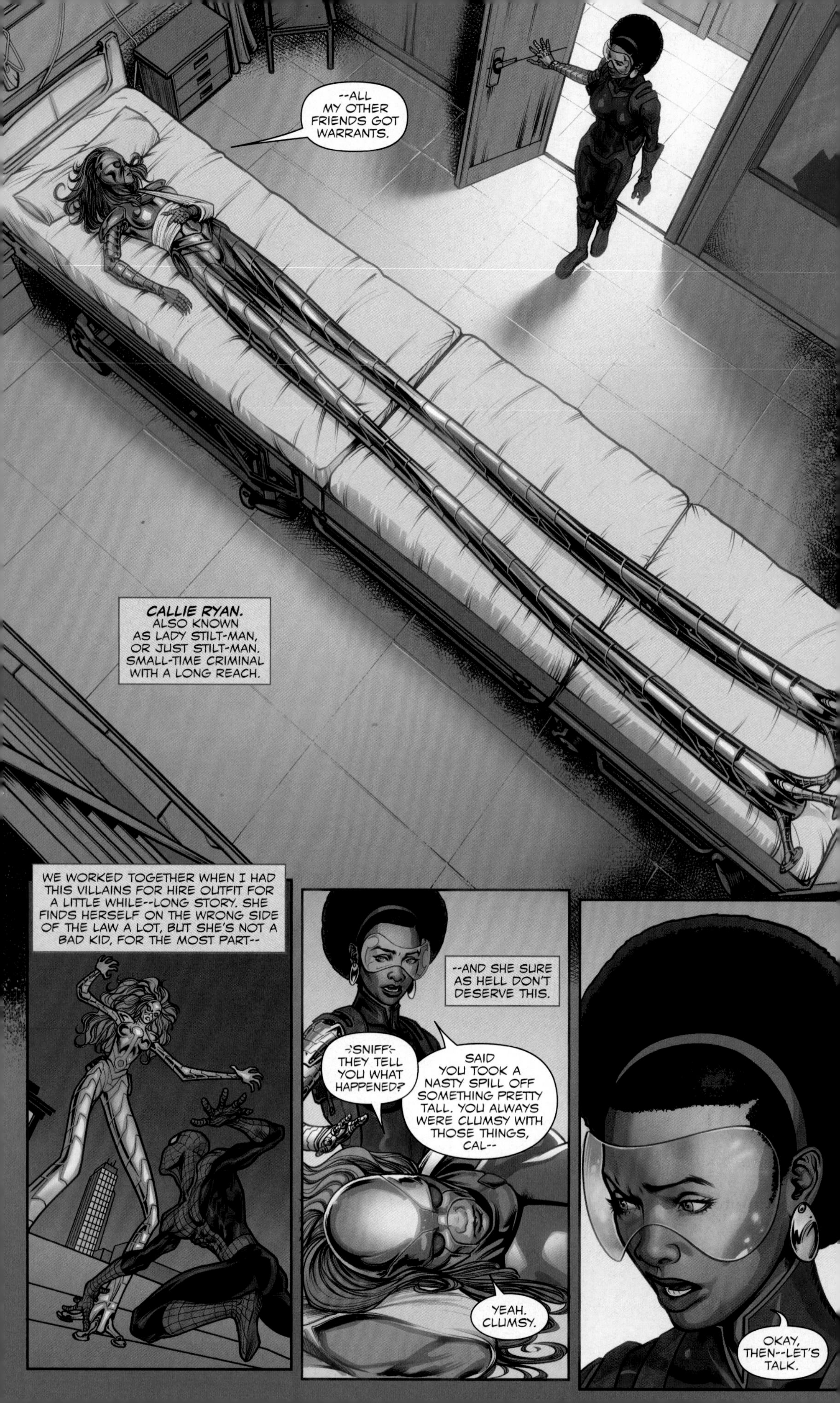
--ALL MY OTHER FRIENDS GOT WARRANTS.
CALLIE RYAN. ALSO KNOWN AS LADY STILT-MAN, OR JUST STILT-MAN. SMALL-TIME CRIMINAL WITH A LONG REACH.
WE WORKED TOGETHER WHEN I HAD THIS VILLAINS FOR HIRE OUTFIT FOR A LITTLE WHILE--LONG STORY. SHE FINDS HERSELF ON THE WRONG SIDE OF THE LAW A LOT, BUT SHE'S NOT A BAD KID, FOR THE MOST PART--
--AND SHE SURE AS HELL DON'T DESERVE THIS.
-SNIFF- THEY TELL YOU WHAT HAPPENED?
SAID YOU TOOK A NASTY SPILL OFF SOMETHING PRETTY TALL. YOU ALWAYS WERE CLUMSY WITH THOSE THINGS, CAL--
YEAH. CLUMSY.
OKAY, THEN--LET'S TALK.

DID YOU SEE IT?

SEE WHAT?

THE VIDEO.

SORRY, I DON'T KNOW WHAT YOU MEAN.

THERE'S A VIDEO. OF ME. AND SOME GUY.

OH, CALLIE...

NO-- YOU DON'T UNDERSTAND--

IT WASN'T ME! I MEAN-- IT LOOKS LIKE ME, AND IT SOUNDS LIKE ME--BUT I WOULD NEVER--

AND THE GUY--I HAVE NO IDEA WHO HE IS, MISTY! I SWEAR TO GOD!

IT'S OKAY, HEY, IT'S OKAY--

--I BELIEVE YOU.

YEAH, WELL-- NOBODY ELSE DOES. MY FAMILY SAW IT, MISTY! DO YOU HAVE ANY IDEA HOW HUMILIATING THAT IS?! EVERY TIME I PUT THIS COSTUME ON, I SEE PEOPLE POINTING UP AT ME, LAUGHING--

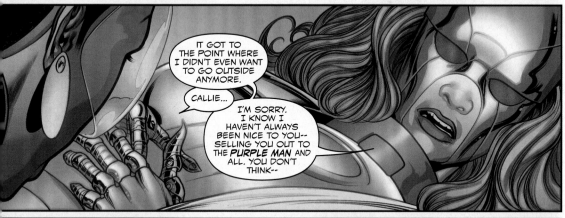

IT GOT TO THE POINT WHERE I DIDN'T EVEN WANT TO GO OUTSIDE ANYMORE.

CALLIE...

I'M SORRY. I KNOW I HAVEN'T ALWAYS BEEN NICE TO YOU-- SELLING YOU OUT TO THE PURPLE MAN AND ALL. YOU DON'T THINK--

YOU DON'T THINK HE HAS ANYTHING TO DO WITH THIS, DO YOU?

I DON'T KNOW, BABY GIRL-- BUT TRUST ME--MISTY KNIGHT IS GONNA FIND OUT. AND WHOEVER IT IS--

"--THEY ARE GONNA HAVE *HELL TO PAY*."

AND ACTUALLY, THERE'S BEEN A *LOT* OF THIS GOING AROUND. YOUR BIGGEST FEAR IS THE CREEPS WITH MIND-CONTROL POWERS. IT'S REAL. IT HAPPENS. BUT THIS SEEMS LIKE SOMETHING ELSE.

FEMALE SUPER HEROES AND VILLAINS GETTING CAUGHT ON TAPE OR IN PICTURES IN... LESS-THAN-FLATTERING POSITIONS--

SEXY SUPER HEROINE
CAUGHT IN TAWDRY TAPE

Heavybreatherharry: Whoa

EXOTIC ALIEN PRINCESS FOOLS AROUND

Grossguy1487: Link to full

SULTRY VILLAINESS BARES ALL IN REVEALING PHOTOS

The_Canadian_Leerer: Fav'd

HOT YOUNG SIDEKICK FINALLY SHOWS ALL

LEAKED VIDEO OF INHUMAN HOTTIE

OsbornWasRight: There's gotta be more out there

THE WOMEN IN QUESTION DENY THE AUTHENTICITY OF THE FOOTAGE, BUT NOBODY BELIEVES THEM BECAUSE-- WELL, HELL, DOES *ANYONE EVER* BELIEVE WOMEN WHEN IT COMES TO THIS STUFF?

BUT HERE'S THE THING: IF ANYONE HAD BOTHERED WITH A LITTLE DETECTIVE WORK-- BECAUSE, YES, THAT'S WHAT *I USED* TO DO-- THE EVIDENCE BACKS THEM UP.

LOOKING AT THE TIMESTAMPS ON SOME OF THESE VIDEOS, THE WOMEN IN QUESTION WERE SOMETIMES OFF-WORLD, IN PRISON, OR EVEN DEAD. SO INSTEAD OF WONDERING WHERE THE VICTIMS FALL IN ALL THIS--

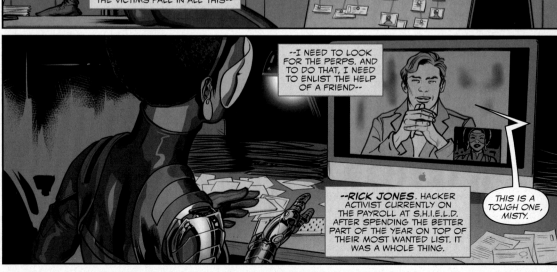

--I NEED TO LOOK FOR THE PERPS. AND TO DO THAT, I NEED TO ENLIST THE HELP OF A FRIEND--

--*RICK JONES.* HACKER ACTIVIST CURRENTLY ON THE PAYROLL AT S.H.I.E.L.D. AFTER SPENDING THE BETTER PART OF THE YEAR ON TOP OF THEIR MOST WANTED LIST. IT WAS A WHOLE THING.

THIS IS A TOUGH ONE, MISTY.

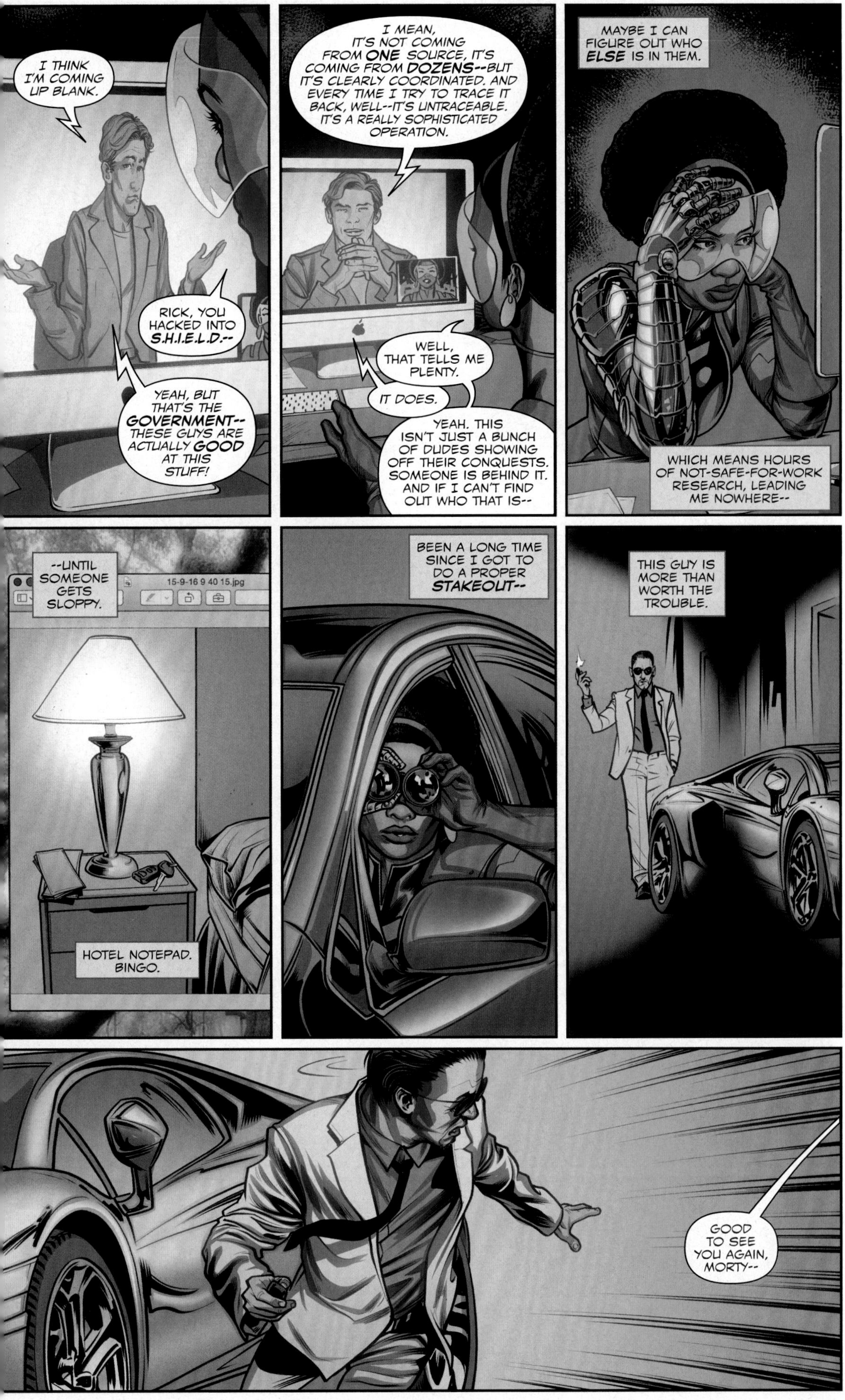
I THINK I'M COMING UP BLANK.
RICK, YOU HACKED INTO S.H.I.E.L.D.--
YEAH, BUT THAT'S THE GOVERNMENT-- THESE GUYS ARE ACTUALLY GOOD AT THIS STUFF!
I MEAN, IT'S NOT COMING FROM ONE SOURCE, IT'S COMING FROM DOZENS--BUT IT'S CLEARLY COORDINATED. AND EVERY TIME I TRY TO TRACE IT BACK, WELL--IT'S UNTRACEABLE. IT'S A REALLY SOPHISTICATED OPERATION.
WELL, THAT TELLS ME PLENTY.
IT DOES.
YEAH. THIS ISN'T JUST A BUNCH OF DUDES SHOWING OFF THEIR CONQUESTS. SOMEONE IS BEHIND IT. AND IF I CAN'T FIND OUT WHO THAT IS--
MAYBE I CAN FIGURE OUT WHO ELSE IS IN THEM.
WHICH MEANS HOURS OF NOT-SAFE-FOR-WORK RESEARCH, LEADING ME NOWHERE--
--UNTIL SOMEONE GETS SLOPPY.
15-9-16 9 40 15.jpg
HOTEL NOTEPAD. BINGO.
BEEN A LONG TIME SINCE I GOT TO DO A PROPER STAKEOUT--
THIS GUY IS MORE THAN WORTH THE TROUBLE.
GOOD TO SEE YOU AGAIN, MORTY--

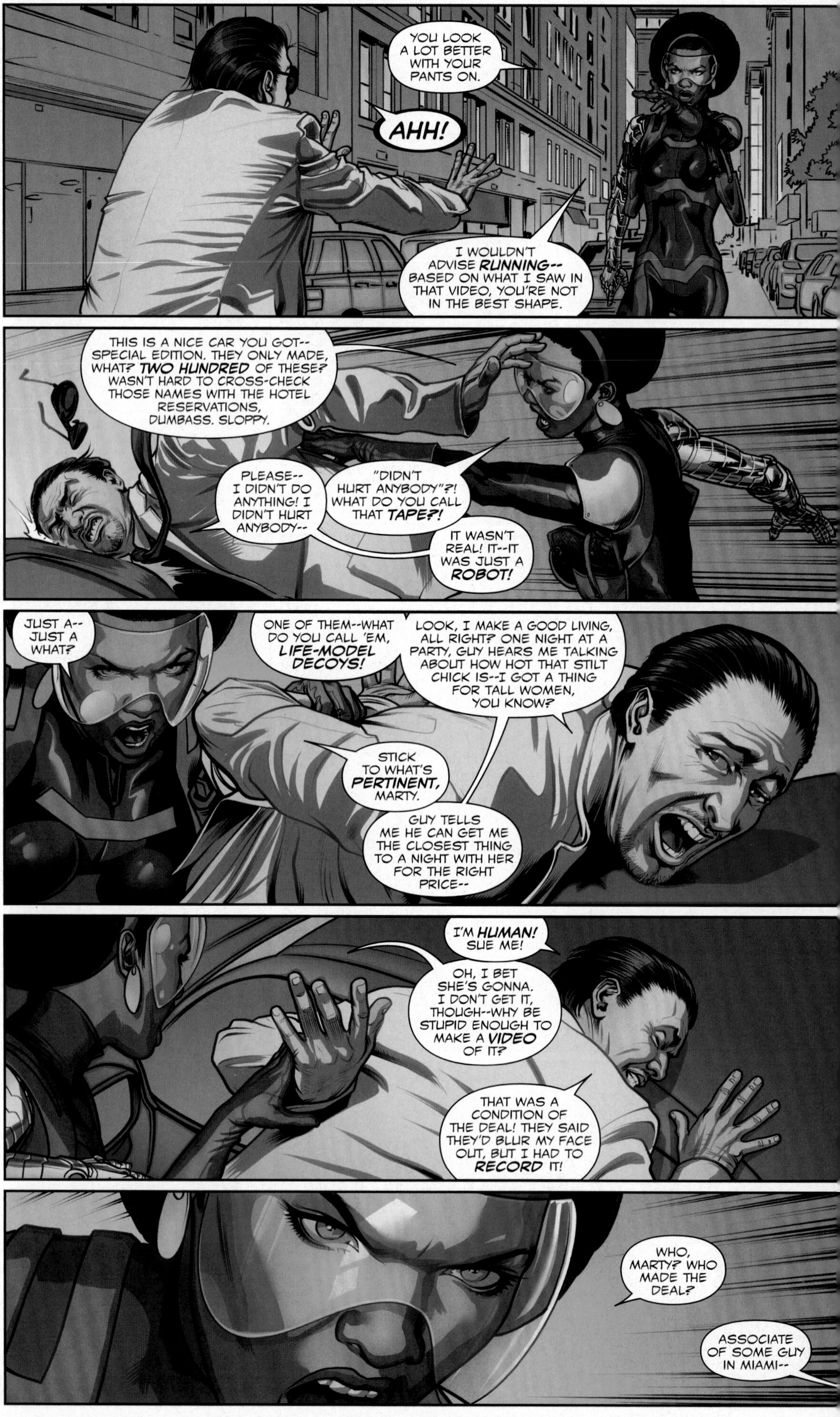
YOU LOOK A LOT BETTER WITH YOUR PANTS ON.
AHH!
I WOULDN'T ADVISE RUNNING-- BASED ON WHAT I SAW IN THAT VIDEO, YOU'RE NOT IN THE BEST SHAPE.
THIS IS A NICE CAR YOU GOT-- SPECIAL EDITION. THEY ONLY MADE, WHAT? TWO HUNDRED OF THESE? WASN'T HARD TO CROSS-CHECK THOSE NAMES WITH THE HOTEL RESERVATIONS, DUMBASS. SLOPPY.
PLEASE-- I DIDN'T DO ANYTHING! I DIDN'T HURT ANYBODY--
"DIDN'T HURT ANYBODY"?! WHAT DO YOU CALL THAT TAPE?!
IT WASN'T REAL! IT--IT WAS JUST A ROBOT!
JUST A-- JUST A WHAT?
ONE OF THEM--WHAT DO YOU CALL 'EM, LIFE-MODEL DECOYS!
LOOK, I MAKE A GOOD LIVING, ALL RIGHT? ONE NIGHT AT A PARTY, GUY HEARS ME TALKING ABOUT HOW HOT THAT STILT CHICK IS--I GOT A THING FOR TALL WOMEN, YOU KNOW?
STICK TO WHAT'S PERTINENT, MARTY.
GUY TELLS ME HE CAN GET ME THE CLOSEST THING TO A NIGHT WITH HER FOR THE RIGHT PRICE--
I'M HUMAN! SUE ME!
OH, I BET SHE'S GONNA. I DON'T GET IT, THOUGH--WHY BE STUPID ENOUGH TO MAKE A VIDEO OF IT?
THAT WAS A CONDITION OF THE DEAL! THEY SAID THEY'D BLUR MY FACE OUT, BUT I HAD TO RECORD IT!
WHO, MARTY? WHO MADE THE DEAL?
ASSOCIATE OF SOME GUY IN MIAMI--

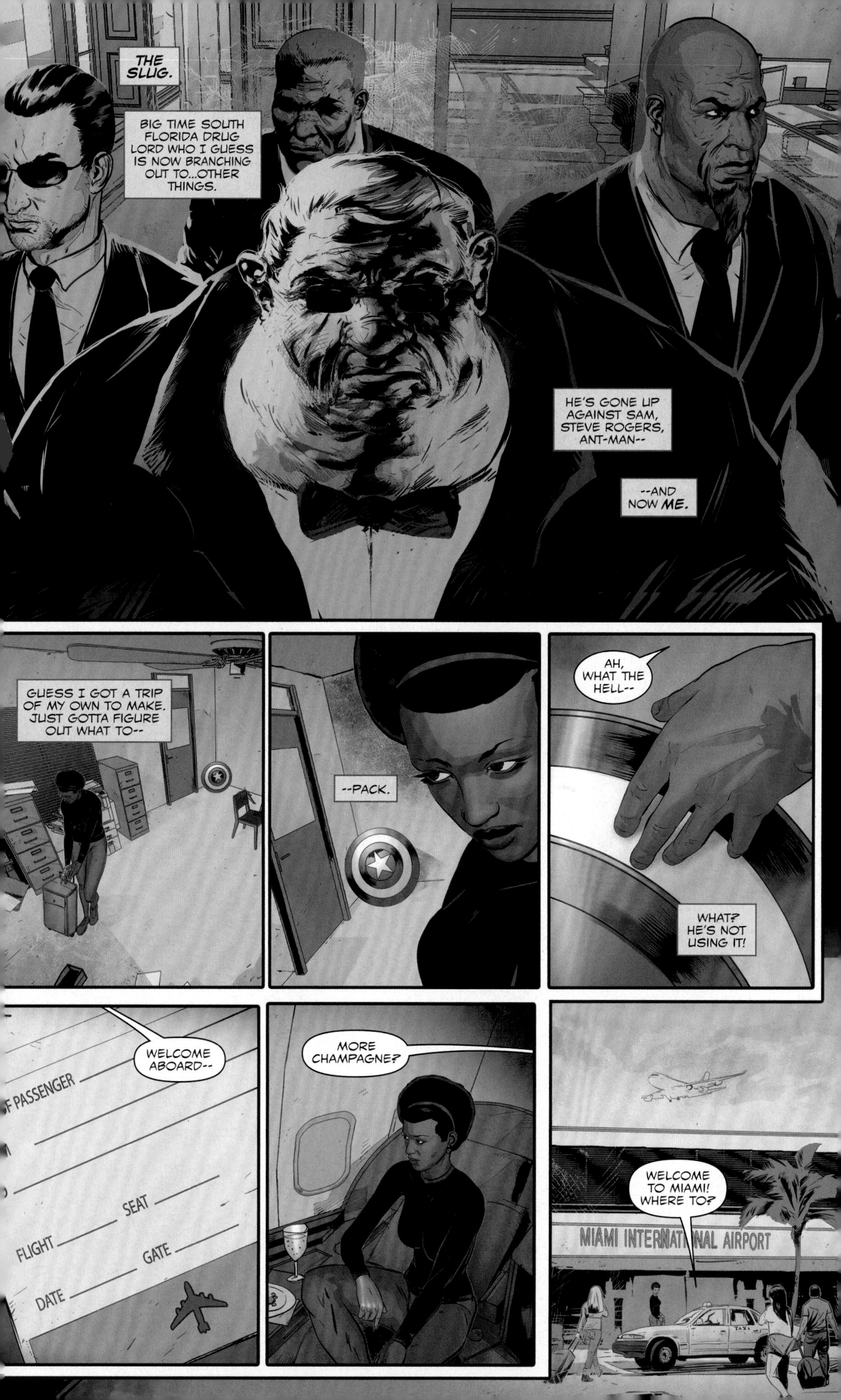

THE SLUG.
BIG TIME SOUTH FLORIDA DRUG LORD WHO I GUESS IS NOW BRANCHING OUT TO...OTHER THINGS.
HE'S GONE UP AGAINST SAM, STEVE ROGERS, ANT-MAN--
--AND NOW ME.
GUESS I GOT A TRIP OF MY OWN TO MAKE. JUST GOTTA FIGURE OUT WHAT TO--
--PACK.
AH, WHAT THE HELL--
WHAT? HE'S NOT USING IT!
WELCOME ABOARD--
F PASSENGER
SEAT
FLIGHT
GATE
DATE
MORE CHAMPAGNE?
WELCOME TO MIAMI! WHERE TO?
MIAMI INTERNATIONAL AIRPORT
TAXI

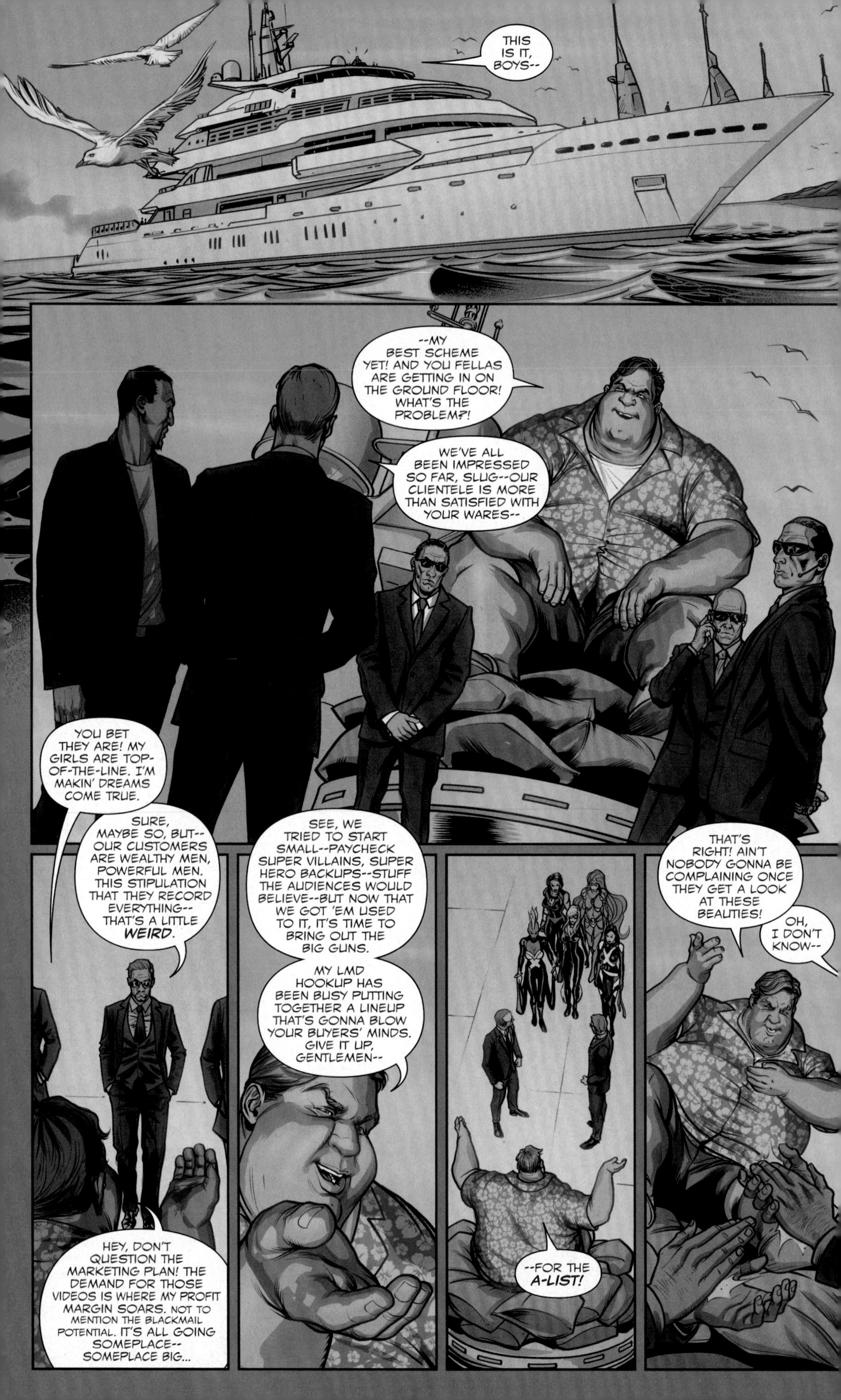

THIS IS IT, BOYS--
--MY BEST SCHEME YET! AND YOU FELLAS ARE GETTING IN ON THE GROUND FLOOR! WHAT'S THE PROBLEM?!
WE'VE ALL BEEN IMPRESSED SO FAR, SLUG--OUR CLIENTELE IS MORE THAN SATISFIED WITH YOUR WARES--
YOU BET THEY ARE! MY GIRLS ARE TOP-OF-THE-LINE. I'M MAKIN' DREAMS COME TRUE.
SURE, MAYBE SO, BUT--OUR CUSTOMERS ARE WEALTHY MEN, POWERFUL MEN. THIS STIPULATION THAT THEY RECORD EVERYTHING--THAT'S A LITTLE WEIRD.
HEY, DON'T QUESTION THE MARKETING PLAN! THE DEMAND FOR THOSE VIDEOS IS WHERE MY PROFIT MARGIN SOARS. NOT TO MENTION THE BLACKMAIL POTENTIAL. IT'S ALL GOING SOMEPLACE--SOMEPLACE BIG...
SEE, WE TRIED TO START SMALL--PAYCHECK SUPER VILLAINS, SUPER HERO BACKUPS--STUFF THE AUDIENCES WOULD BELIEVE--BUT NOW THAT WE GOT 'EM USED TO IT, IT'S TIME TO BRING OUT THE BIG GUNS.
MY LMD HOOKUP HAS BEEN BUSY PUTTING TOGETHER A LINEUP THAT'S GONNA BLOW YOUR BUYERS' MINDS. GIVE IT UP, GENTLEMEN--
--FOR THE A-LIST!
THAT'S RIGHT! AIN'T NOBODY GONNA BE COMPLAINING ONCE THEY GET A LOOK AT THESE BEAUTIES!
OH, I DON'T KNOW--

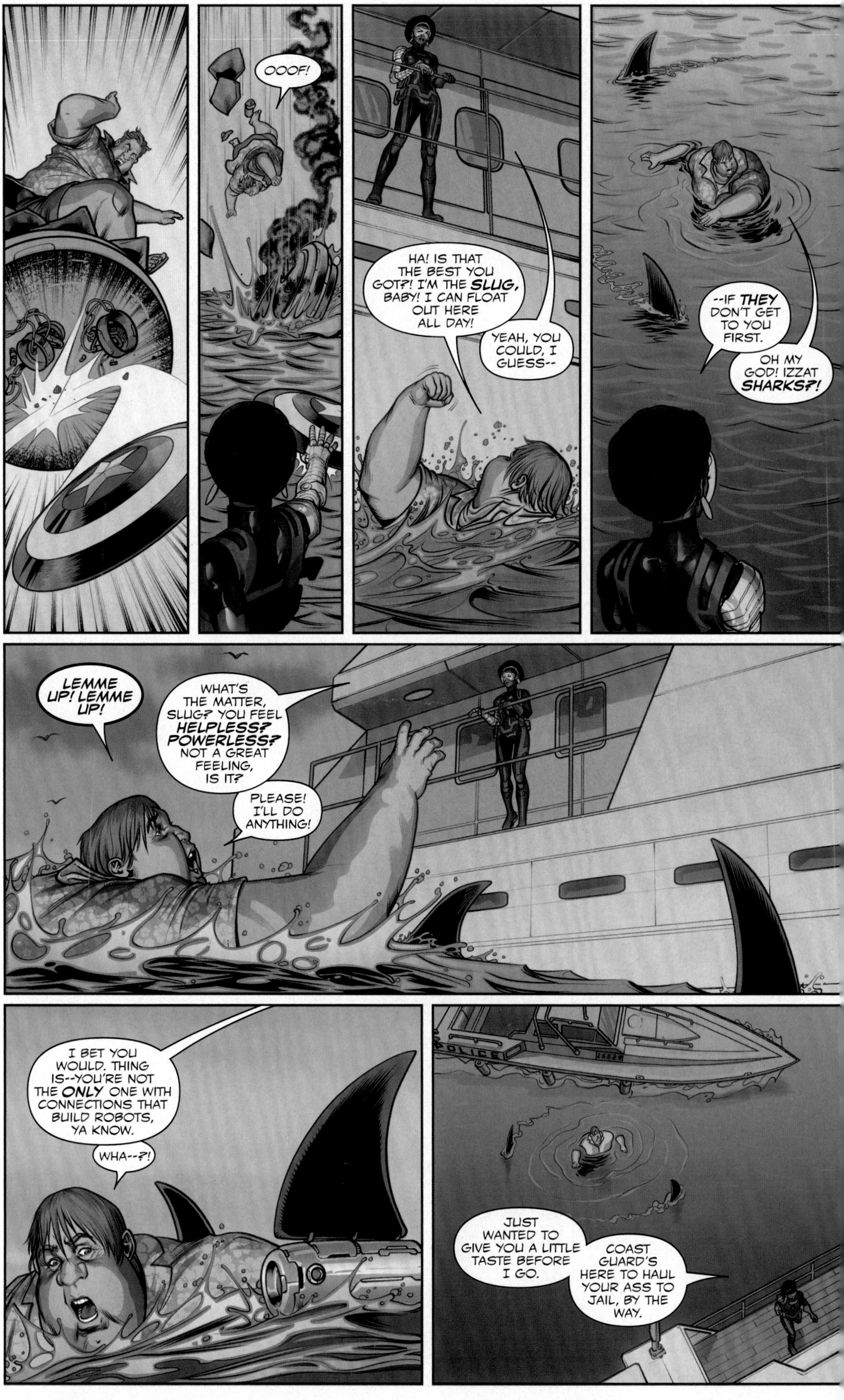
OOOF!
HA! IS THAT THE BEST YOU GOT?! I'M THE SLUG, BABY! I CAN FLOAT OUT HERE ALL DAY!
YEAH, YOU COULD, I GUESS--
--IF THEY DON'T GET TO YOU FIRST.
OH MY GOD! IZZAT SHARKS?!
LEMME UP! LEMME UP!
WHAT'S THE MATTER, SLUG? YOU FEEL HELPLESS? POWERLESS? NOT A GREAT FEELING, IS IT?
PLEASE! I'LL DO ANYTHING!
I BET YOU WOULD. THING IS--YOU'RE NOT THE ONLY ONE WITH CONNECTIONS THAT BUILD ROBOTS, YA KNOW.
WHA--?!
JUST WANTED TO GIVE YOU A LITTLE TASTE BEFORE I GO.
COAST GUARD'S HERE TO HAUL YOUR ASS TO JAIL, BY THE WAY.

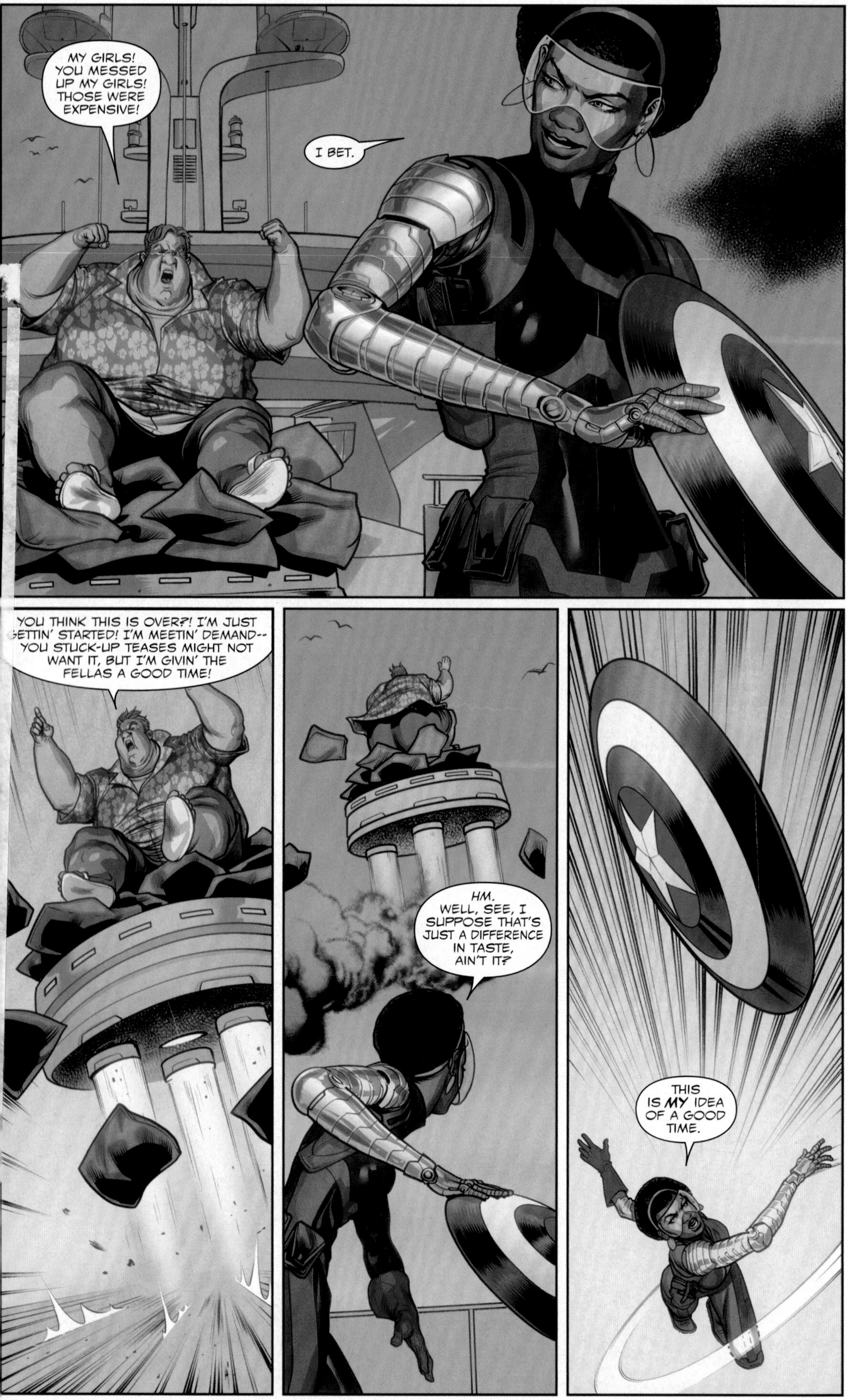
MY GIRLS! YOU MESSED UP MY GIRLS! THOSE WERE EXPENSIVE!
I BET.
YOU THINK THIS IS OVER?! I'M JUST GETTIN' STARTED! I'M MEETIN' DEMAND-- YOU STUCK-UP TEASES MIGHT NOT WANT IT, BUT I'M GIVIN' THE FELLAS A GOOD TIME!
HM. WELL, SEE, I SUPPOSE THAT'S JUST A DIFFERENCE IN TASTE, AIN'T IT?
THIS IS MY IDEA OF A GOOD TIME.

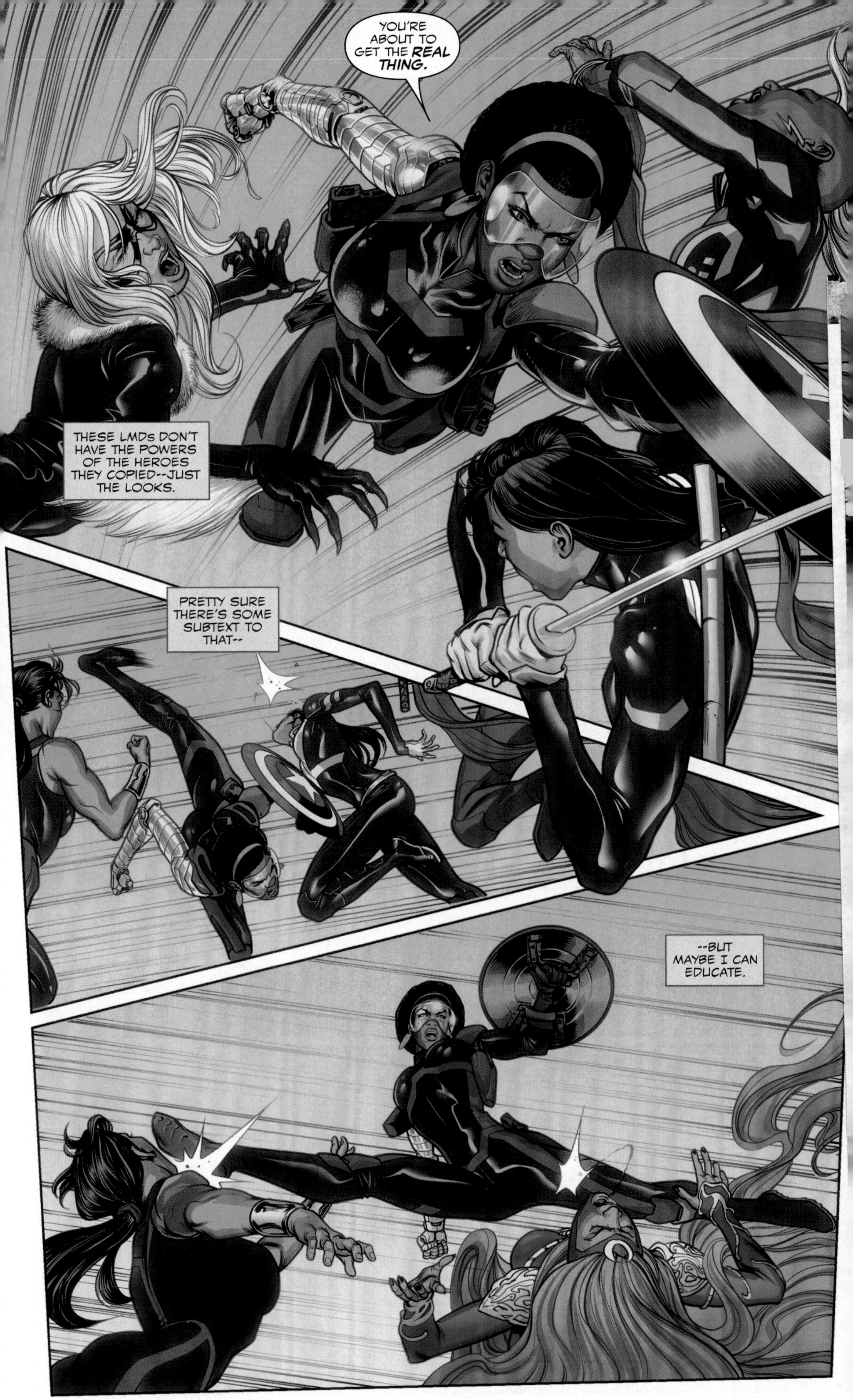
YOU'RE ABOUT TO GET THE REAL THING.
THESE LMDs DON'T HAVE THE POWERS OF THE HEROES THEY COPIED--JUST THE LOOKS.
PRETTY SURE THERE'S SOME SUBTEXT TO THAT--
--BUT MAYBE I CAN EDUCATE.

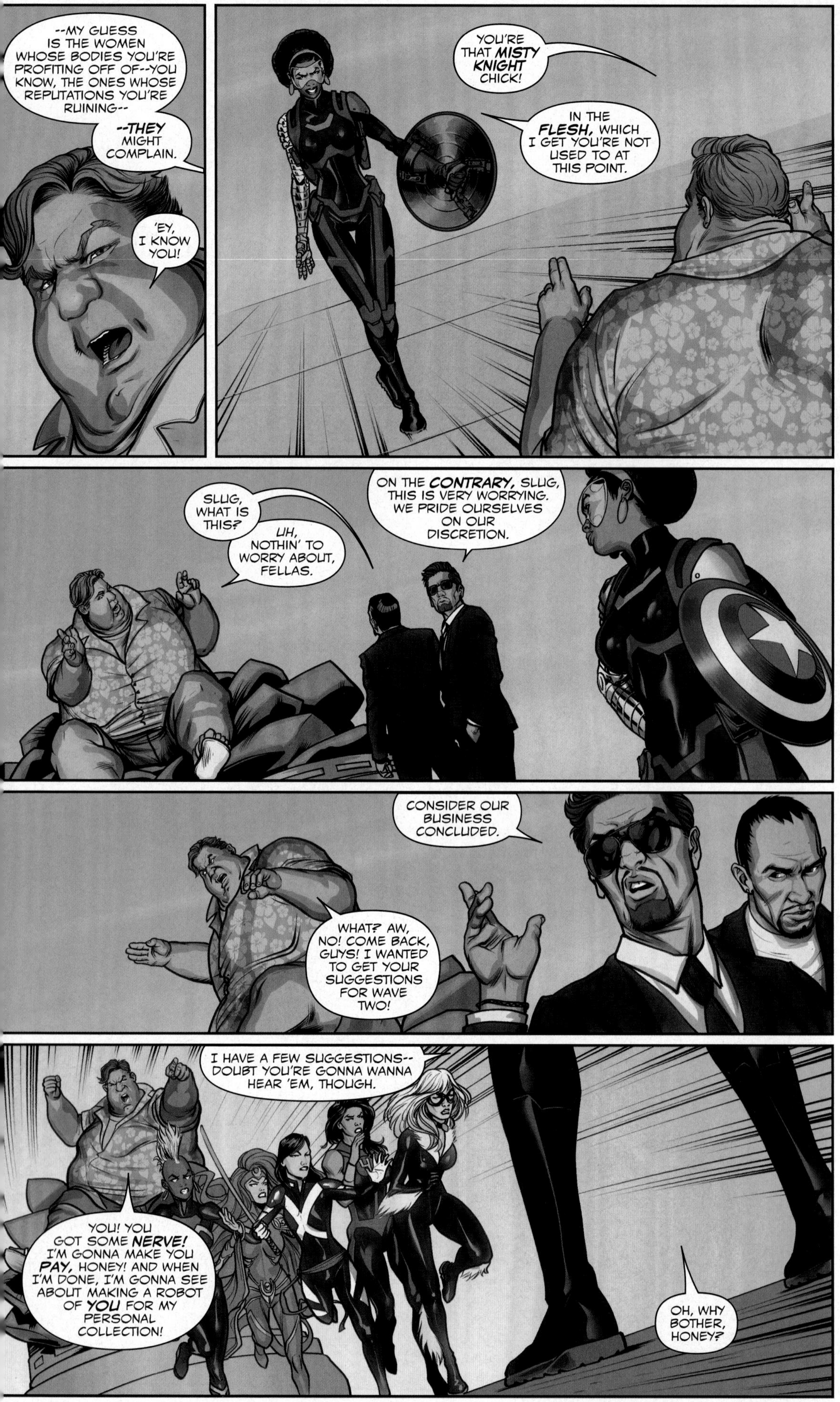
--MY GUESS IS THE WOMEN WHOSE BODIES YOU'RE PROFITING OFF OF--YOU KNOW, THE ONES WHOSE REPUTATIONS YOU'RE RUINING--
--THEY MIGHT COMPLAIN.
'EY, I KNOW YOU!
YOU'RE THAT MISTY KNIGHT CHICK!
IN THE FLESH, WHICH I GET YOU'RE NOT USED TO AT THIS POINT.
SLUG, WHAT IS THIS?
UH, NOTHIN' TO WORRY ABOUT, FELLAS.
ON THE CONTRARY, SLUG, THIS IS VERY WORRYING. WE PRIDE OURSELVES ON OUR DISCRETION.
CONSIDER OUR BUSINESS CONCLUDED.
WHAT? AW, NO! COME BACK, GUYS! I WANTED TO GET YOUR SUGGESTIONS FOR WAVE TWO!
I HAVE A FEW SUGGESTIONS--DOUBT YOU'RE GONNA WANNA HEAR 'EM, THOUGH.
YOU! YOU GOT SOME NERVE! I'M GONNA MAKE YOU PAY, HONEY! AND WHEN I'M DONE, I'M GONNA SEE ABOUT MAKING A ROBOT OF YOU FOR MY PERSONAL COLLECTION!
OH, WHY BOTHER, HONEY?

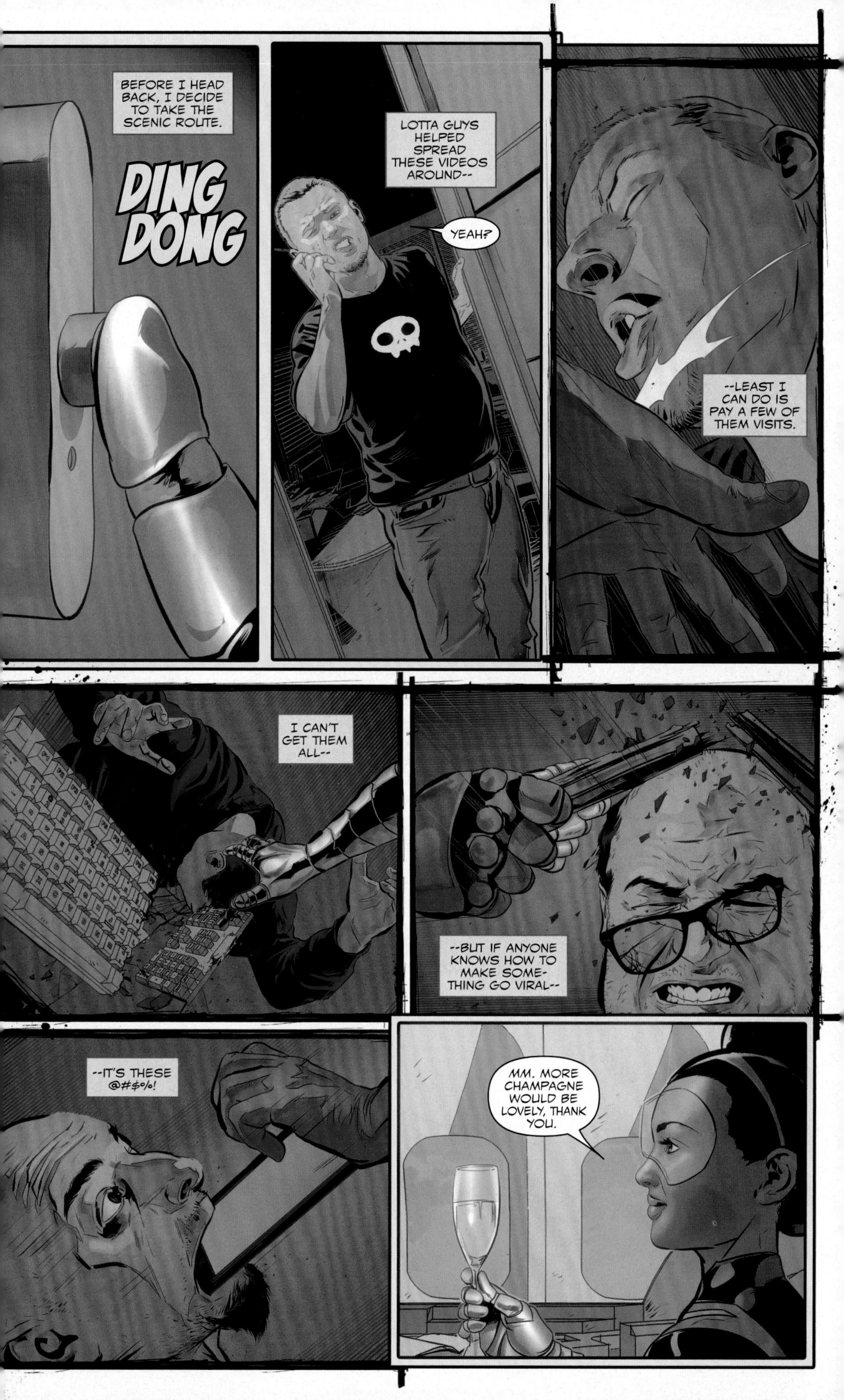
BEFORE I HEAD BACK, I DECIDE TO TAKE THE SCENIC ROUTE.
DING DONG
LOTTA GUYS HELPED SPREAD THESE VIDEOS AROUND--
YEAH?
--LEAST I CAN DO IS PAY A FEW OF THEM VISITS.
I CAN'T GET THEM ALL--
--BUT IF ANYONE KNOWS HOW TO MAKE SOME-THING GO VIRAL--
--IT'S THESE @#$%!
MM. MORE CHAMPAGNE WOULD BE LOVELY, THANK YOU.

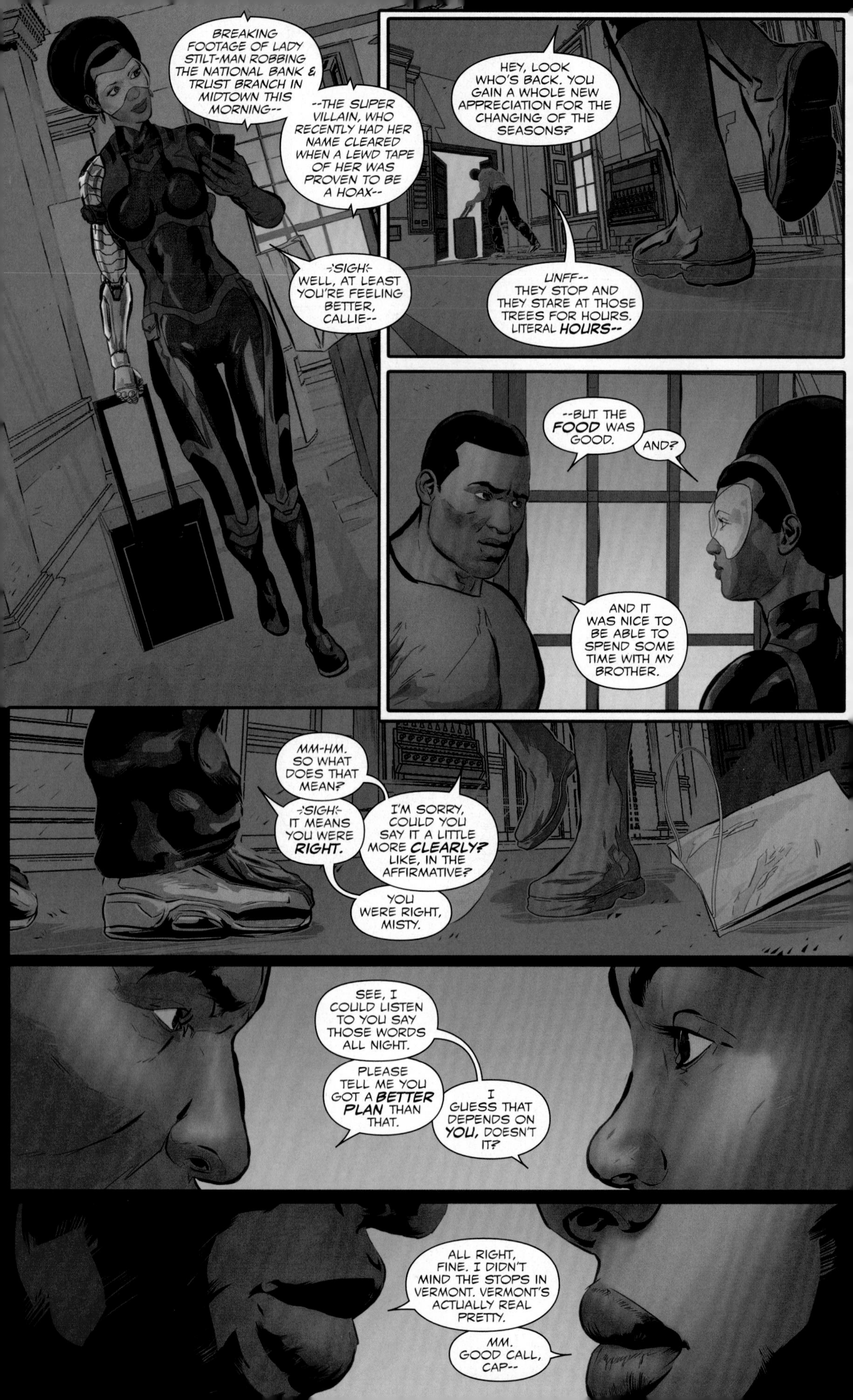
BREAKING FOOTAGE OF LADY STILT-MAN ROBBING THE NATIONAL BANK & TRUST BRANCH IN MIDTOWN THIS MORNING--
--THE SUPER VILLAIN, WHO RECENTLY HAD HER NAME CLEARED WHEN A LEWD TAPE OF HER WAS PROVEN TO BE A HOAX--
-SIGH- WELL, AT LEAST YOU'RE FEELING BETTER, CALLIE--
HEY, LOOK WHO'S BACK. YOU GAIN A WHOLE NEW APPRECIATION FOR THE CHANGING OF THE SEASONS?
UNFF-- THEY STOP AND THEY STARE AT THOSE TREES FOR HOURS. LITERAL HOURS--
--BUT THE FOOD WAS GOOD.
AND?
AND IT WAS NICE TO BE ABLE TO SPEND SOME TIME WITH MY BROTHER.
MM-HM. SO WHAT DOES THAT MEAN?
-SIGH- IT MEANS YOU WERE RIGHT.
I'M SORRY, COULD YOU SAY IT A LITTLE MORE CLEARLY? LIKE, IN THE AFFIRMATIVE?
YOU WERE RIGHT, MISTY.
SEE, I COULD LISTEN TO YOU SAY THOSE WORDS ALL NIGHT.
PLEASE TELL ME YOU GOT A BETTER PLAN THAN THAT.
I GUESS THAT DEPENDS ON YOU, DOESN'T IT?
ALL RIGHT, FINE. I DIDN'T MIND THE STOPS IN VERMONT. VERMONT'S ACTUALLY REAL PRETTY.
MM. GOOD CALL, CAP--

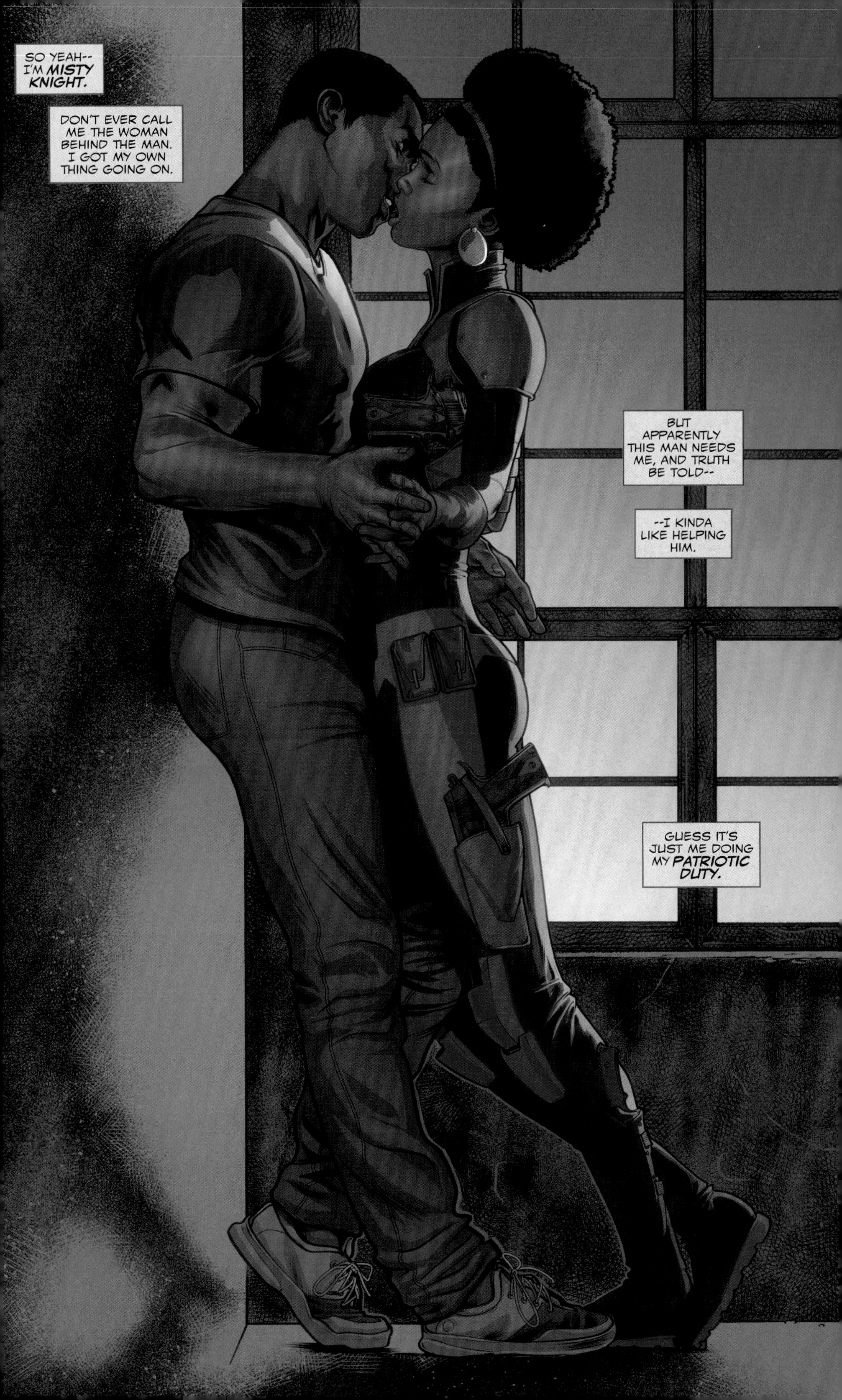
SO YEAH-- I'M **MISTY KNIGHT.**
DON'T EVER CALL ME THE WOMAN BEHIND THE MAN. I GOT MY OWN THING GOING ON.
BUT APPARENTLY THIS MAN NEEDS ME, AND TRUTH BE TOLD--
--I KINDA LIKE HELPING HIM.
GUESS IT'S JUST ME DOING MY **PATRIOTIC DUTY.**

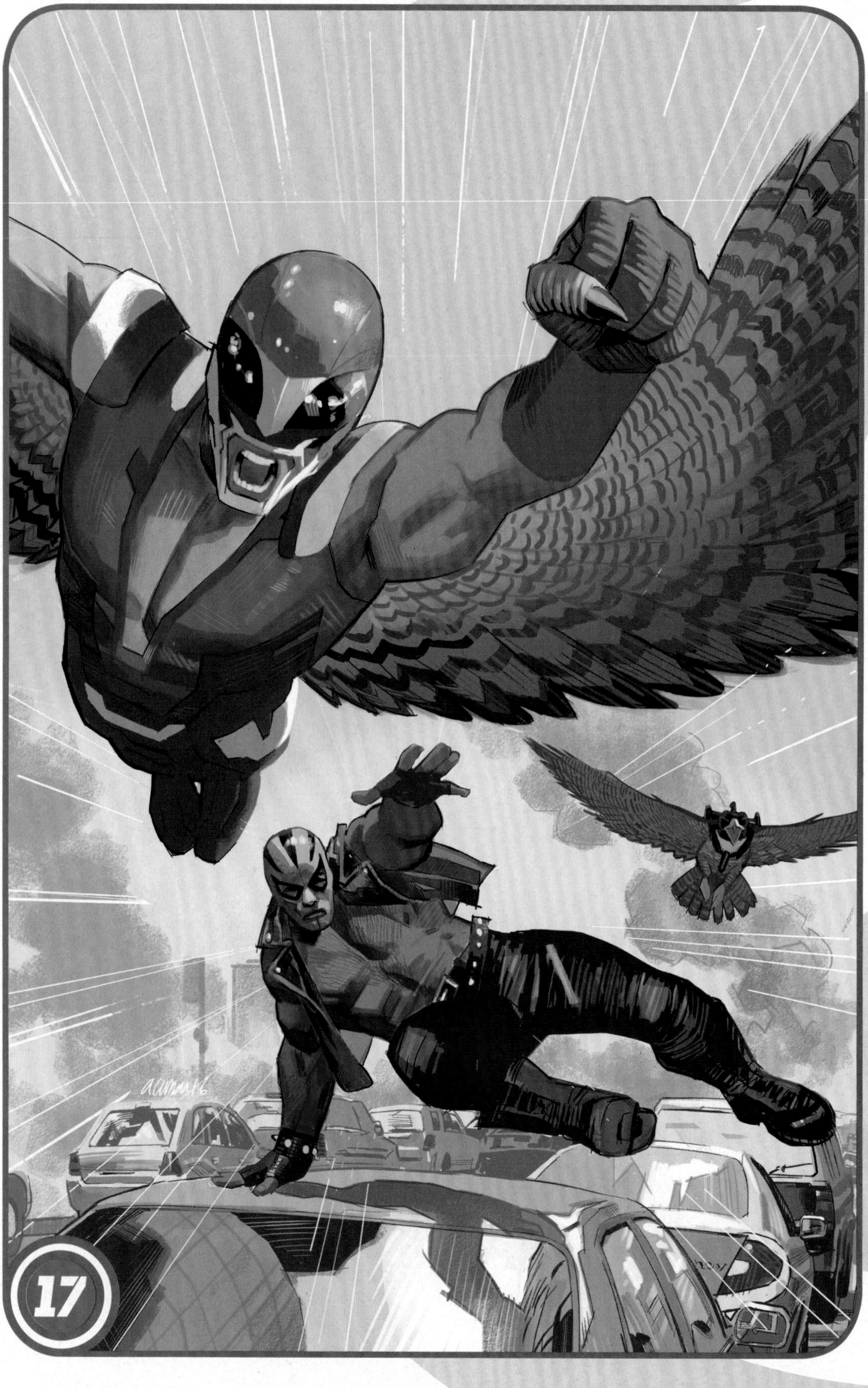
17

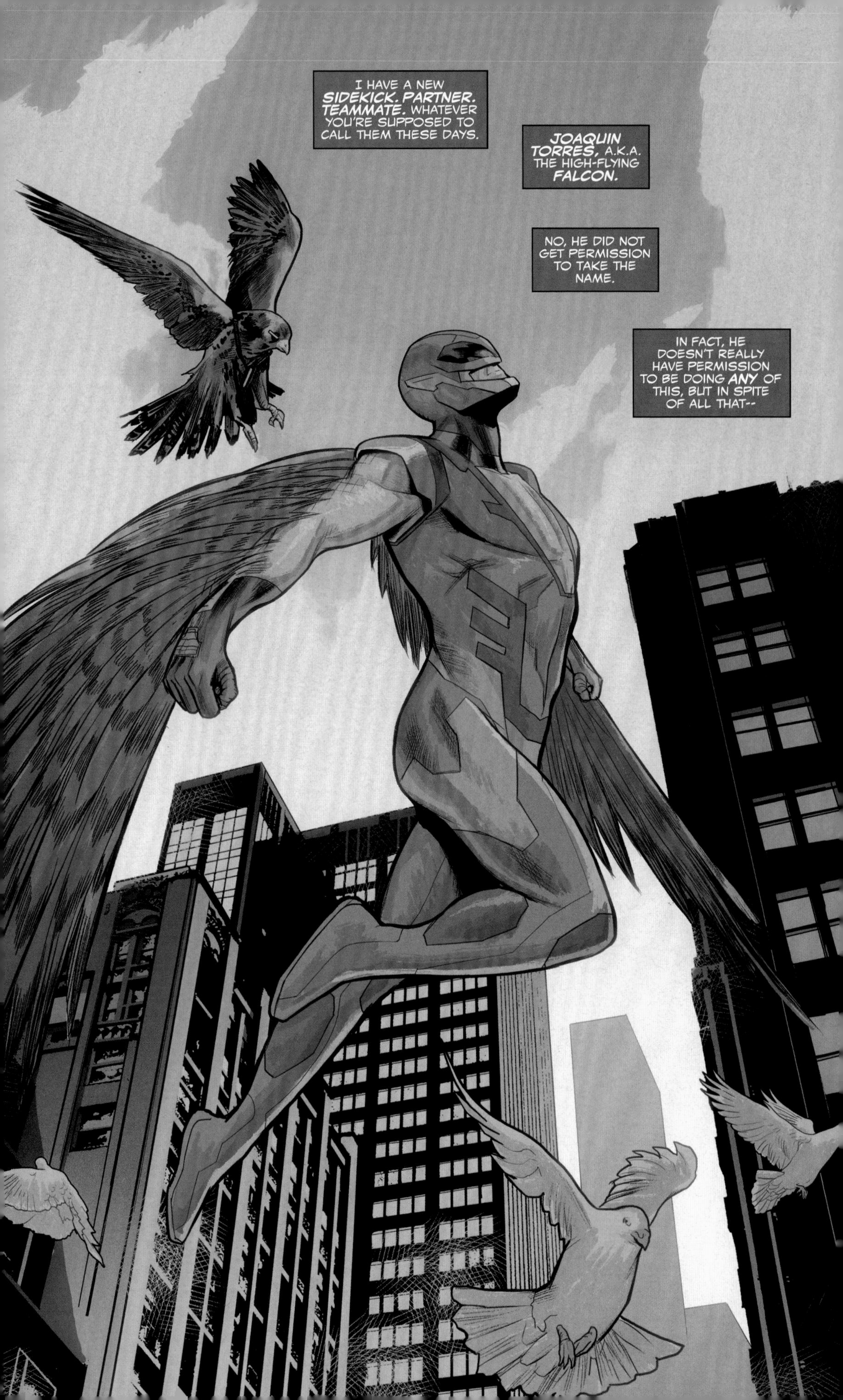
I HAVE A NEW SIDEKICK. PARTNER. TEAMMATE. WHATEVER YOU'RE SUPPOSED TO CALL THEM THESE DAYS.
JOAQUIN TORRES, A.K.A. THE HIGH-FLYING FALCON.
NO, HE DID NOT GET PERMISSION TO TAKE THE NAME.
IN FACT, HE DOESN'T REALLY HAVE PERMISSION TO BE DOING ANY OF THIS, BUT IN SPITE OF ALL THAT--

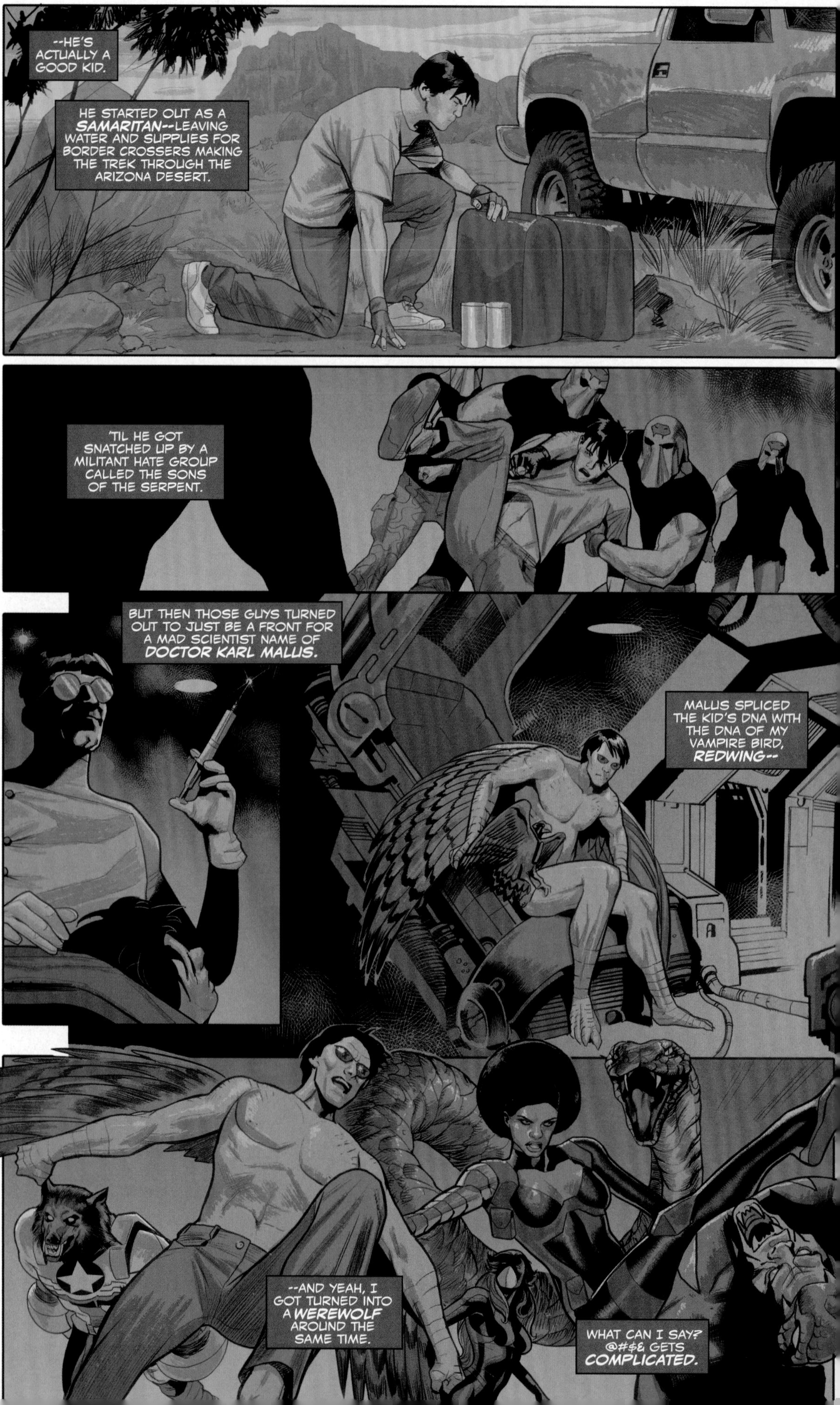
--HE'S ACTUALLY A GOOD KID.
HE STARTED OUT AS A SAMARITAN--LEAVING WATER AND SUPPLIES FOR BORDER CROSSERS MAKING THE TREK THROUGH THE ARIZONA DESERT.
'TIL HE GOT SNATCHED UP BY A MILITANT HATE GROUP CALLED THE SONS OF THE SERPENT.
BUT THEN THOSE GUYS TURNED OUT TO JUST BE A FRONT FOR A MAD SCIENTIST NAME OF DOCTOR KARL MALUS.
MALUS SPLICED THE KID'S DNA WITH THE DNA OF MY VAMPIRE BIRD, REDWING--
--AND YEAH, I GOT TURNED INTO A WEREWOLF AROUND THE SAME TIME.
WHAT CAN I SAY? @#$& GETS COMPLICATED.

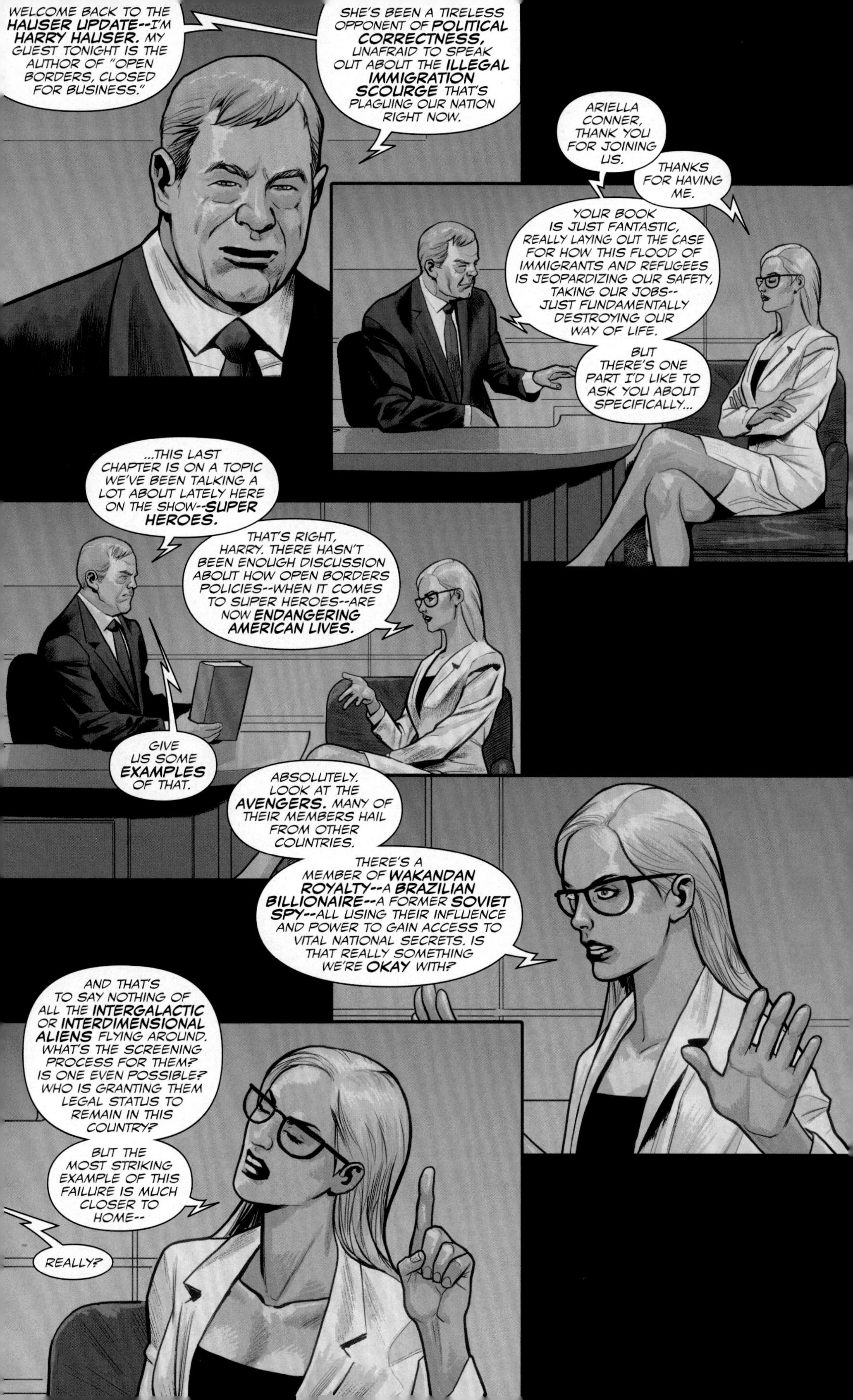
WELCOME BACK TO THE HAUSER UPDATE--I'M HARRY HAUSER. MY GUEST TONIGHT IS THE AUTHOR OF "OPEN BORDERS, CLOSED FOR BUSINESS."
SHE'S BEEN A TIRELESS OPPONENT OF POLITICAL CORRECTNESS, UNAFRAID TO SPEAK OUT ABOUT THE ILLEGAL IMMIGRATION SCOURGE THAT'S PLAGUING OUR NATION RIGHT NOW.
ARIELLA CONNER, THANK YOU FOR JOINING US.
THANKS FOR HAVING ME.
YOUR BOOK IS JUST FANTASTIC, REALLY LAYING OUT THE CASE FOR HOW THIS FLOOD OF IMMIGRANTS AND REFUGEES IS JEOPARDIZING OUR SAFETY, TAKING OUR JOBS-- JUST FUNDAMENTALLY DESTROYING OUR WAY OF LIFE.
BUT THERE'S ONE PART I'D LIKE TO ASK YOU ABOUT SPECIFICALLY...
...THIS LAST CHAPTER IS ON A TOPIC WE'VE BEEN TALKING A LOT ABOUT LATELY HERE ON THE SHOW--SUPER HEROES.
THAT'S RIGHT, HARRY. THERE HASN'T BEEN ENOUGH DISCUSSION ABOUT HOW OPEN BORDERS POLICIES--WHEN IT COMES TO SUPER HEROES--ARE NOW ENDANGERING AMERICAN LIVES.
GIVE US SOME EXAMPLES OF THAT.
ABSOLUTELY. LOOK AT THE AVENGERS. MANY OF THEIR MEMBERS HAIL FROM OTHER COUNTRIES.
THERE'S A MEMBER OF WAKANDAN ROYALTY--A BRAZILIAN BILLIONAIRE--A FORMER SOVIET SPY--ALL USING THEIR INFLUENCE AND POWER TO GAIN ACCESS TO VITAL NATIONAL SECRETS. IS THAT REALLY SOMETHING WE'RE OKAY WITH?
AND THAT'S TO SAY NOTHING OF ALL THE INTERGALACTIC OR INTERDIMENSIONAL ALIENS FLYING AROUND. WHAT'S THE SCREENING PROCESS FOR THEM? IS ONE EVEN POSSIBLE? WHO IS GRANTING THEM LEGAL STATUS TO REMAIN IN THIS COUNTRY?
BUT THE MOST STRIKING EXAMPLE OF THIS FAILURE IS MUCH CLOSER TO HOME--
REALLY?

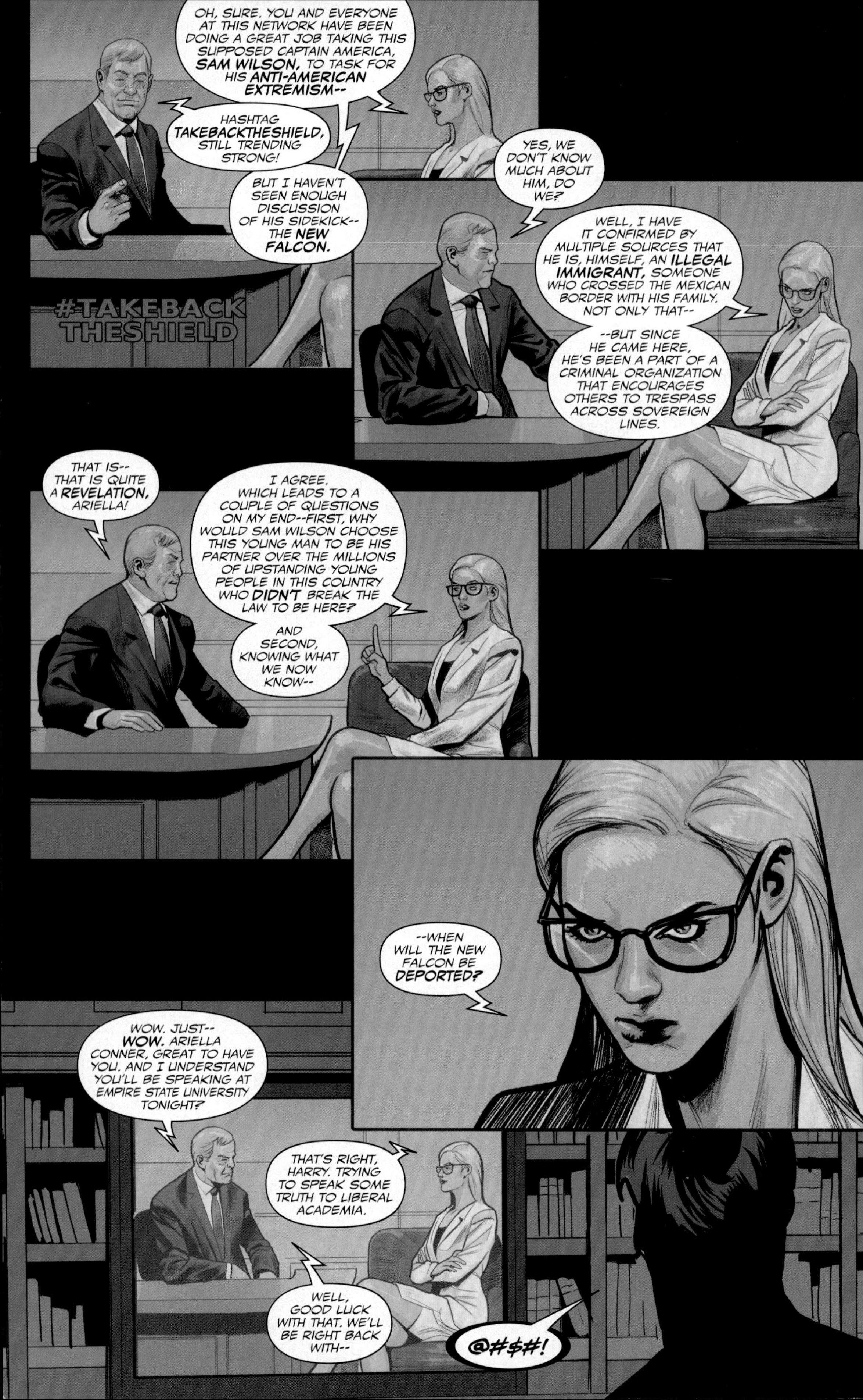
OH, SURE. YOU AND EVERYONE AT THIS NETWORK HAVE BEEN DOING A GREAT JOB TAKING THIS SUPPOSED CAPTAIN AMERICA, SAM WILSON, TO TASK FOR HIS ANTI-AMERICAN EXTREMISM--
HASHTAG TAKEBACKTHESHIELD, STILL TRENDING STRONG!
BUT I HAVEN'T SEEN ENOUGH DISCUSSION OF HIS SIDEKICK-- THE NEW FALCON.
#TAKEBACK THESHIELD
YES, WE DON'T KNOW MUCH ABOUT HIM, DO WE?
WELL, I HAVE IT CONFIRMED BY MULTIPLE SOURCES THAT HE IS, HIMSELF, AN ILLEGAL IMMIGRANT, SOMEONE WHO CROSSED THE MEXICAN BORDER WITH HIS FAMILY. NOT ONLY THAT--
--BUT SINCE HE CAME HERE, HE'S BEEN A PART OF A CRIMINAL ORGANIZATION THAT ENCOURAGES OTHERS TO TRESPASS ACROSS SOVEREIGN LINES.
THAT IS-- THAT IS QUITE A REVELATION, ARIELLA!
I AGREE. WHICH LEADS TO A COUPLE OF QUESTIONS ON MY END--FIRST, WHY WOULD SAM WILSON CHOOSE THIS YOUNG MAN TO BE HIS PARTNER OVER THE MILLIONS OF UPSTANDING YOUNG PEOPLE IN THIS COUNTRY WHO DIDN'T BREAK THE LAW TO BE HERE?
AND SECOND, KNOWING WHAT WE NOW KNOW--
--WHEN WILL THE NEW FALCON BE DEPORTED?
WOW. JUST-- WOW. ARIELLA CONNER, GREAT TO HAVE YOU. AND I UNDERSTAND YOU'LL BE SPEAKING AT EMPIRE STATE UNIVERSITY TONIGHT?
THAT'S RIGHT, HARRY. TRYING TO SPEAK SOME TRUTH TO LIBERAL ACADEMIA.
WELL, GOOD LUCK WITH THAT. WE'LL BE RIGHT BACK WITH--
@#$#!

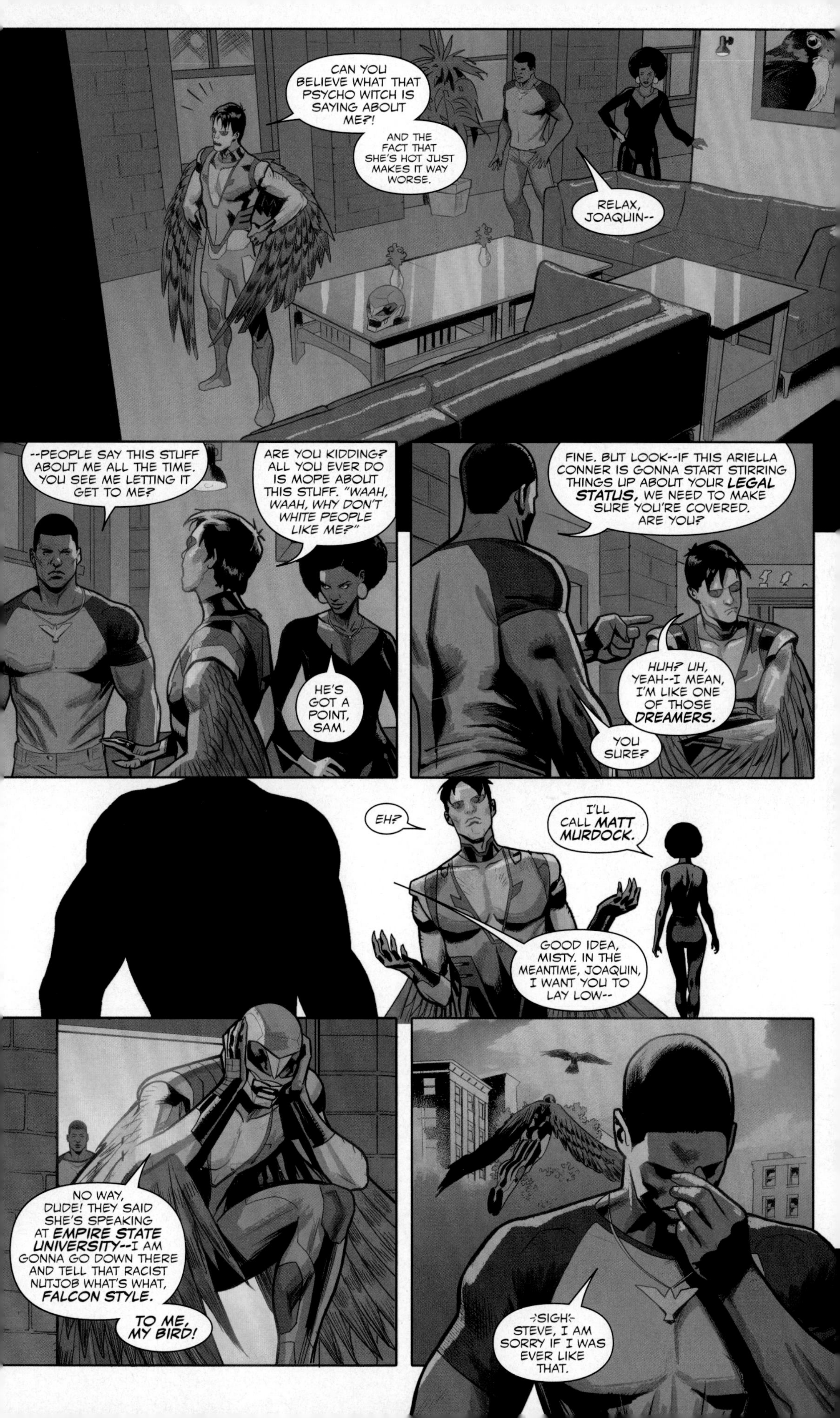
CAN YOU BELIEVE WHAT THAT PSYCHO WITCH IS SAYING ABOUT ME?!
AND THE FACT THAT SHE'S HOT JUST MAKES IT WAY WORSE.
RELAX, JOAQUIN--
--PEOPLE SAY THIS STUFF ABOUT ME ALL THE TIME. YOU SEE ME LETTING IT GET TO ME?
ARE YOU KIDDING? ALL YOU EVER DO IS MOPE ABOUT THIS STUFF. "WAAH, WAAH, WHY DON'T WHITE PEOPLE LIKE ME?"
HE'S GOT A POINT, SAM.
FINE. BUT LOOK--IF THIS ARIELLA CONNER IS GONNA START STIRRING THINGS UP ABOUT YOUR LEGAL STATUS, WE NEED TO MAKE SURE YOU'RE COVERED. ARE YOU?
HUH? UH, YEAH--I MEAN, I'M LIKE ONE OF THOSE DREAMERS.
YOU SURE?
EH?
I'LL CALL MATT MURDOCK.
GOOD IDEA, MISTY. IN THE MEANTIME, JOAQUIN, I WANT YOU TO LAY LOW--
NO WAY, DUDE! THEY SAID SHE'S SPEAKING AT EMPIRE STATE UNIVERSITY--I AM GONNA GO DOWN THERE AND TELL THAT RACIST NUTJOB WHAT'S WHAT, FALCON STYLE.
TO ME, MY BIRD!
-SIGH- STEVE, I AM SORRY IF I WAS EVER LIKE THAT.

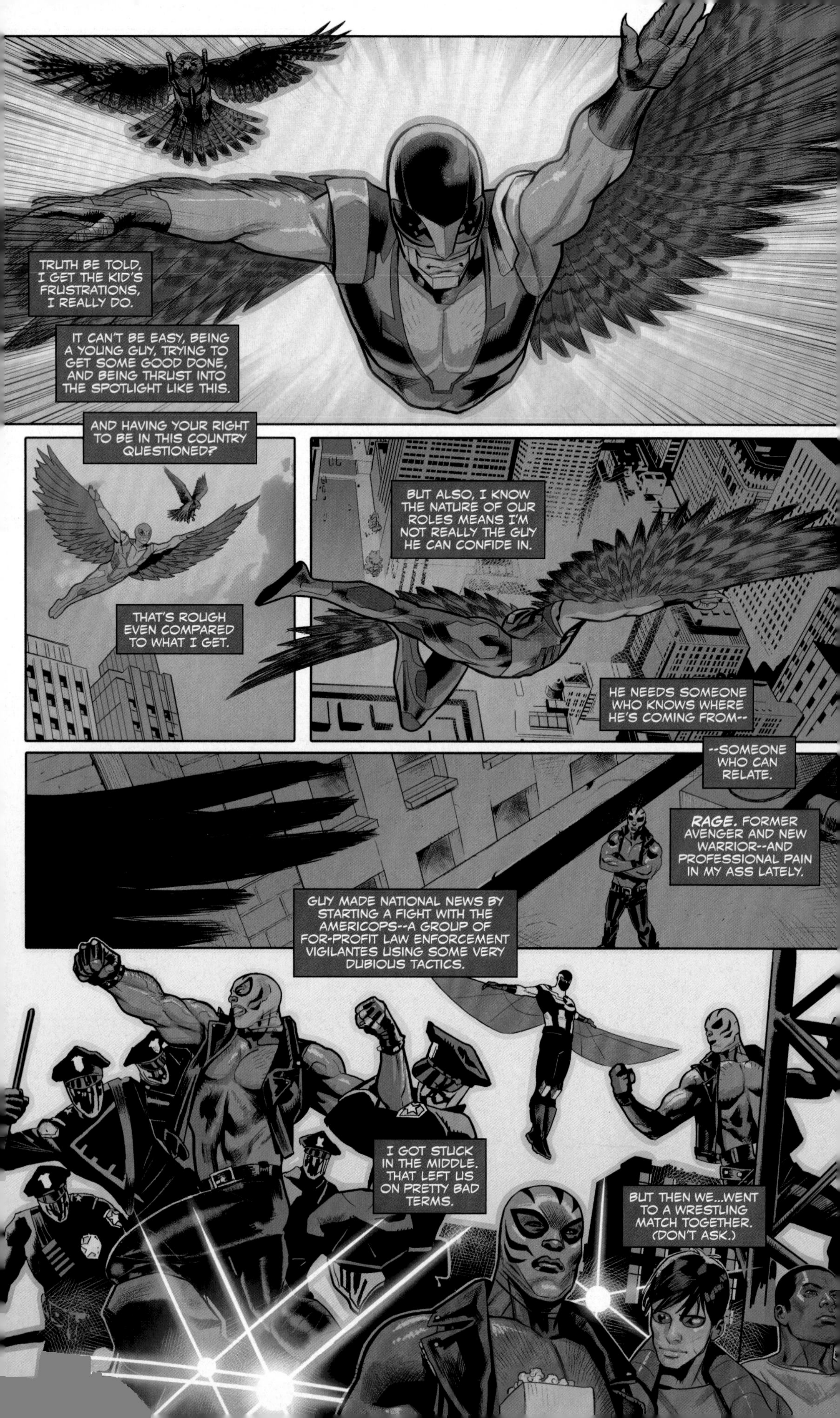
TRUTH BE TOLD, I GET THE KID'S FRUSTRATIONS, I REALLY DO.
IT CAN'T BE EASY, BEING A YOUNG GUY, TRYING TO GET SOME GOOD DONE, AND BEING THRUST INTO THE SPOTLIGHT LIKE THIS.
AND HAVING YOUR RIGHT TO BE IN THIS COUNTRY QUESTIONED?
THAT'S ROUGH EVEN COMPARED TO WHAT I GET.
BUT ALSO, I KNOW THE NATURE OF OUR ROLES MEANS I'M NOT REALLY THE GUY HE CAN CONFIDE IN.
HE NEEDS SOMEONE WHO KNOWS WHERE HE'S COMING FROM--
--SOMEONE WHO CAN RELATE.
RAGE. FORMER AVENGER AND NEW WARRIOR--AND PROFESSIONAL PAIN IN MY ASS LATELY.
GUY MADE NATIONAL NEWS BY STARTING A FIGHT WITH THE AMERICOPS--A GROUP OF FOR-PROFIT LAW ENFORCEMENT VIGILANTES USING SOME VERY DUBIOUS TACTICS.
I GOT STUCK IN THE MIDDLE. THAT LEFT US ON PRETTY BAD TERMS.
BUT THEN WE...WENT TO A WRESTLING MATCH TOGETHER. (DON'T ASK.)

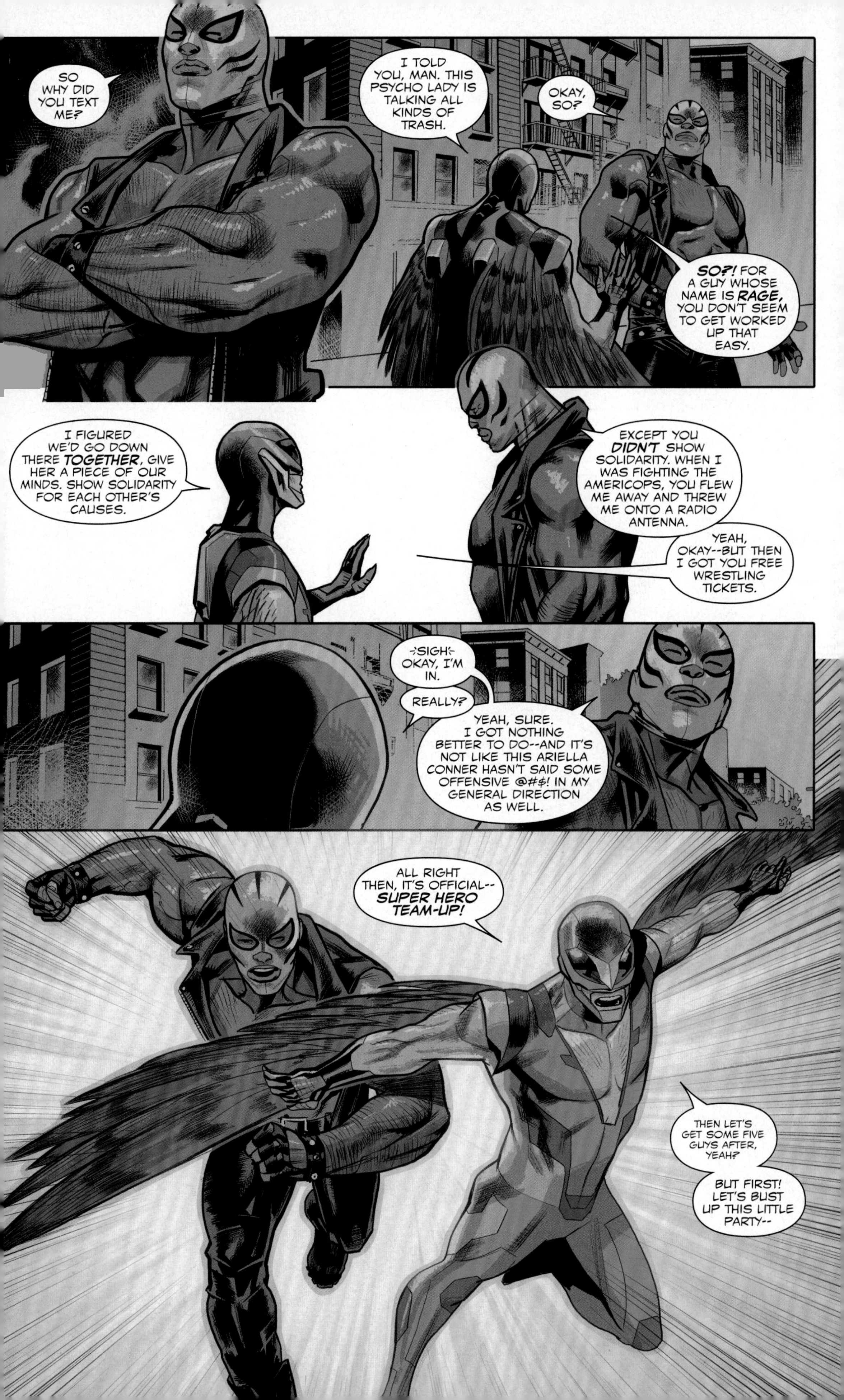
SO WHY DID YOU TEXT ME?
I TOLD YOU, MAN. THIS PSYCHO LADY IS TALKING ALL KINDS OF TRASH.
OKAY, SO?
SO?! FOR A GUY WHOSE NAME IS RAGE, YOU DON'T SEEM TO GET WORKED UP THAT EASY.
I FIGURED WE'D GO DOWN THERE TOGETHER, GIVE HER A PIECE OF OUR MINDS. SHOW SOLIDARITY FOR EACH OTHER'S CAUSES.
EXCEPT YOU DIDN'T SHOW SOLIDARITY. WHEN I WAS FIGHTING THE AMERICOPS, YOU FLEW ME AWAY AND THREW ME ONTO A RADIO ANTENNA.
YEAH, OKAY--BUT THEN I GOT YOU FREE WRESTLING TICKETS.
-SIGH- OKAY, I'M IN.
REALLY?
YEAH, SURE. I GOT NOTHING BETTER TO DO--AND IT'S NOT LIKE THIS ARIELLA CONNER HASN'T SAID SOME OFFENSIVE @#$! IN MY GENERAL DIRECTION AS WELL.
ALL RIGHT THEN, IT'S OFFICIAL-- SUPER HERO TEAM-UP!
THEN LET'S GET SOME FIVE GUYS AFTER, YEAH?
BUT FIRST! LET'S BUST UP THIS LITTLE PARTY--

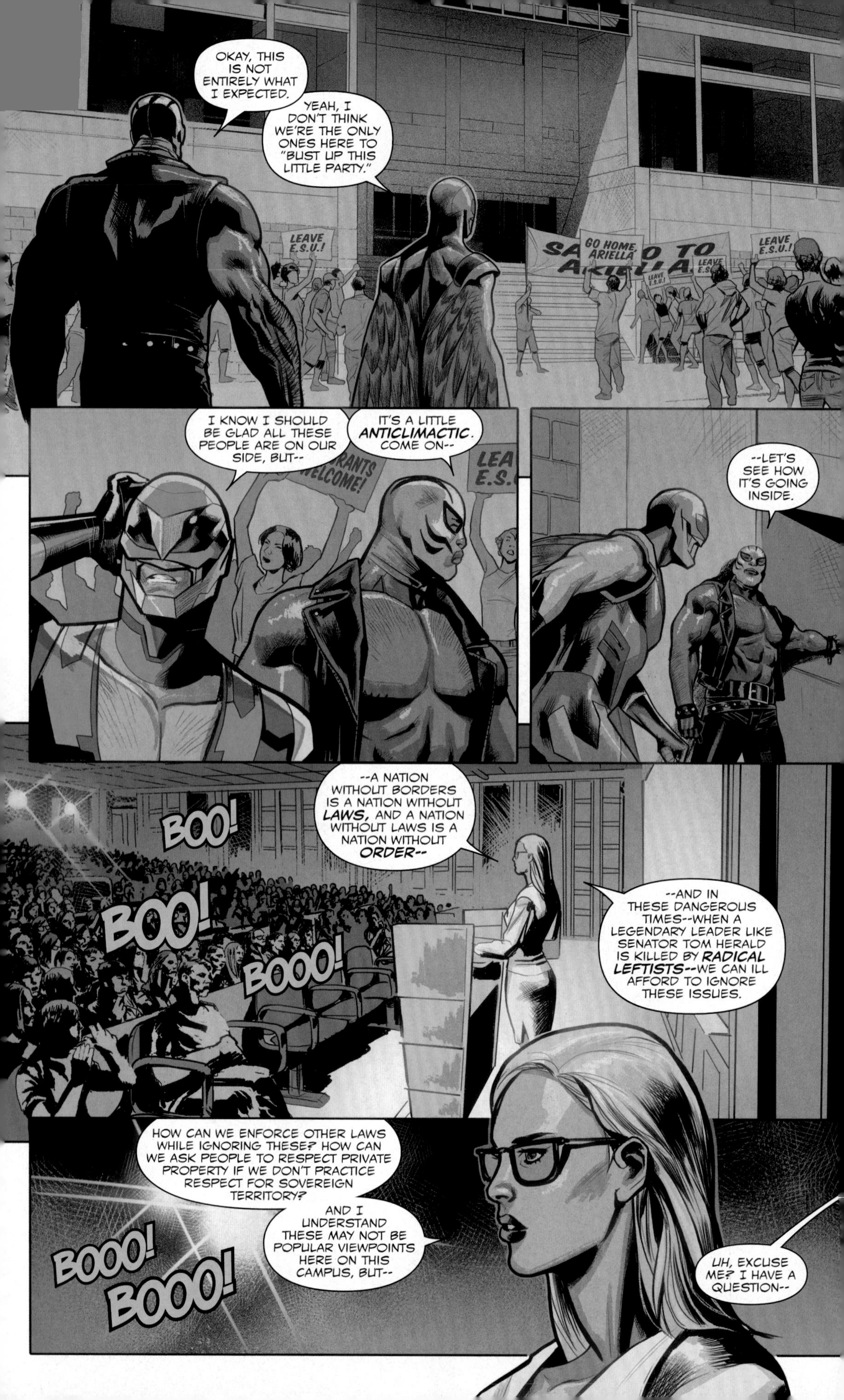
OKAY, THIS IS NOT ENTIRELY WHAT I EXPECTED.
YEAH, I DON'T THINK WE'RE THE ONLY ONES HERE TO "BUST UP THIS LITTLE PARTY."
LEAVE E.S.U.!
GO HOME, ARIELLA
LEAVE E.S.U.!
I KNOW I SHOULD BE GLAD ALL THESE PEOPLE ARE ON OUR SIDE, BUT--
IT'S A LITTLE ANTICLIMACTIC. COME ON--
--LET'S SEE HOW IT'S GOING INSIDE.
--A NATION WITHOUT BORDERS IS A NATION WITHOUT LAWS, AND A NATION WITHOUT LAWS IS A NATION WITHOUT ORDER--
BOO!
BOO!
BOOO!
--AND IN THESE DANGEROUS TIMES--WHEN A LEGENDARY LEADER LIKE SENATOR TOM HERALD IS KILLED BY RADICAL LEFTISTS--WE CAN ILL AFFORD TO IGNORE THESE ISSUES.
HOW CAN WE ENFORCE OTHER LAWS WHILE IGNORING THESE? HOW CAN WE ASK PEOPLE TO RESPECT PRIVATE PROPERTY IF WE DON'T PRACTICE RESPECT FOR SOVEREIGN TERRITORY?
AND I UNDERSTAND THESE MAY NOT BE POPULAR VIEWPOINTS HERE ON THIS CAMPUS, BUT--
BOOO!
BOOO!
UH, EXCUSE ME? I HAVE A QUESTION--

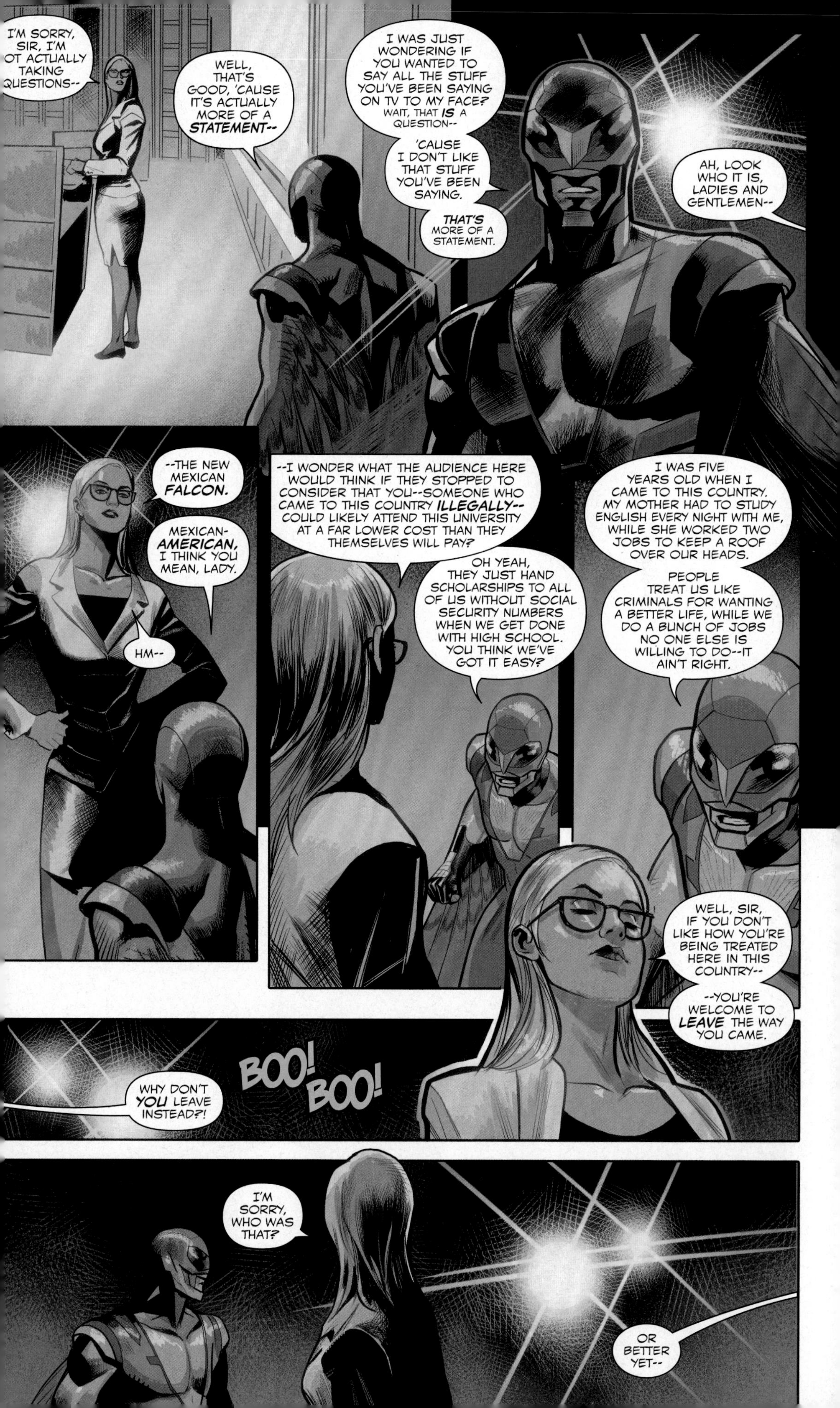
I'M SORRY, SIR, I'M OT ACTUALLY TAKING QUESTIONS--
WELL, THAT'S GOOD, 'CAUSE IT'S ACTUALLY MORE OF A STATEMENT--
I WAS JUST WONDERING IF YOU WANTED TO SAY ALL THE STUFF YOU'VE BEEN SAYING ON TV TO MY FACE? WAIT, THAT IS A QUESTION--
'CAUSE I DON'T LIKE THAT STUFF YOU'VE BEEN SAYING.
THAT'S MORE OF A STATEMENT.
AH, LOOK WHO IT IS, LADIES AND GENTLEMEN--
--THE NEW MEXICAN FALCON.
MEXICAN-AMERICAN, I THINK YOU MEAN, LADY.
HM--
--I WONDER WHAT THE AUDIENCE HERE WOULD THINK IF THEY STOPPED TO CONSIDER THAT YOU--SOMEONE WHO CAME TO THIS COUNTRY ILLEGALLY--COULD LIKELY ATTEND THIS UNIVERSITY AT A FAR LOWER COST THAN THEY THEMSELVES WILL PAY?
OH YEAH, THEY JUST HAND SCHOLARSHIPS TO ALL OF US WITHOUT SOCIAL SECURITY NUMBERS WHEN WE GET DONE WITH HIGH SCHOOL. YOU THINK WE'VE GOT IT EASY?
I WAS FIVE YEARS OLD WHEN I CAME TO THIS COUNTRY. MY MOTHER HAD TO STUDY ENGLISH EVERY NIGHT WITH ME, WHILE SHE WORKED TWO JOBS TO KEEP A ROOF OVER OUR HEADS.
PEOPLE TREAT US LIKE CRIMINALS FOR WANTING A BETTER LIFE, WHILE WE DO A BUNCH OF JOBS NO ONE ELSE IS WILLING TO DO--IT AIN'T RIGHT.
WELL, SIR, IF YOU DON'T LIKE HOW YOU'RE BEING TREATED HERE IN THIS COUNTRY--
--YOU'RE WELCOME TO LEAVE THE WAY YOU CAME.
WHY DON'T YOU LEAVE INSTEAD?!
BOO! BOO!
I'M SORRY, WHO WAS THAT?
OR BETTER YET--

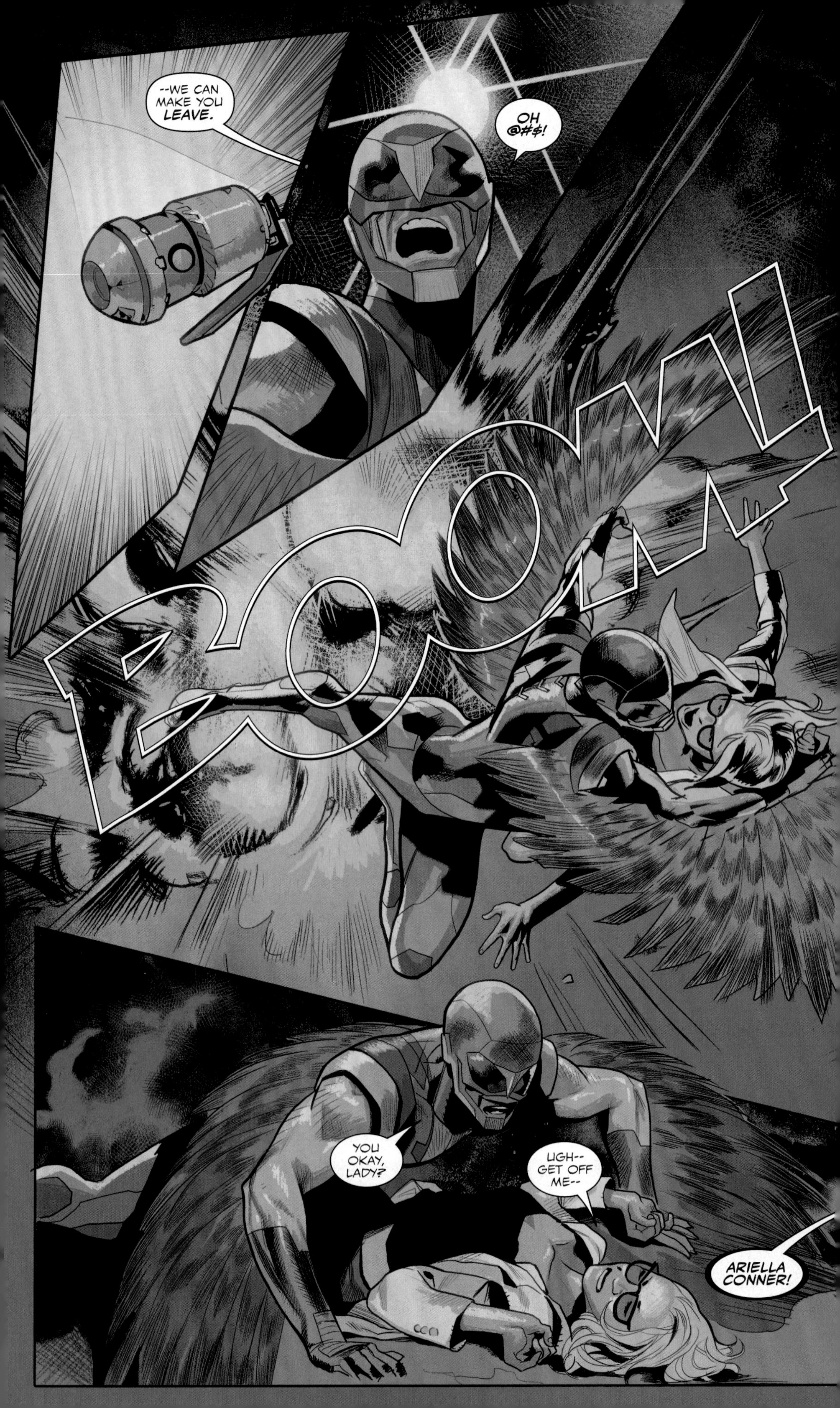
--WE CAN MAKE YOU LEAVE.
OH @#$!
BOOM!
YOU OKAY, LADY?
UGH-- GET OFF ME--
ARIELLA CONNER!

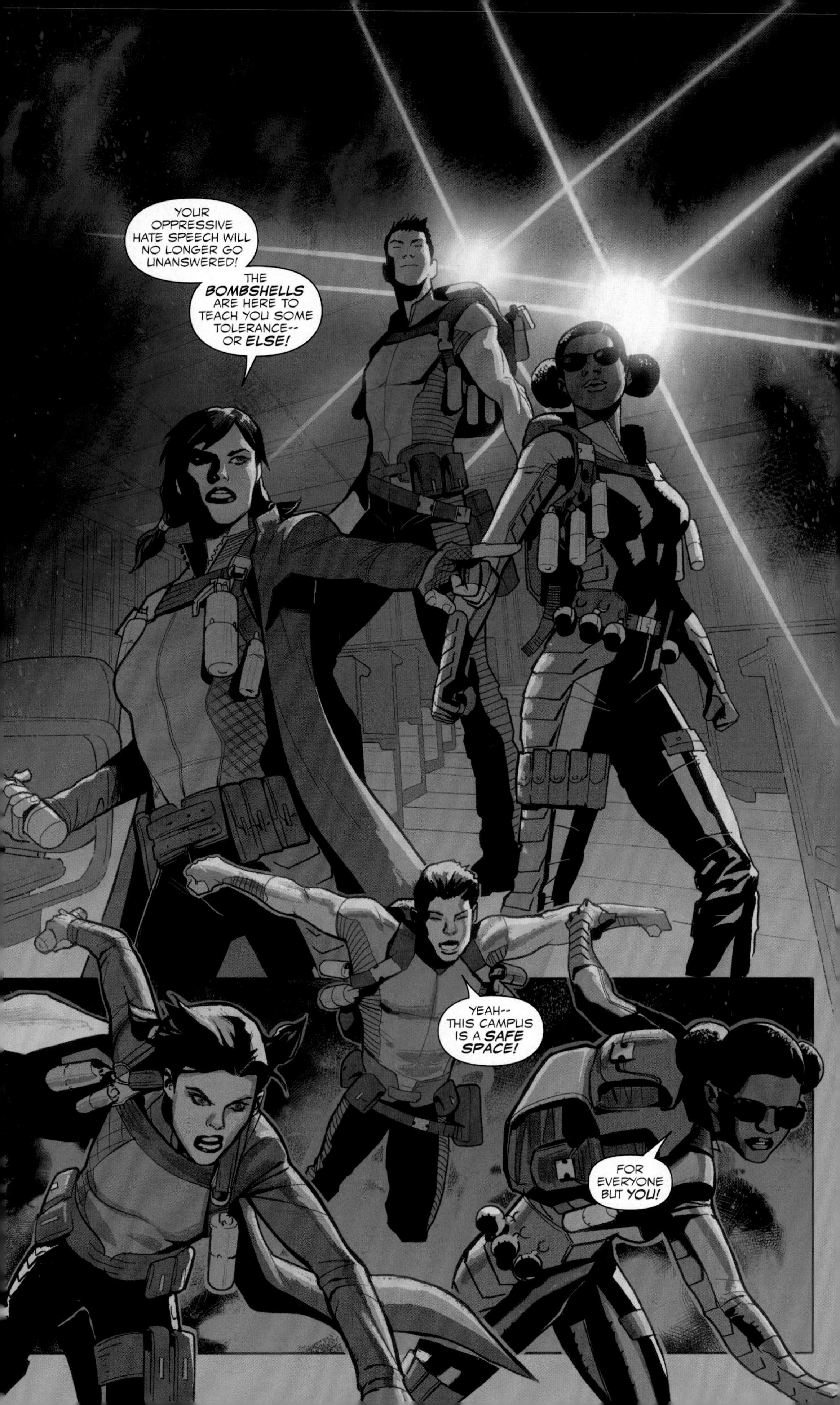
YOUR OPPRESSIVE HATE SPEECH WILL NO LONGER GO UNANSWERED!
THE **BOMBSHELLS** ARE HERE TO TEACH YOU SOME TOLERANCE-- OR **ELSE!**
YEAH-- THIS CAMPUS IS A **SAFE SPACE!**
FOR EVERYONE BUT **YOU!**

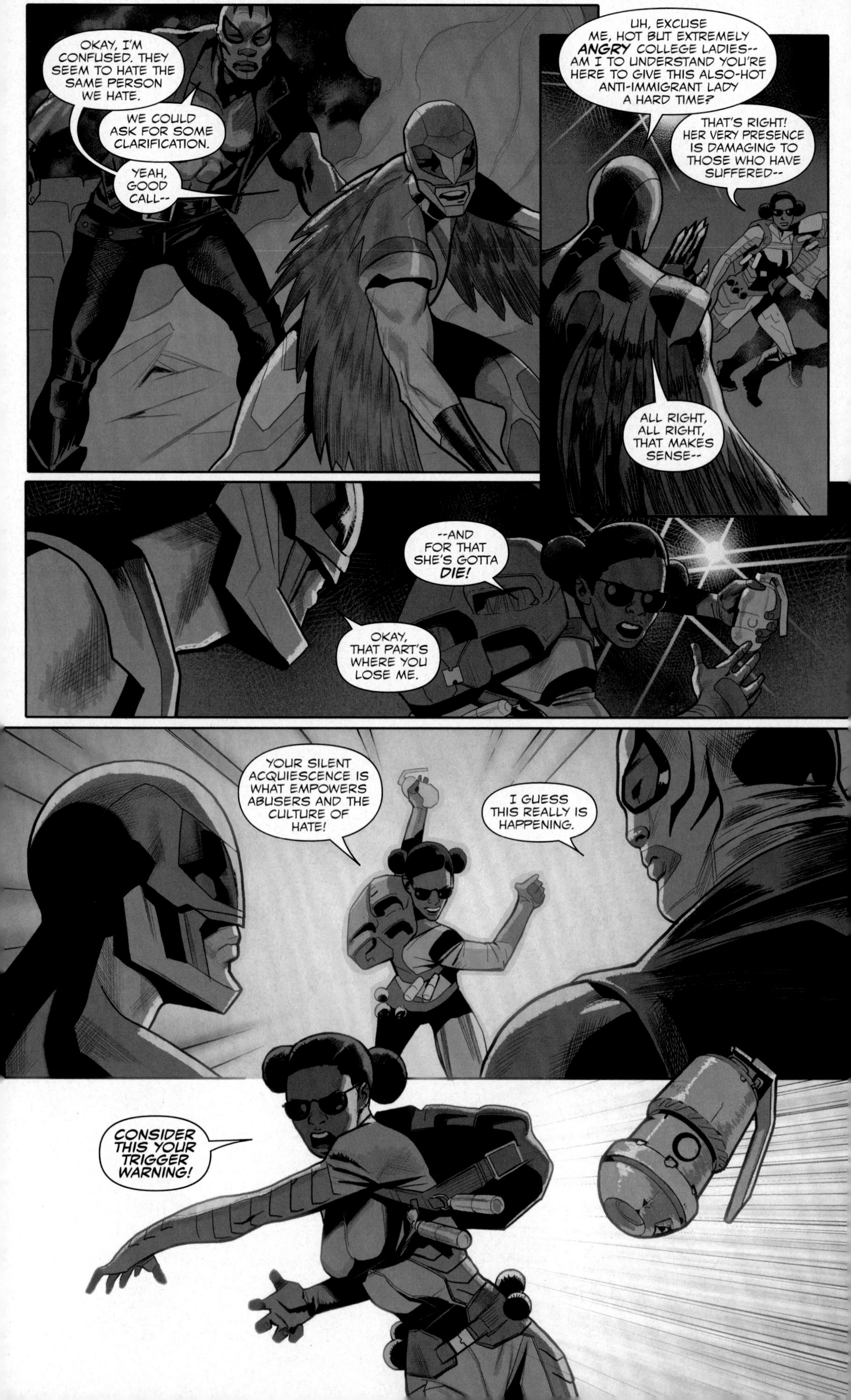
OKAY, I'M CONFUSED. THEY SEEM TO HATE THE SAME PERSON WE HATE.
WE COULD ASK FOR SOME CLARIFICATION.
YEAH, GOOD CALL--
UH, EXCUSE ME, HOT BUT EXTREMELY ANGRY COLLEGE LADIES-- AM I TO UNDERSTAND YOU'RE HERE TO GIVE THIS ALSO-HOT ANTI-IMMIGRANT LADY A HARD TIME?
THAT'S RIGHT! HER VERY PRESENCE IS DAMAGING TO THOSE WHO HAVE SUFFERED--
ALL RIGHT, ALL RIGHT, THAT MAKES SENSE--
--AND FOR THAT SHE'S GOTTA DIE!
OKAY, THAT PART'S WHERE YOU LOSE ME.
YOUR SILENT ACQUIESCENCE IS WHAT EMPOWERS ABUSERS AND THE CULTURE OF HATE!
I GUESS THIS REALLY IS HAPPENING.
CONSIDER THIS YOUR TRIGGER WARNING!

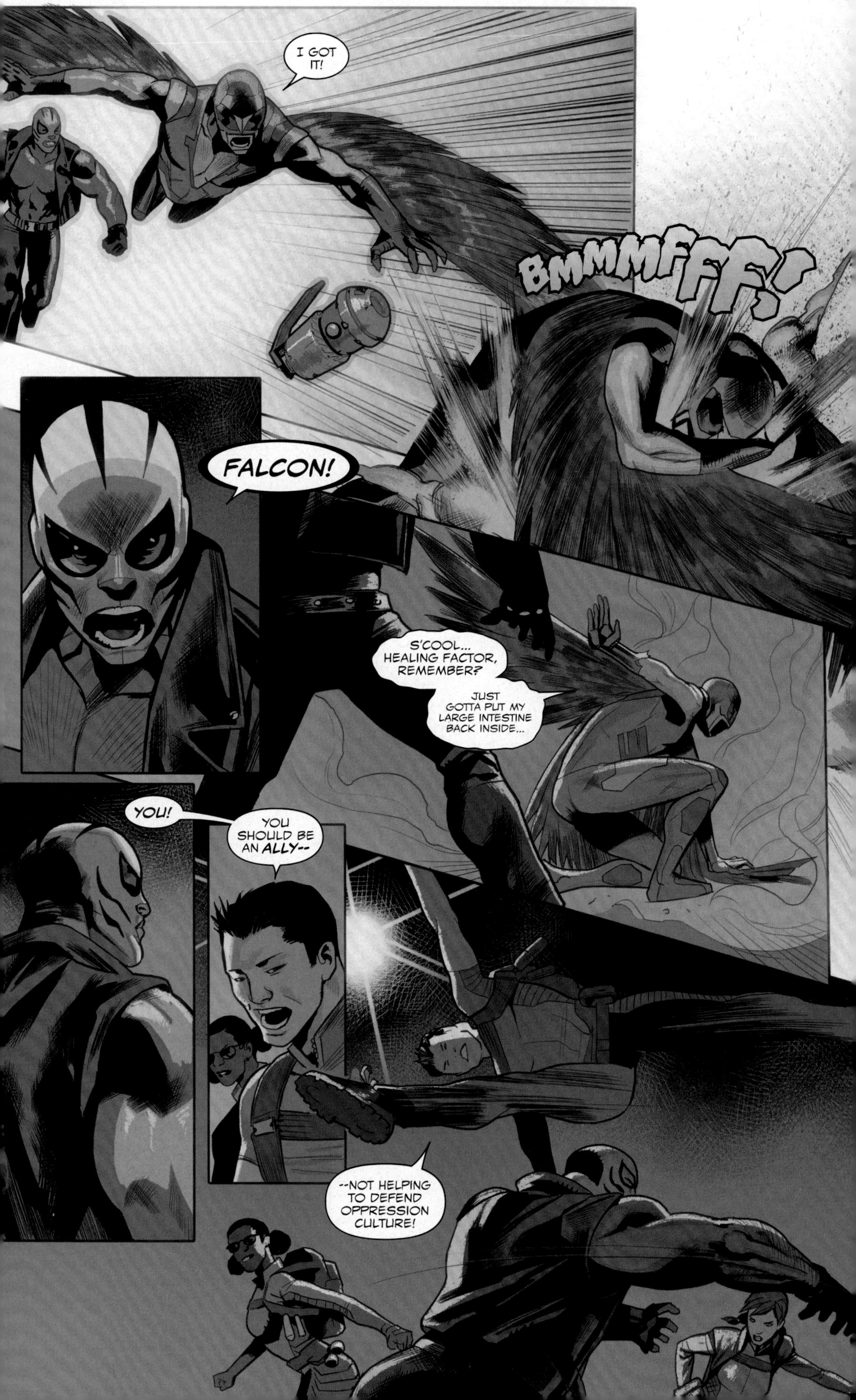
I GOT IT!
BMMMFFF!
FALCON!
S'COOL... HEALING FACTOR, REMEMBER?
JUST GOTTA PUT MY LARGE INTESTINE BACK INSIDE...
YOU!
YOU SHOULD BE AN ALLY--
--NOT HELPING TO DEFEND OPPRESSION CULTURE!

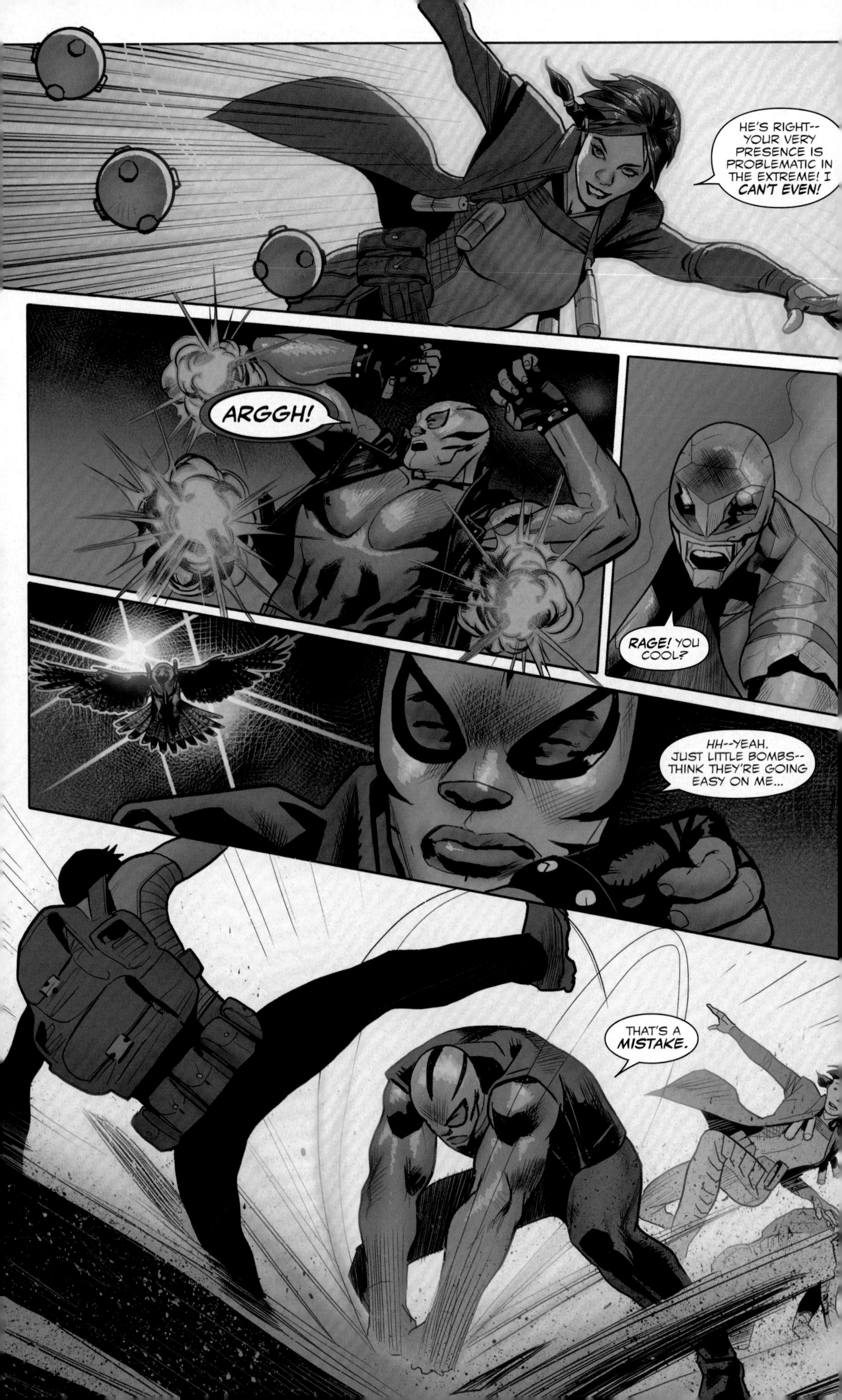
HE'S RIGHT-- YOUR VERY PRESENCE IS PROBLEMATIC IN THE EXTREME! I CAN'T EVEN!
ARGGH!
RAGE! YOU COOL?
HH--YEAH. JUST LITTLE BOMBS-- THINK THEY'RE GOING EASY ON ME...
THAT'S A MISTAKE.

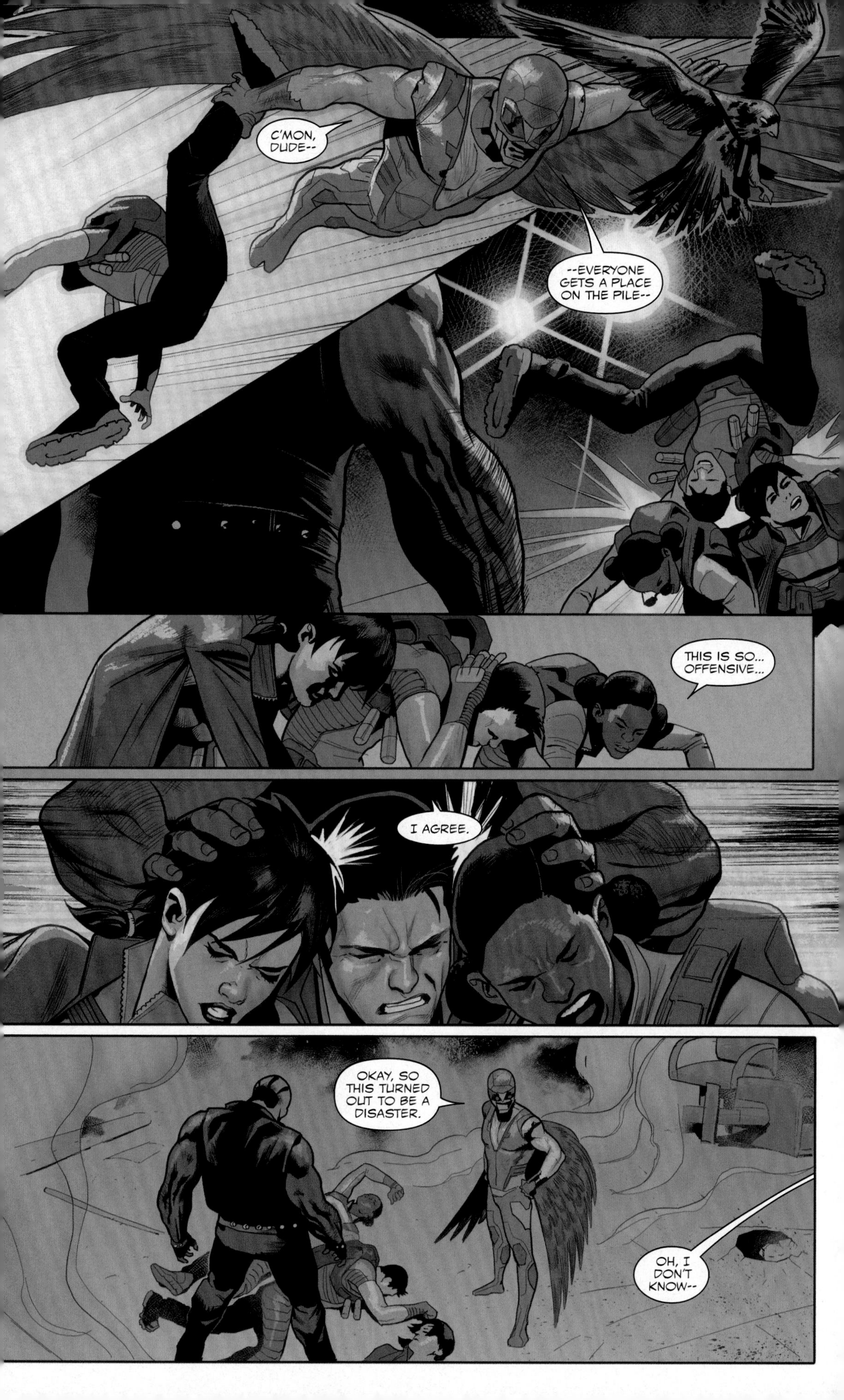
C'MON, DUDE--
--EVERYONE GETS A PLACE ON THE PILE--
THIS IS SO... OFFENSIVE...
I AGREE.
OKAY, SO THIS TURNED OUT TO BE A DISASTER.
OH, I DON'T KNOW--

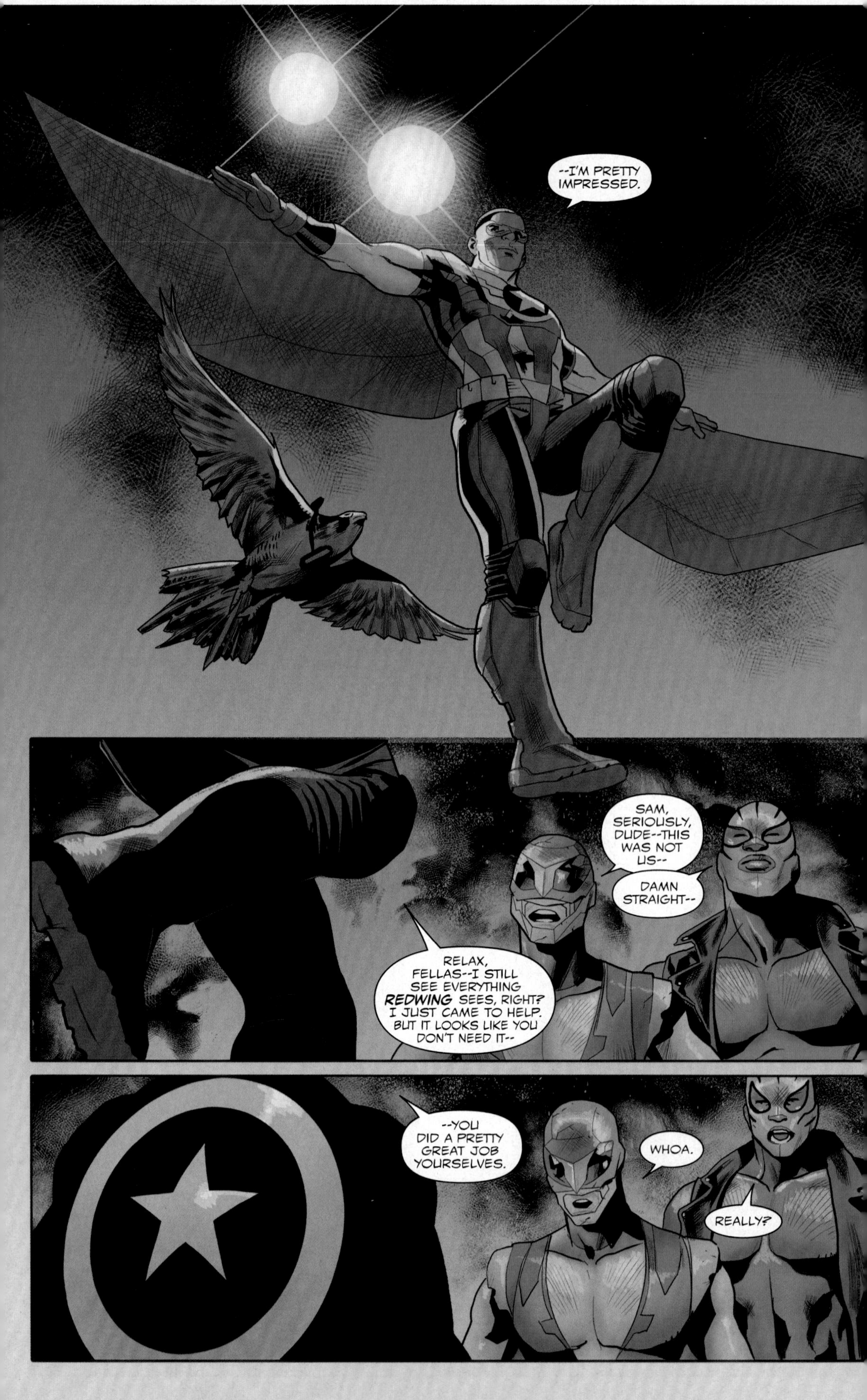

--I'M PRETTY IMPRESSED.
SAM, SERIOUSLY, DUDE--THIS WAS NOT US--
DAMN STRAIGHT--
RELAX, FELLAS--I STILL SEE EVERYTHING REDWING SEES, RIGHT? I JUST CAME TO HELP. BUT IT LOOKS LIKE YOU DON'T NEED IT--
--YOU DID A PRETTY GREAT JOB YOURSELVES.
WHOA.
REALLY?

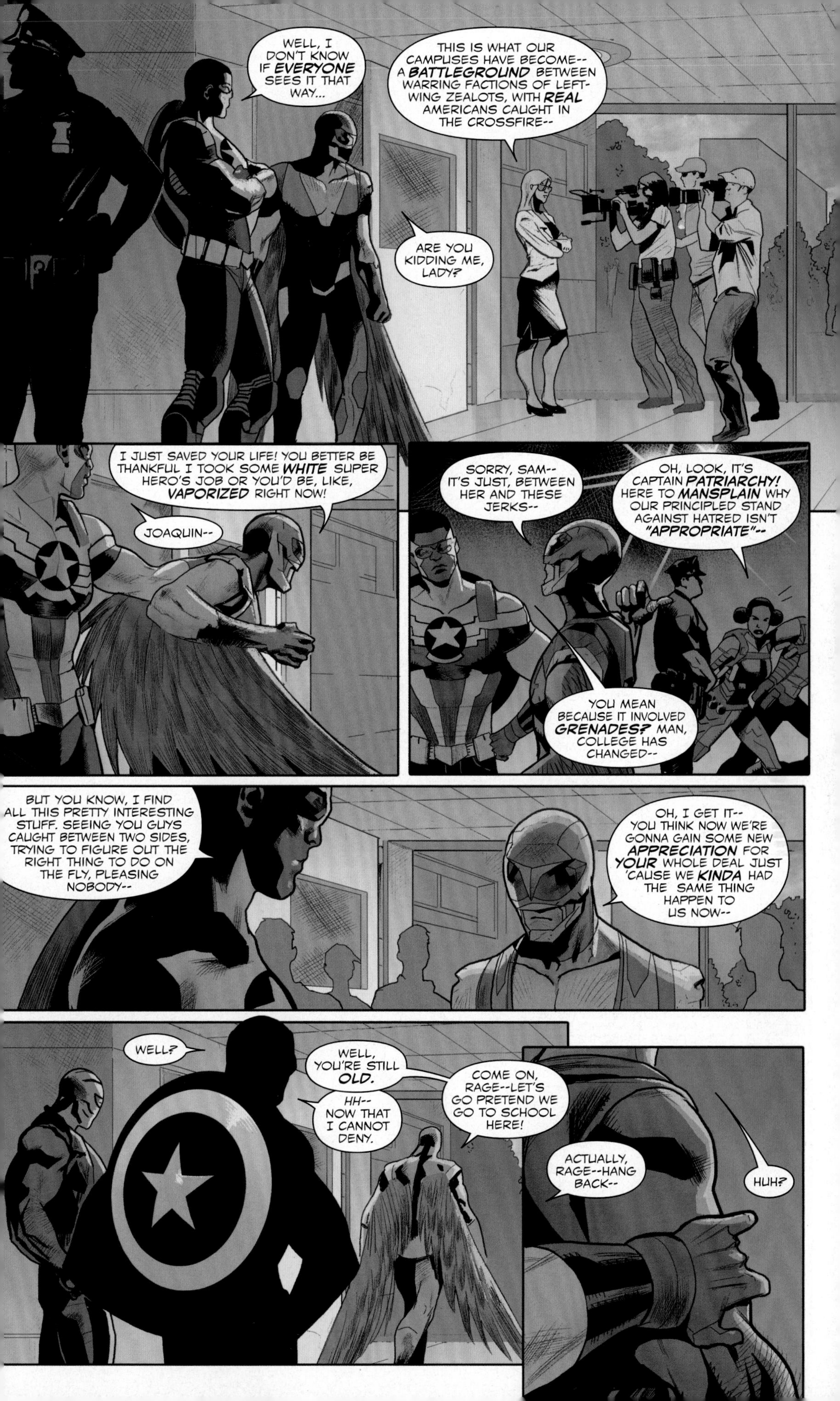
WELL, I DON'T KNOW IF EVERYONE SEES IT THAT WAY...
THIS IS WHAT OUR CAMPUSES HAVE BECOME-- A BATTLEGROUND BETWEEN WARRING FACTIONS OF LEFT-WING ZEALOTS, WITH REAL AMERICANS CAUGHT IN THE CROSSFIRE--
ARE YOU KIDDING ME, LADY?
I JUST SAVED YOUR LIFE! YOU BETTER BE THANKFUL I TOOK SOME WHITE SUPER HERO'S JOB OR YOU'D BE, LIKE, VAPORIZED RIGHT NOW!
JOAQUIN--
SORRY, SAM-- IT'S JUST, BETWEEN HER AND THESE JERKS--
OH, LOOK, IT'S CAPTAIN PATRIARCHY! HERE TO MANSPLAIN WHY OUR PRINCIPLED STAND AGAINST HATRED ISN'T "APPROPRIATE"--
YOU MEAN BECAUSE IT INVOLVED GRENADES? MAN, COLLEGE HAS CHANGED--
BUT YOU KNOW, I FIND ALL THIS PRETTY INTERESTING STUFF. SEEING YOU GUYS CAUGHT BETWEEN TWO SIDES, TRYING TO FIGURE OUT THE RIGHT THING TO DO ON THE FLY, PLEASING NOBODY--
OH, I GET IT-- YOU THINK NOW WE'RE GONNA GAIN SOME NEW APPRECIATION FOR YOUR WHOLE DEAL JUST 'CAUSE WE KINDA HAD THE SAME THING HAPPEN TO US NOW--
WELL?
WELL, YOU'RE STILL OLD.
HH-- NOW THAT I CANNOT DENY.
COME ON, RAGE--LET'S GO PRETEND WE GO TO SCHOOL HERE!
ACTUALLY, RAGE--HANG BACK--
HUH?

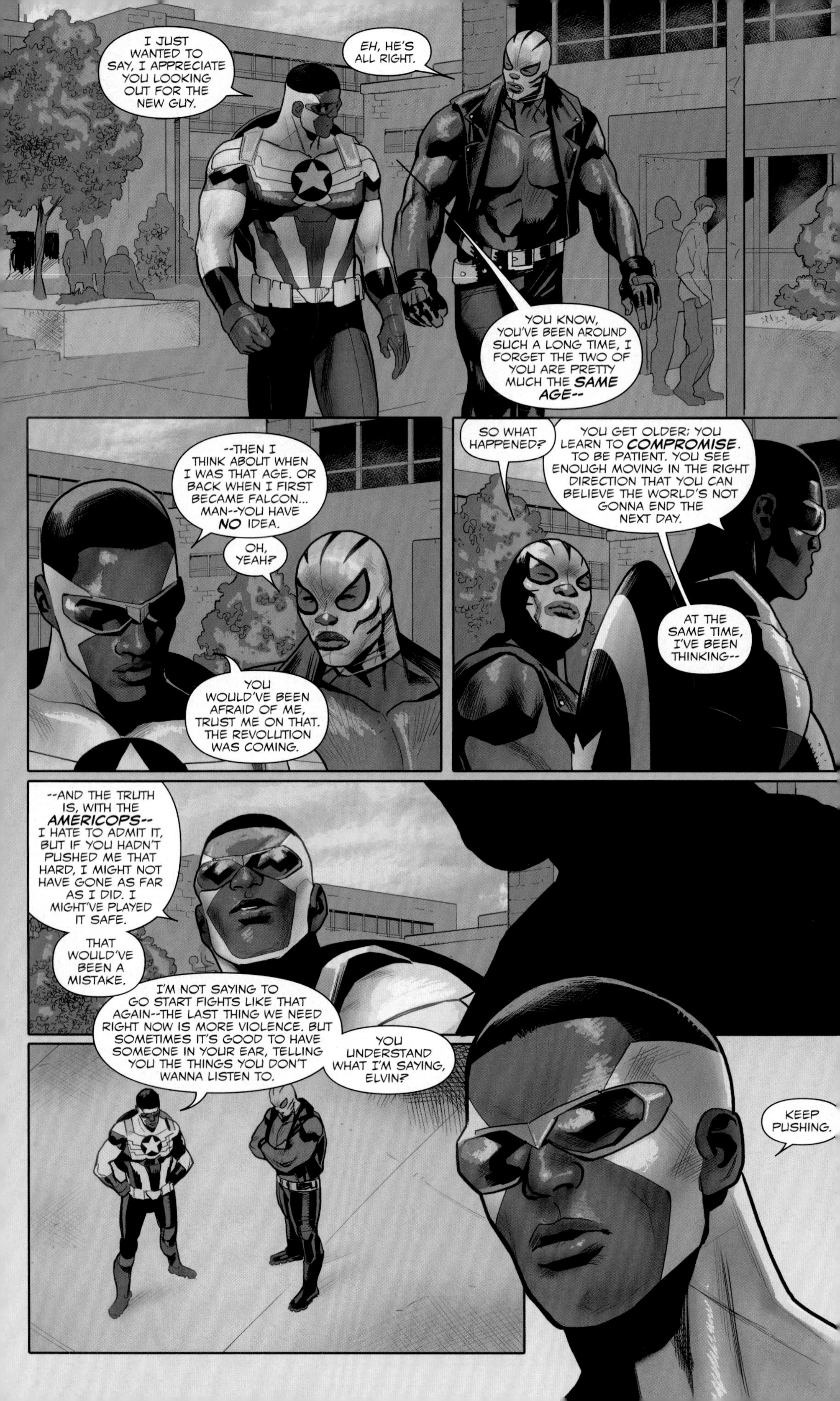

I JUST WANTED TO SAY, I APPRECIATE YOU LOOKING OUT FOR THE NEW GUY.
EH, HE'S ALL RIGHT.
YOU KNOW, YOU'VE BEEN AROUND SUCH A LONG TIME, I FORGET THE TWO OF YOU ARE PRETTY MUCH THE SAME AGE--
--THEN I THINK ABOUT WHEN I WAS THAT AGE. OR BACK WHEN I FIRST BECAME FALCON... MAN--YOU HAVE NO IDEA.
OH, YEAH?
YOU WOULD'VE BEEN AFRAID OF ME, TRUST ME ON THAT. THE REVOLUTION WAS COMING.
SO WHAT HAPPENED?
YOU GET OLDER; YOU LEARN TO COMPROMISE. TO BE PATIENT. YOU SEE ENOUGH MOVING IN THE RIGHT DIRECTION THAT YOU CAN BELIEVE THE WORLD'S NOT GONNA END THE NEXT DAY.
AT THE SAME TIME, I'VE BEEN THINKING--
--AND THE TRUTH IS, WITH THE AMERICOPS-- I HATE TO ADMIT IT, BUT IF YOU HADN'T PUSHED ME THAT HARD, I MIGHT NOT HAVE GONE AS FAR AS I DID. I MIGHT'VE PLAYED IT SAFE.
THAT WOULD'VE BEEN A MISTAKE.
I'M NOT SAYING TO GO START FIGHTS LIKE THAT AGAIN--THE LAST THING WE NEED RIGHT NOW IS MORE VIOLENCE. BUT SOMETIMES IT'S GOOD TO HAVE SOMEONE IN YOUR EAR, TELLING YOU THE THINGS YOU DON'T WANNA LISTEN TO.
YOU UNDERSTAND WHAT I'M SAYING, ELVIN?
KEEP PUSHING.

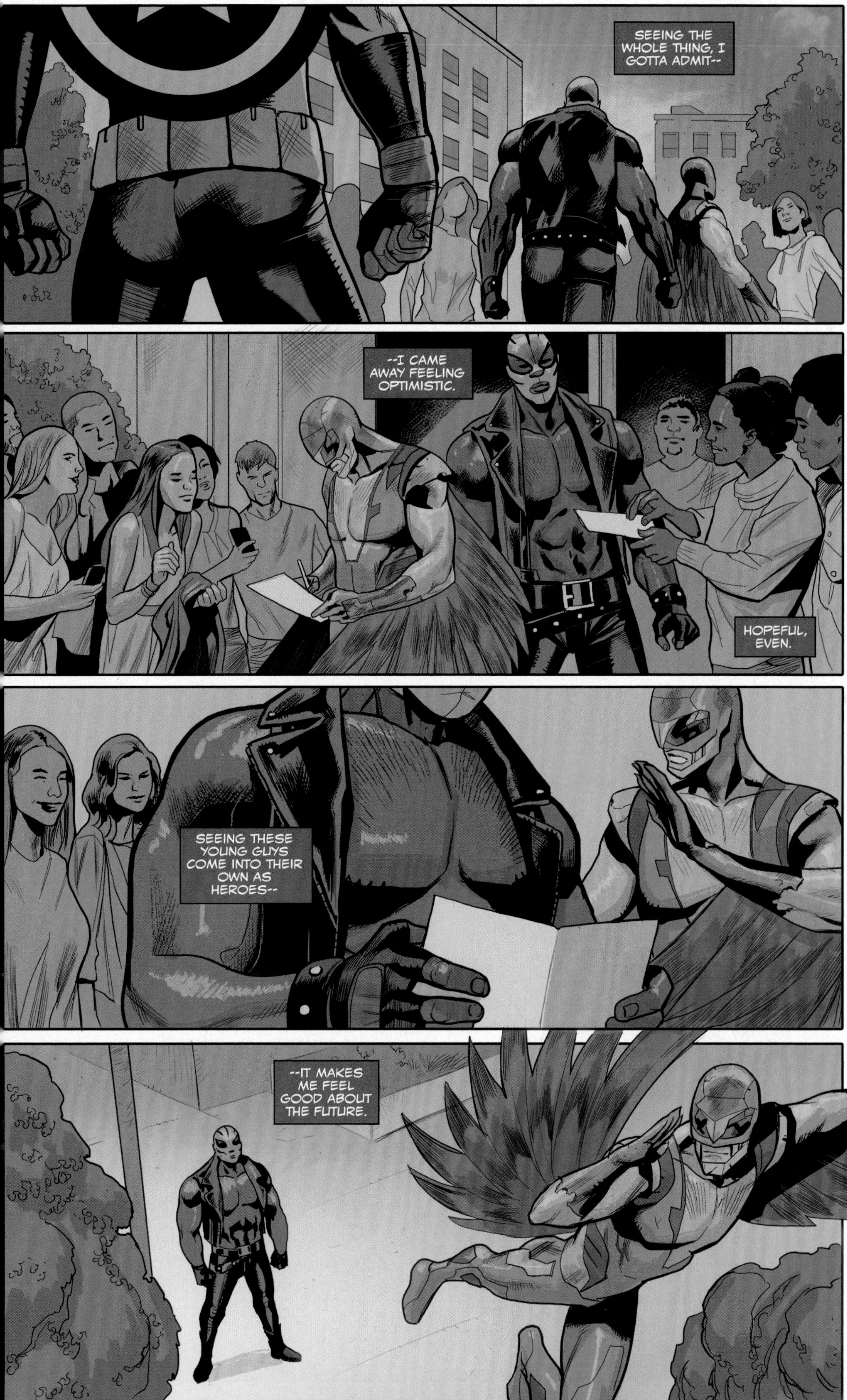
SEEING THE WHOLE THING, I GOTTA ADMIT--
--I CAME AWAY FEELING OPTIMISTIC.
HOPEFUL, EVEN.
SEEING THESE YOUNG GUYS COME INTO THEIR OWN AS HEROES--
--IT MAKES ME FEEL GOOD ABOUT THE FUTURE.

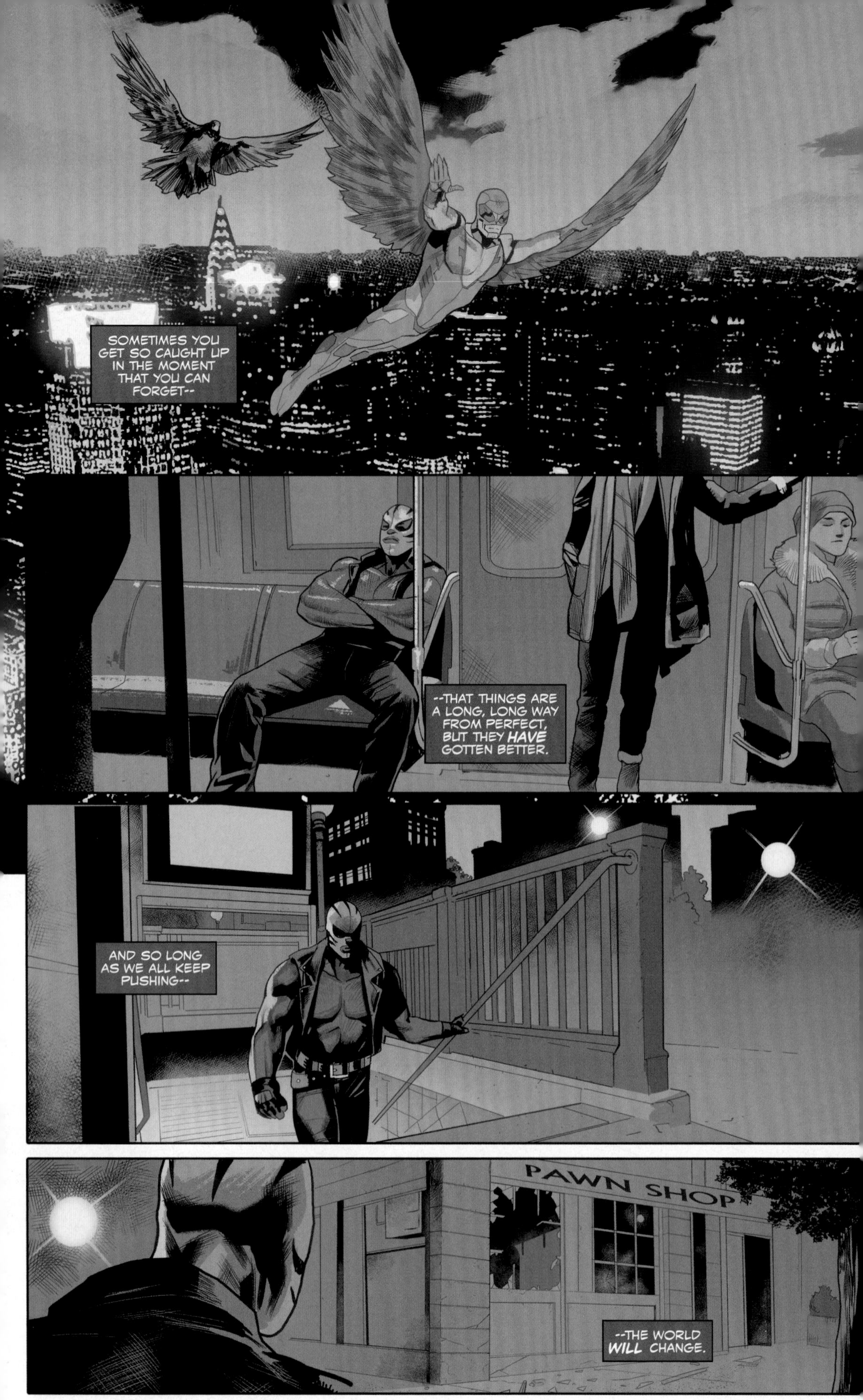
SOMETIMES YOU GET SO CAUGHT UP IN THE MOMENT THAT YOU CAN FORGET--
--THAT THINGS ARE A LONG, LONG WAY FROM PERFECT, BUT THEY HAVE GOTTEN BETTER.
AND SO LONG AS WE ALL KEEP PUSHING--
PAWN SHOP
--THE WORLD WILL CHANGE.

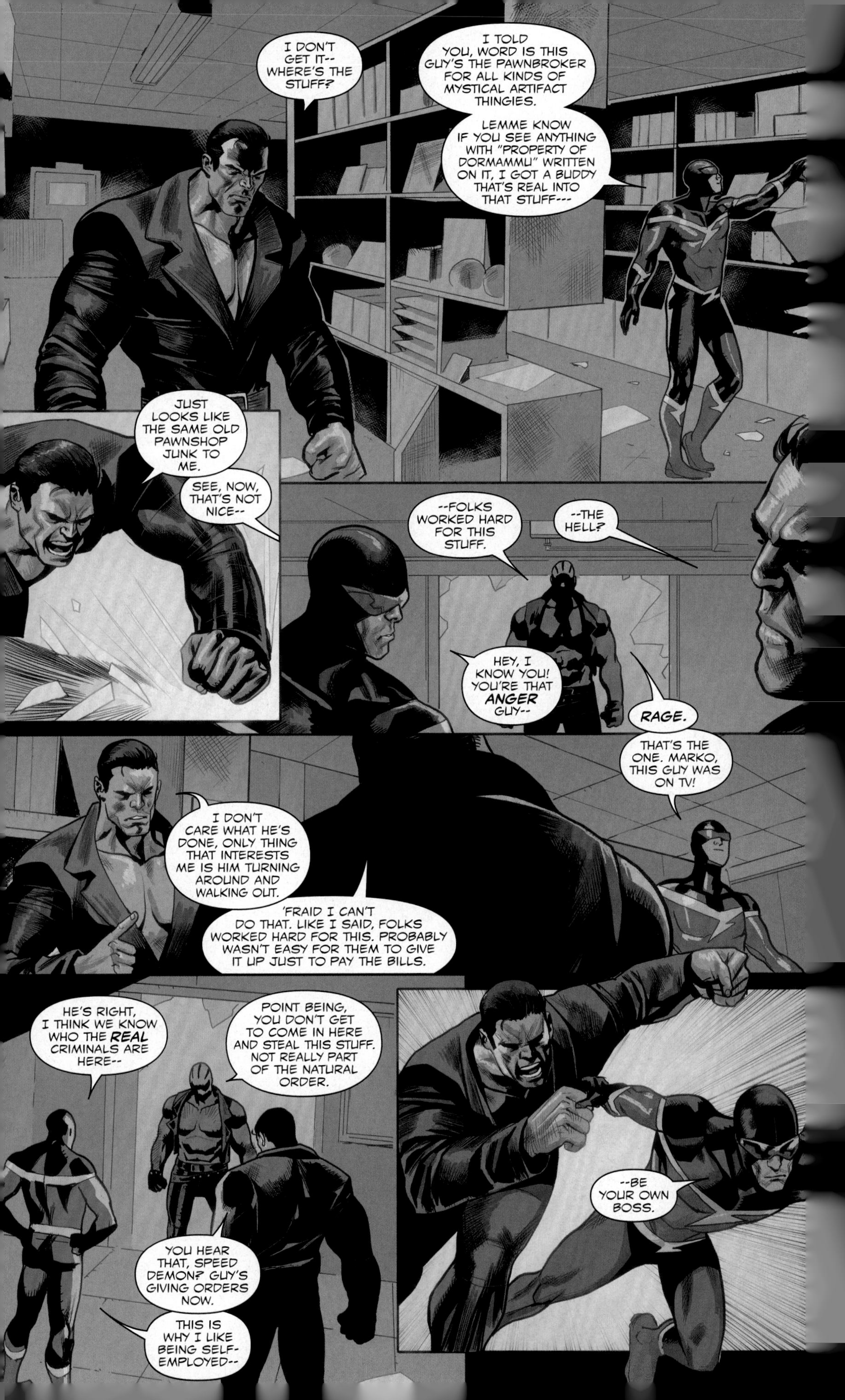
I DON'T GET IT-- WHERE'S THE STUFF?
I TOLD YOU, WORD IS THIS GUY'S THE PAWNBROKER FOR ALL KINDS OF MYSTICAL ARTIFACT THINGIES.
LEMME KNOW IF YOU SEE ANYTHING WITH "PROPERTY OF DORMAMMU" WRITTEN ON IT, I GOT A BUDDY THAT'S REAL INTO THAT STUFF---
JUST LOOKS LIKE THE SAME OLD PAWNSHOP JUNK TO ME.
SEE, NOW, THAT'S NOT NICE--
--FOLKS WORKED HARD FOR THIS STUFF.
--THE HELL?
HEY, I KNOW YOU! YOU'RE THAT ANGER GUY--
RAGE.
THAT'S THE ONE. MARKO, THIS GUY WAS ON TV!
I DON'T CARE WHAT HE'S DONE, ONLY THING THAT INTERESTS ME IS HIM TURNING AROUND AND WALKING OUT.
'FRAID I CAN'T DO THAT. LIKE I SAID, FOLKS WORKED HARD FOR THIS. PROBABLY WASN'T EASY FOR THEM TO GIVE IT UP JUST TO PAY THE BILLS.
HE'S RIGHT, I THINK WE KNOW WHO THE REAL CRIMINALS ARE HERE--
POINT BEING, YOU DON'T GET TO COME IN HERE AND STEAL THIS STUFF. NOT REALLY PART OF THE NATURAL ORDER.
YOU HEAR THAT, SPEED DEMON? GUY'S GIVING ORDERS NOW.
THIS IS WHY I LIKE BEING SELF-EMPLOYED--
--BE YOUR OWN BOSS.

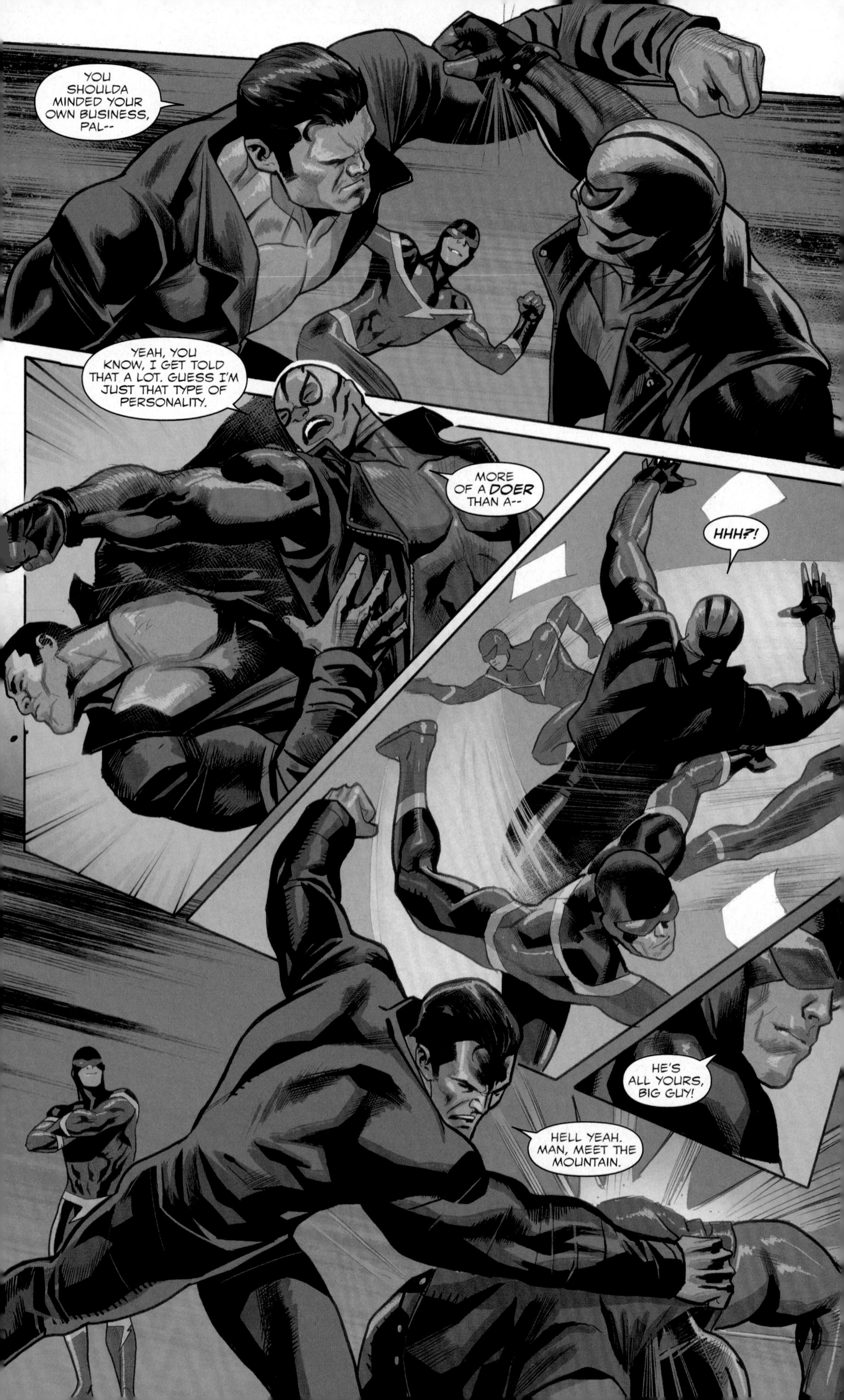
YOU SHOULDA MINDED YOUR OWN BUSINESS, PAL--
YEAH, YOU KNOW, I GET TOLD THAT A LOT. GUESS I'M JUST THAT TYPE OF PERSONALITY.
MORE OF A DOER THAN A--
HHH?!
HE'S ALL YOURS, BIG GUY!
HELL YEAH. MAN, MEET THE MOUNTAIN.

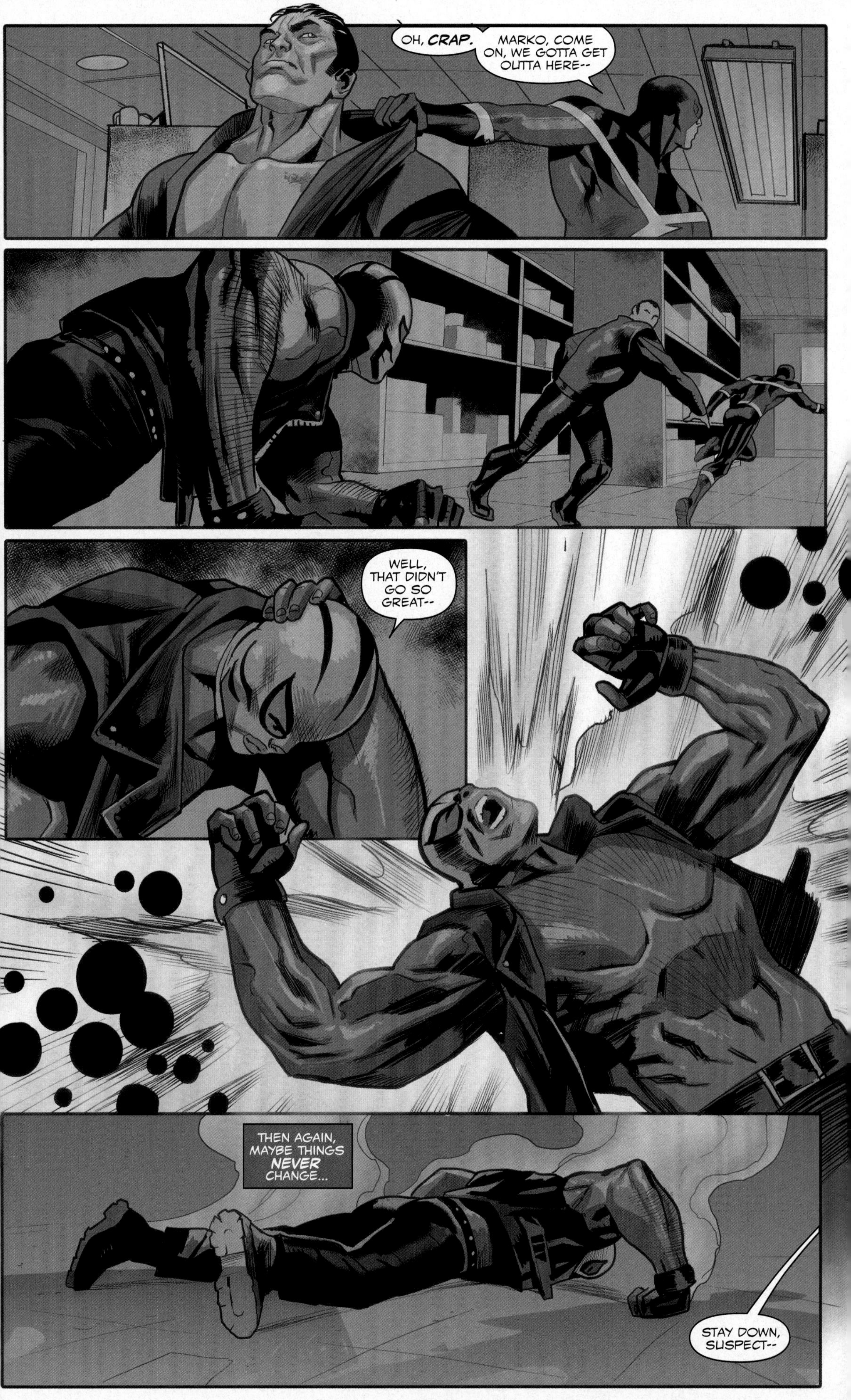
OH, CRAP.
MARKO, COME ON, WE GOTTA GET OUTTA HERE--
WELL, THAT DIDN'T GO SO GREAT--
THEN AGAIN, MAYBE THINGS NEVER CHANGE...
STAY DOWN, SUSPECT--

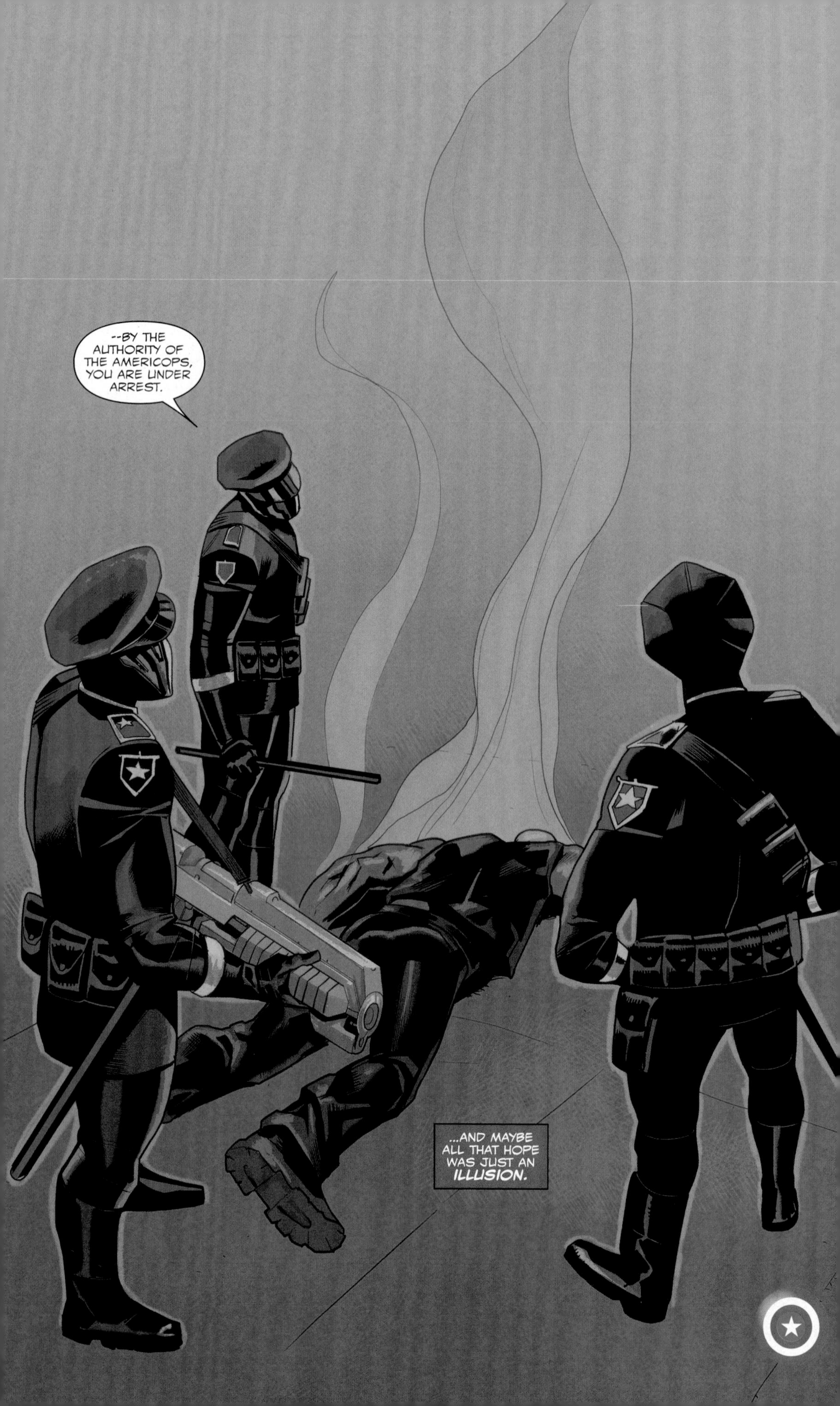
--BY THE AUTHORITY OF THE AMERICOPS, YOU ARE UNDER ARREST.
...AND MAYBE ALL THAT HOPE WAS JUST AN ILLUSION.

In this classic story, Steve Rogers – in his identity as "The Captain" – battles the Serpent Society, and Demolition Man has his first super-hero fight with Battle Star.

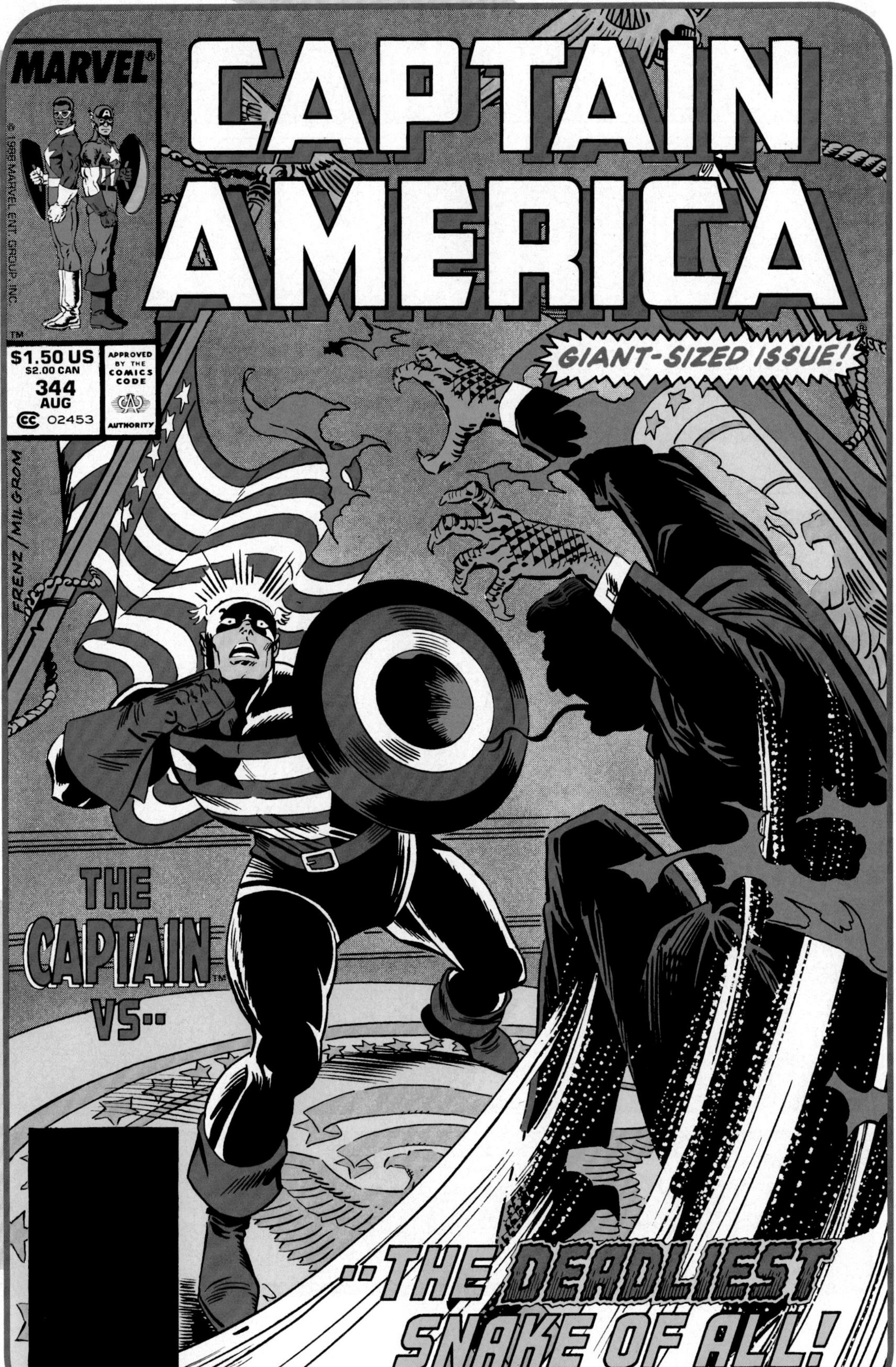

MARVEL
CAPTAIN AMERICA
© 1988 MARVEL ENT. GROUP, INC.
$1.50 US
$2.00 CAN
344
AUG
02453
APPROVED BY THE COMICS CODE AUTHORITY
GIANT-SIZED ISSUE!
FRENZ / MILGROM
THE CAPTAIN VS--
--THE DEADLIEST SNAKE OF ALL!

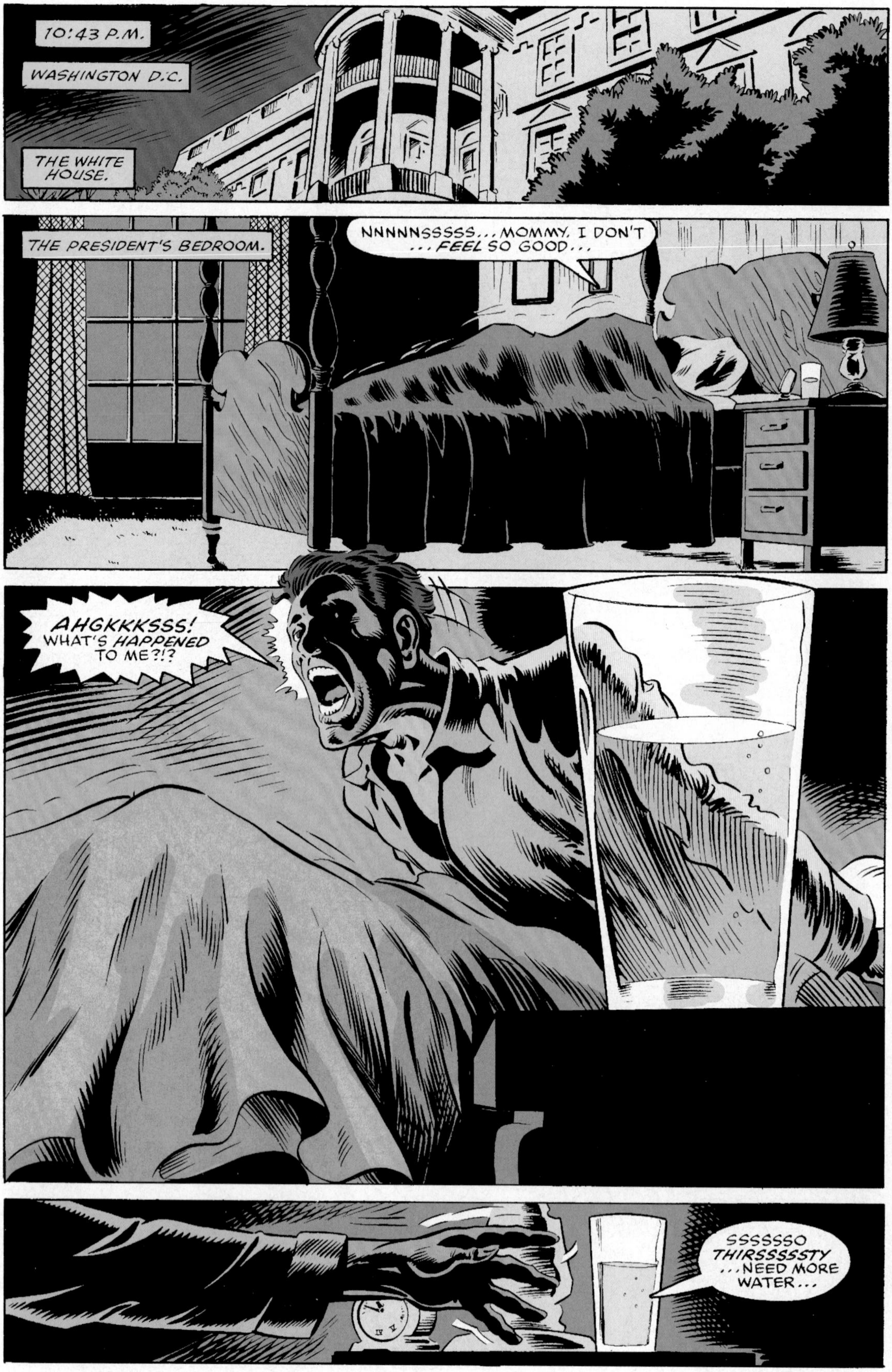
10:43 P.M.
WASHINGTON D.C.
THE WHITE HOUSE.
THE PRESIDENT'S BEDROOM.
NNNNNSSSSS... MOMMY, I DON'T ...FEEL SO GOOD...
AHGKKKSSS! WHAT'S HAPPENED TO ME?!?
SSSSSSO THIRSSSSSTY ...NEED MORE WATER...

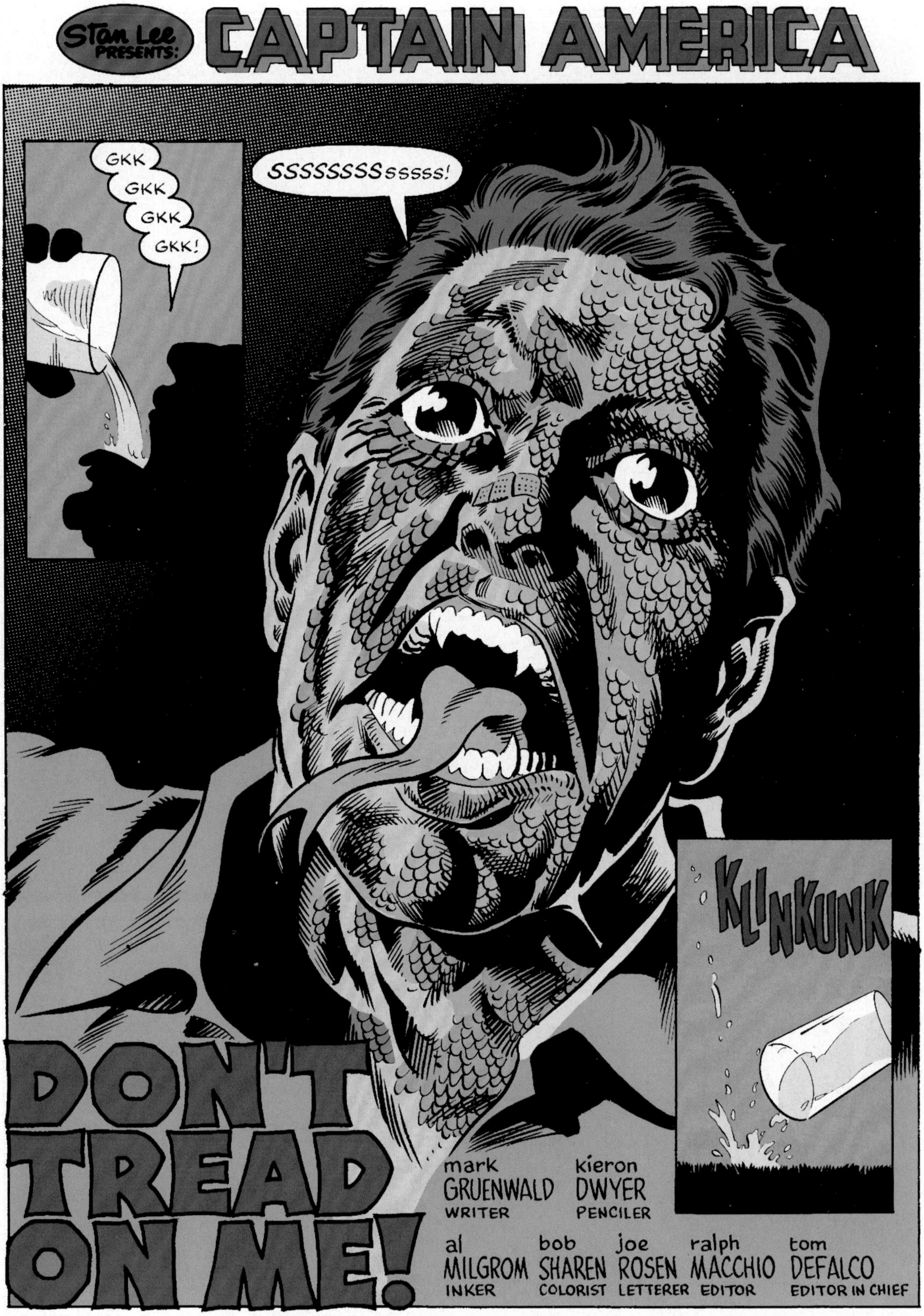

Stan Lee PRESENTS: CAPTAIN AMERICA
GKK GKK GKK GKK!
SSSSSSSSsssss!
KLINKUNK
DON'T TREAD ON ME!
mark GRUENWALD WRITER
kieron DWYER PENCILER
al MILGROM INKER
bob SHAREN COLORIST
joe ROSEN LETTERER
ralph MACCHIO EDITOR
tom DEFALCO EDITOR IN CHIEF

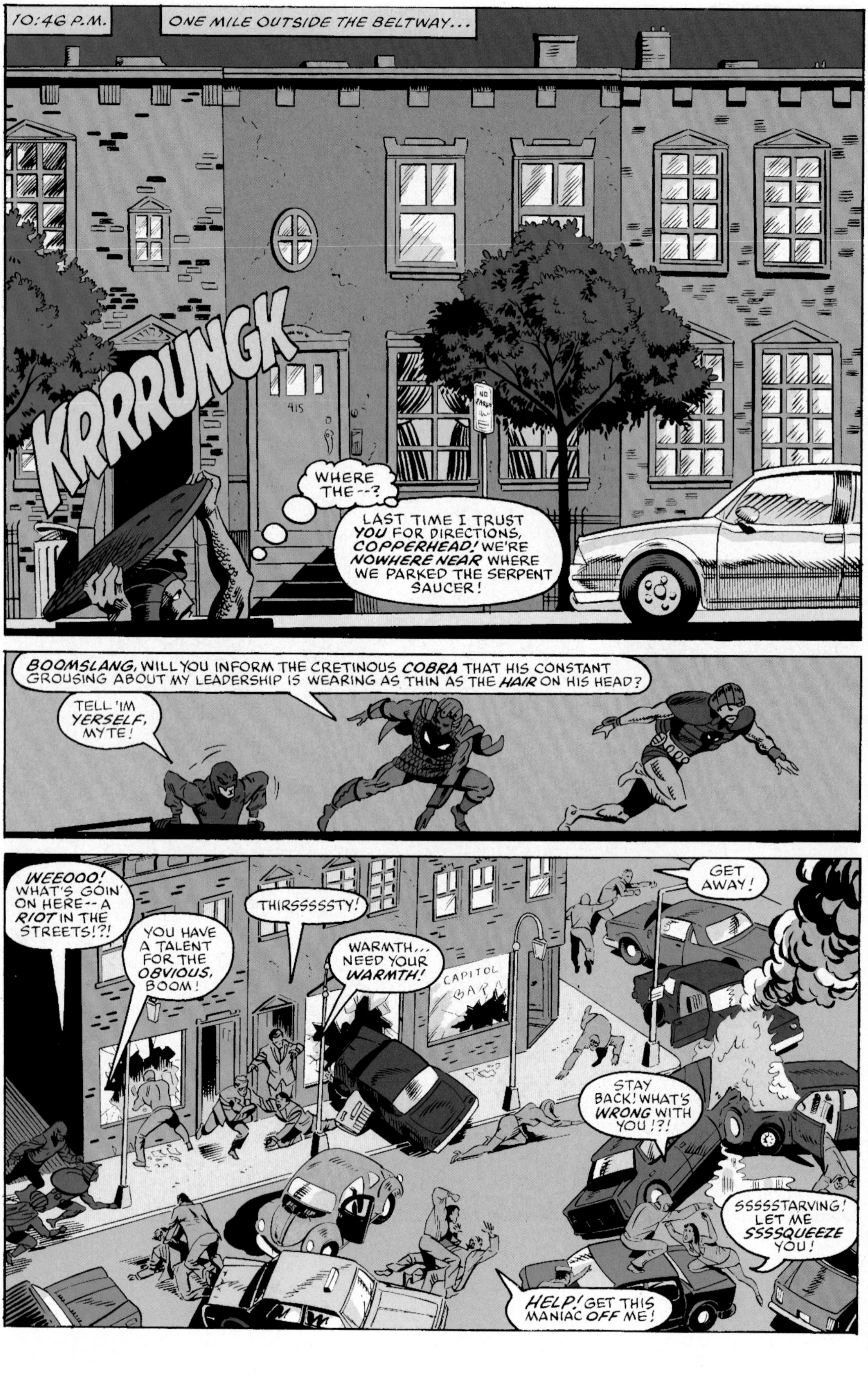

10:46 P.M.
ONE MILE OUTSIDE THE BELTWAY...
KRRRUNGK
415
NO PARKING
WHERE THE--?
LAST TIME I TRUST YOU FOR DIRECTIONS, COPPERHEAD! WE'RE NOWHERE NEAR WHERE WE PARKED THE SERPENT SAUCER!
BOOMSLANG, WILL YOU INFORM THE CRETINOUS COBRA THAT HIS CONSTANT GROUSING ABOUT MY LEADERSHIP IS WEARING AS THIN AS THE HAIR ON HIS HEAD?
TELL 'IM YERSELF, MYTE!
WEEOOO! WHAT'S GOIN' ON HERE-- A RIOT IN THE STREETS!?!
YOU HAVE A TALENT FOR THE OBVIOUS, BOOM!
THIRSSSSSTY!
WARMTH... NEED YOUR WARMTH!
CAPITOL BAR
GET AWAY!
STAY BACK! WHAT'S WRONG WITH YOU!?!
SSSSSTARVING! LET ME SSSSQUEEZE YOU!
HELP! GET THIS MANIAC OFF ME!

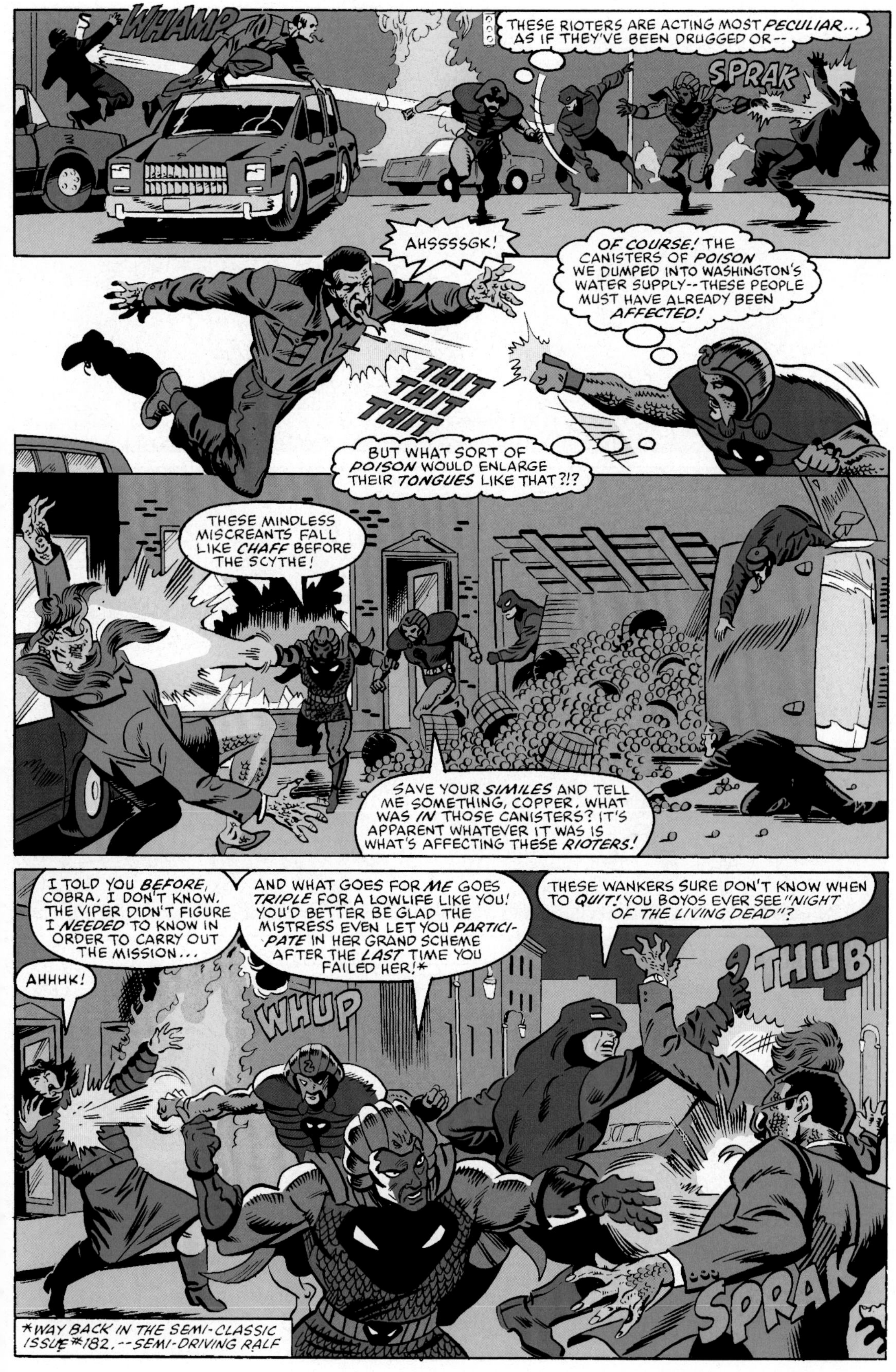
WHAMP
THESE RIOTERS ARE ACTING MOST PECULIAR... AS IF THEY'VE BEEN DRUGGED OR--
SPRAK
AHSSSSGK!
OF COURSE! THE CANISTERS OF POISON WE DUMPED INTO WASHINGTON'S WATER SUPPLY--THESE PEOPLE MUST HAVE ALREADY BEEN AFFECTED!
THIT THIT THIT
BUT WHAT SORT OF POISON WOULD ENLARGE THEIR TONGUES LIKE THAT?!?
THESE MINDLESS MISCREANTS FALL LIKE CHAFF BEFORE THE SCYTHE!
SAVE YOUR SIMILES AND TELL ME SOMETHING, COPPER. WHAT WAS IN THOSE CANISTERS? IT'S APPARENT WHATEVER IT WAS IS WHAT'S AFFECTING THESE RIOTERS!
I TOLD YOU BEFORE, COBRA. I DON'T KNOW. THE VIPER DIDN'T FIGURE I NEEDED TO KNOW IN ORDER TO CARRY OUT THE MISSION...
AND WHAT GOES FOR ME GOES TRIPLE FOR A LOWLIFE LIKE YOU! YOU'D BETTER BE GLAD THE MISTRESS EVEN LET YOU PARTICIPATE IN HER GRAND SCHEME AFTER THE LAST TIME YOU FAILED HER!*
THESE WANKERS SURE DON'T KNOW WHEN TO QUIT! YOU BOYOS EVER SEE "NIGHT OF THE LIVING DEAD"?
AHHHK!
THUB
WHUP
SPRAK
*WAY BACK IN THE SEMI-CLASSIC ISSUE #182. --SEMI-DRIVING RALF

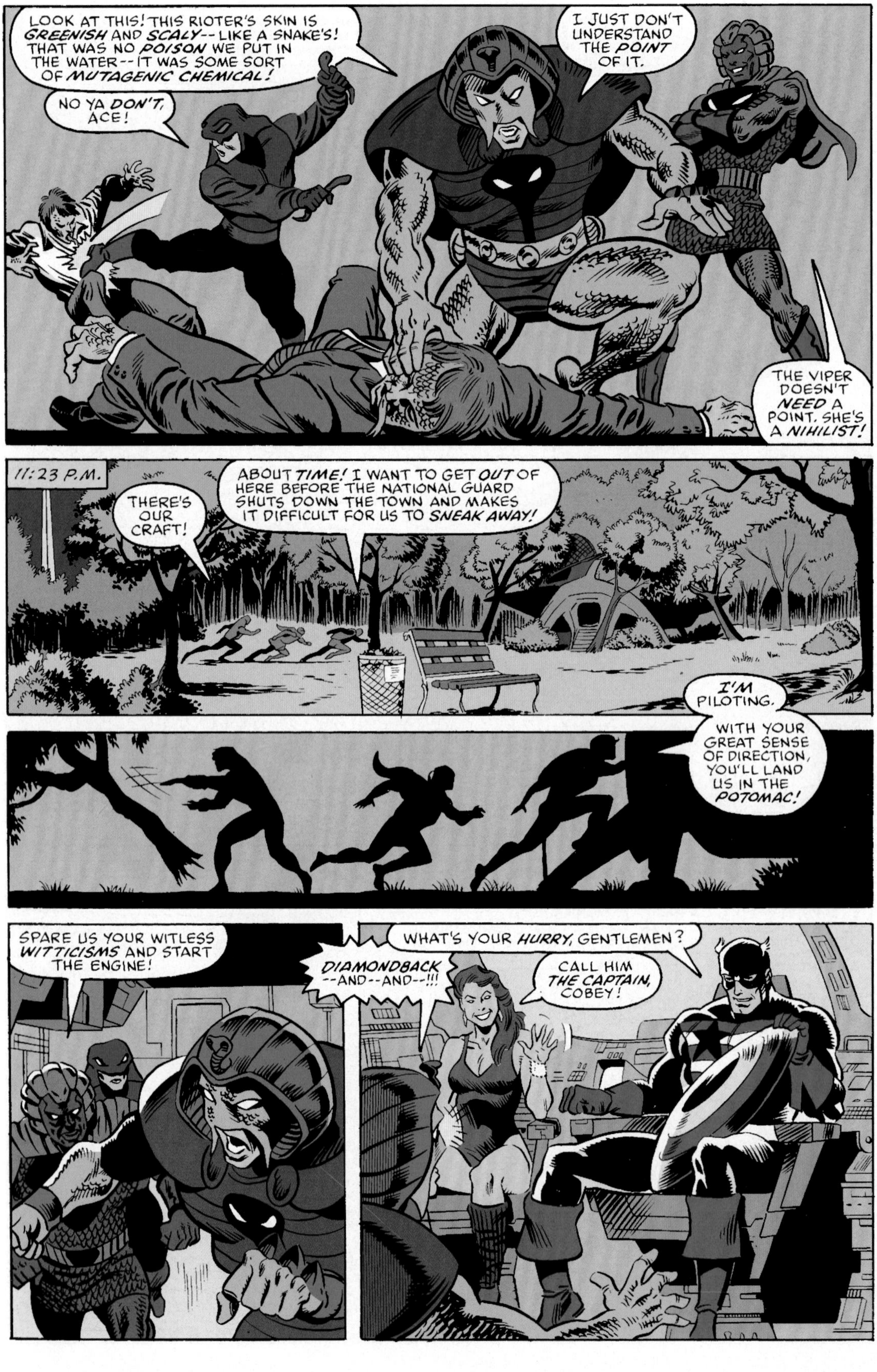
LOOK AT THIS! THIS RIOTER'S SKIN IS GREENISH AND SCALY-- LIKE A SNAKE'S! THAT WAS NO POISON WE PUT IN THE WATER--IT WAS SOME SORT OF MUTAGENIC CHEMICAL!
NO YA DON'T, ACE!
I JUST DON'T UNDERSTAND THE POINT OF IT.
THE VIPER DOESN'T NEED A POINT. SHE'S A NIHILIST!
11:23 P.M.
THERE'S OUR CRAFT!
ABOUT TIME! I WANT TO GET OUT OF HERE BEFORE THE NATIONAL GUARD SHUTS DOWN THE TOWN AND MAKES IT DIFFICULT FOR US TO SNEAK AWAY!
I'M PILOTING.
WITH YOUR GREAT SENSE OF DIRECTION, YOU'LL LAND US IN THE POTOMAC!
SPARE US YOUR WITLESS WITTICISMS AND START THE ENGINE!
WHAT'S YOUR HURRY, GENTLEMEN?
DIAMONDBACK --AND--AND--!!!
CALL HIM THE CAPTAIN, COBEY!

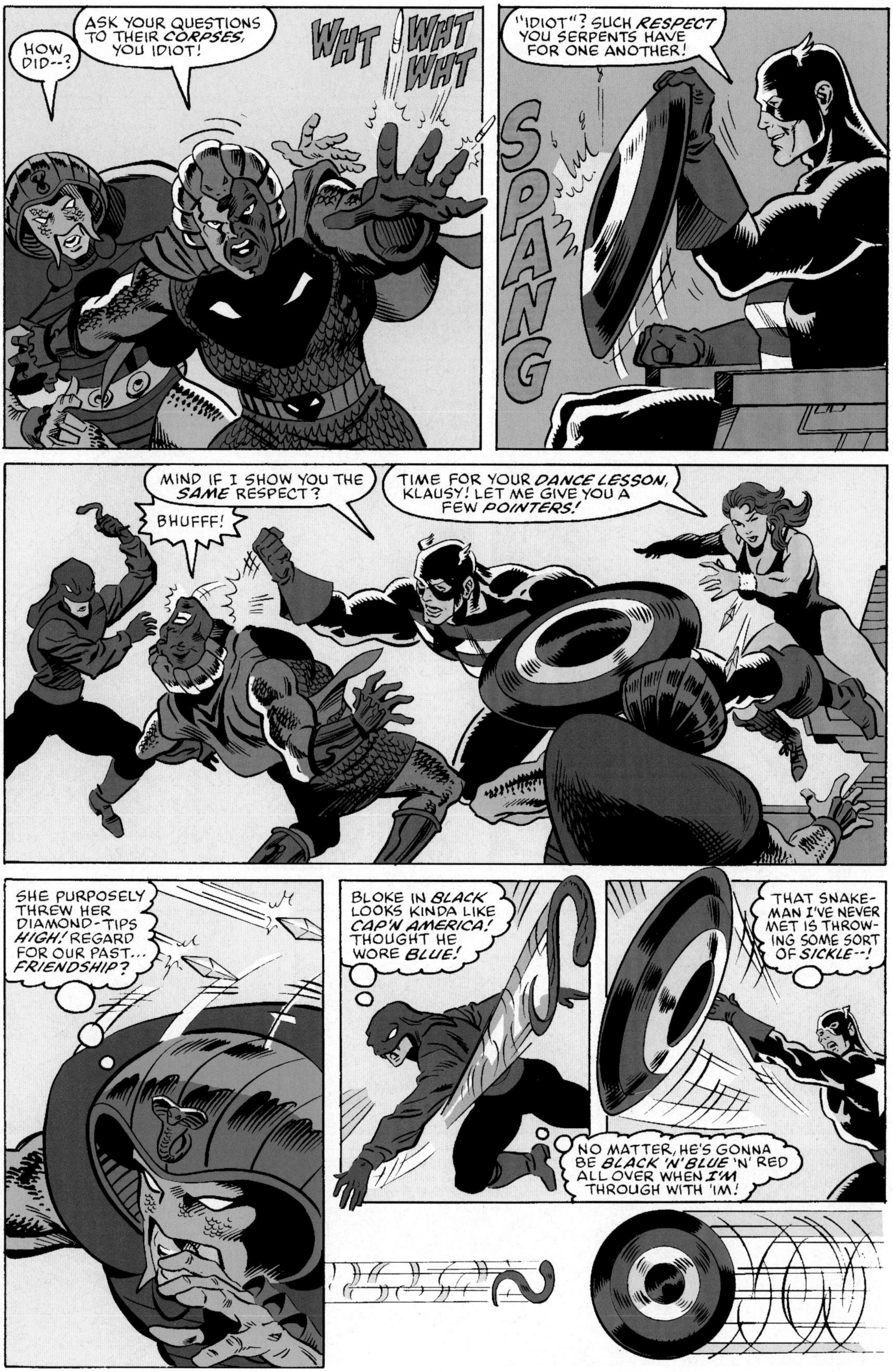
HOW DID--?
ASK YOUR QUESTIONS TO THEIR CORPSES, YOU IDIOT!
WHT WHT WHT
"IDIOT"? SUCH RESPECT YOU SERPENTS HAVE FOR ONE ANOTHER!
SPANG
MIND IF I SHOW YOU THE SAME RESPECT?
BHUFFF!
TIME FOR YOUR DANCE LESSON, KLAUSY! LET ME GIVE YOU A FEW POINTERS!
SHE PURPOSELY THREW HER DIAMOND-TIPS HIGH! REGARD FOR OUR PAST... FRIENDSHIP?
BLOKE IN BLACK LOOKS KINDA LIKE CAP'N AMERICA! THOUGHT HE WORE BLUE!
THAT SNAKE-MAN I'VE NEVER MET IS THROWING SOME SORT OF SICKLE--!
NO MATTER, HE'S GONNA BE BLACK 'N' BLUE 'N' RED ALL OVER WHEN I'M THROUGH WITH 'IM!

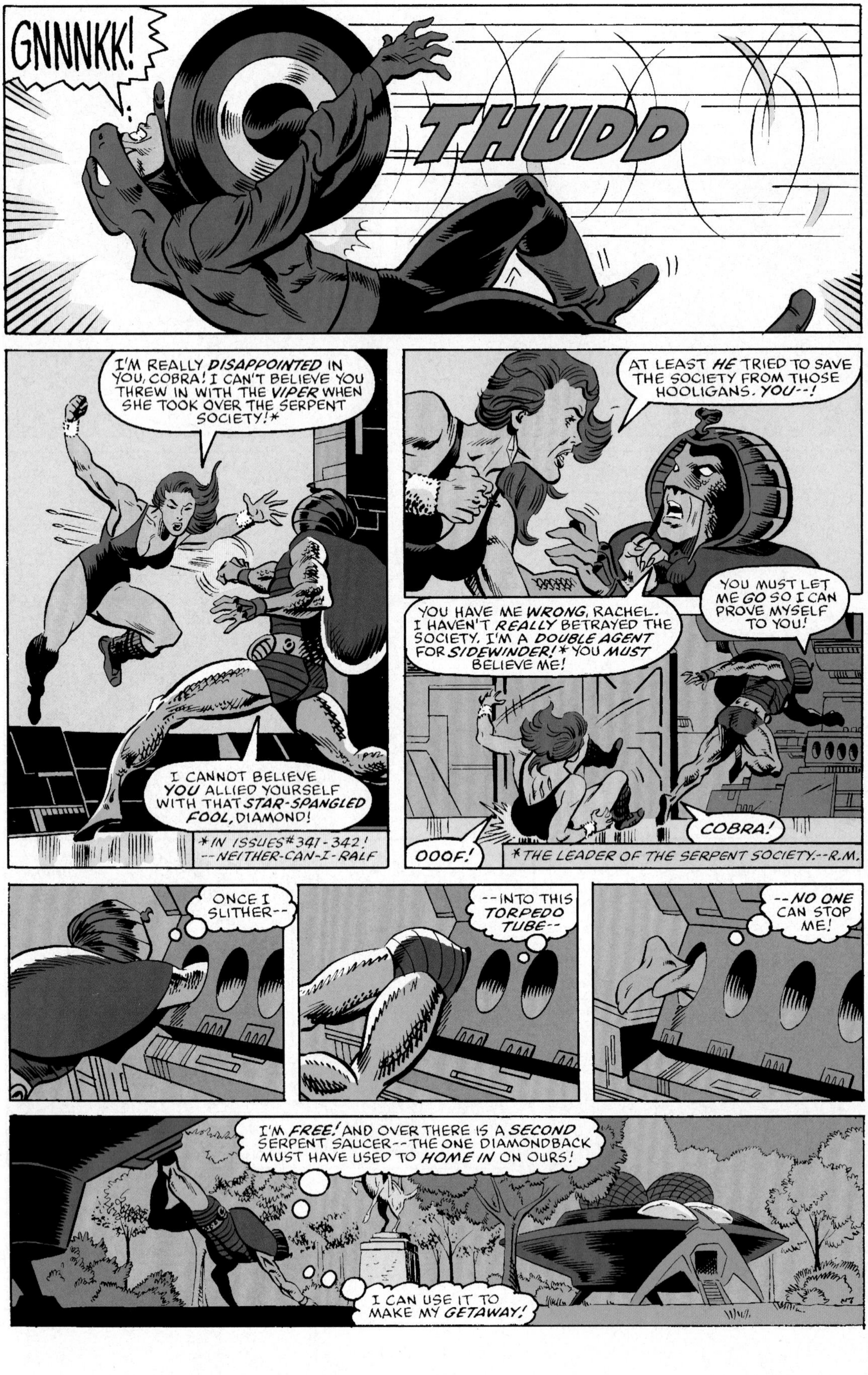

GNNNKK!
THUDD
I'M REALLY DISAPPOINTED IN YOU, COBRA! I CAN'T BELIEVE YOU THREW IN WITH THE VIPER WHEN SHE TOOK OVER THE SERPENT SOCIETY!*
I CANNOT BELIEVE YOU ALLIED YOURSELF WITH THAT STAR-SPANGLED FOOL, DIAMOND!
*IN ISSUES #341-342! --NEITHER-CAN-I-RALF
AT LEAST HE TRIED TO SAVE THE SOCIETY FROM THOSE HOOLIGANS. YOU--!
YOU HAVE ME WRONG, RACHEL. I HAVEN'T REALLY BETRAYED THE SOCIETY. I'M A DOUBLE AGENT FOR SIDEWINDER!* YOU MUST BELIEVE ME!
YOU MUST LET ME GO SO I CAN PROVE MYSELF TO YOU!
OOOF!
COBRA!
*THE LEADER OF THE SERPENT SOCIETY.--R.M.
ONCE I SLITHER--
--INTO THIS TORPEDO TUBE--
--NO ONE CAN STOP ME!
I'M FREE! AND OVER THERE IS A SECOND SERPENT SAUCER--THE ONE DIAMONDBACK MUST HAVE USED TO HOME IN ON OURS!
I CAN USE IT TO MAKE MY GETAWAY!

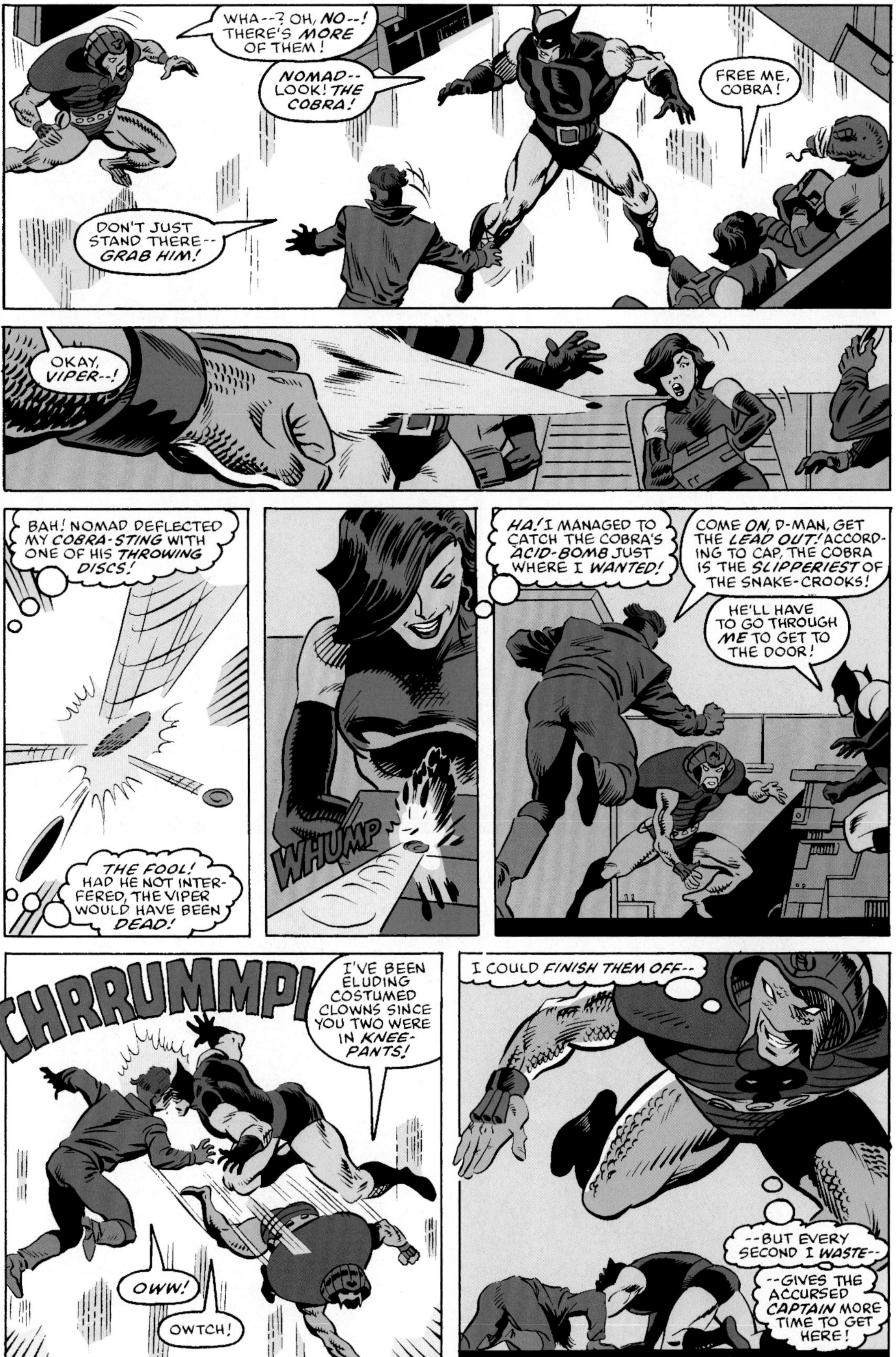
WHA--? OH, NO--! THERE'S MORE OF THEM!
NOMAD-- LOOK! THE COBRA!
FREE ME, COBRA!
DON'T JUST STAND THERE-- GRAB HIM!
OKAY, VIPER--!
BAH! NOMAD DEFLECTED MY COBRA-STING WITH ONE OF HIS THROWING DISCS!
THE FOOL! HAD HE NOT INTERFERED, THE VIPER WOULD HAVE BEEN DEAD!
WHUMP
HA! I MANAGED TO CATCH THE COBRA'S ACID-BOMB JUST WHERE I WANTED!
COME ON, D-MAN, GET THE LEAD OUT! ACCORDING TO CAP, THE COBRA IS THE SLIPPERIEST OF THE SNAKE-CROOKS!
HE'LL HAVE TO GO THROUGH ME TO GET TO THE DOOR!
CHRRUMMP!
I'VE BEEN ELUDING COSTUMED CLOWNS SINCE YOU TWO WERE IN KNEE-PANTS!
OWW!
OWTCH!
I COULD FINISH THEM OFF--
--BUT EVERY SECOND I WASTE--
--GIVES THE ACCURSED CAPTAIN MORE TIME TO GET HERE!

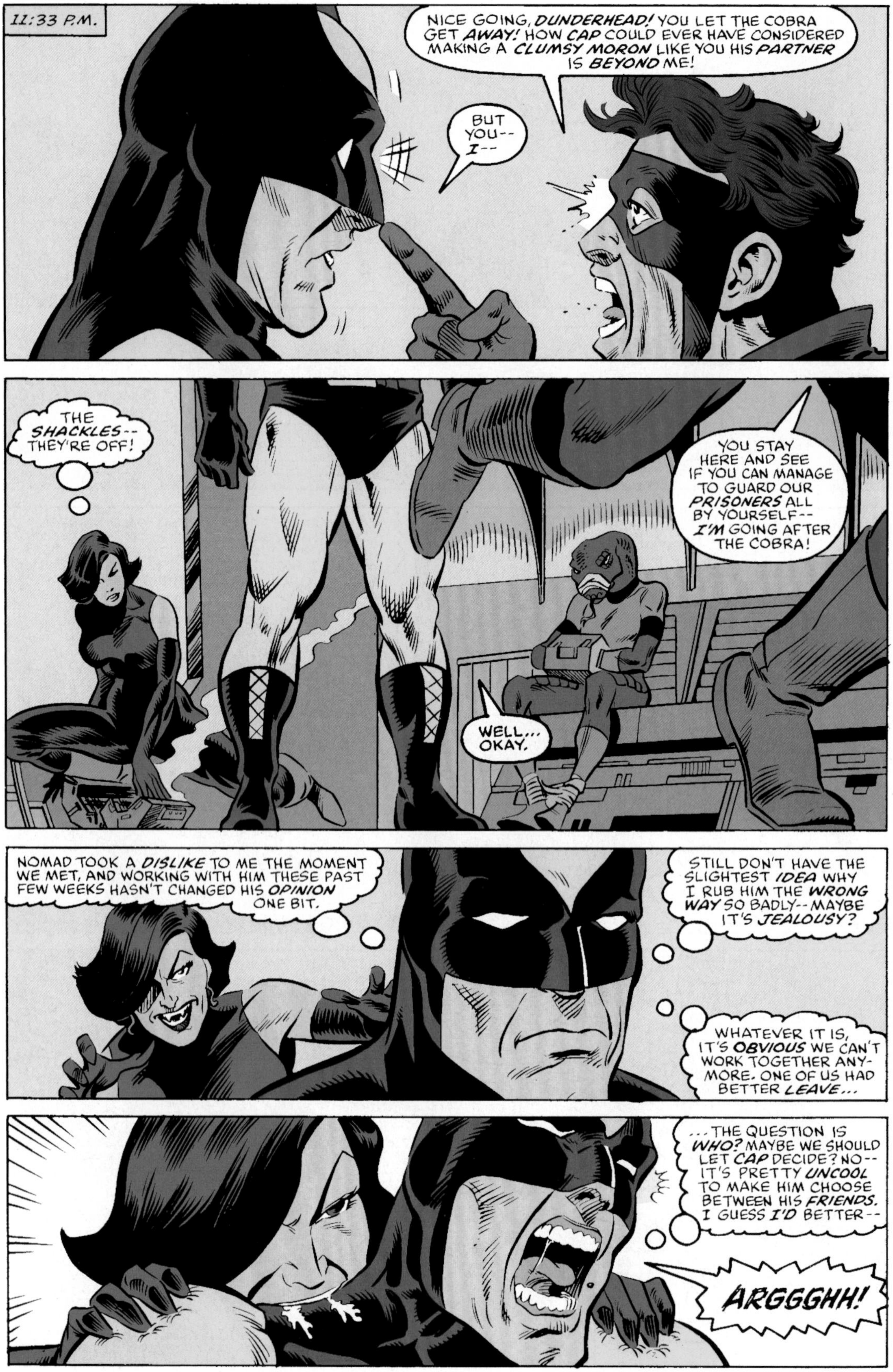
11:33 P.M.
NICE GOING, DUNDERHEAD! YOU LET THE COBRA GET AWAY! HOW CAP COULD EVER HAVE CONSIDERED MAKING A CLUMSY MORON LIKE YOU HIS PARTNER IS BEYOND ME!
BUT YOU-- I--
THE SHACKLES-- THEY'RE OFF!
YOU STAY HERE AND SEE IF YOU CAN MANAGE TO GUARD OUR PRISONERS ALL BY YOURSELF-- I'M GOING AFTER THE COBRA!
WELL... OKAY.
NOMAD TOOK A DISLIKE TO ME THE MOMENT WE MET, AND WORKING WITH HIM THESE PAST FEW WEEKS HASN'T CHANGED HIS OPINION ONE BIT.
STILL DON'T HAVE THE SLIGHTEST IDEA WHY I RUB HIM THE WRONG WAY SO BADLY--MAYBE IT'S JEALOUSY?
WHATEVER IT IS, IT'S OBVIOUS WE CAN'T WORK TOGETHER ANY-MORE. ONE OF US HAD BETTER LEAVE...
...THE QUESTION IS WHO? MAYBE WE SHOULD LET CAP DECIDE? NO-- IT'S PRETTY UNCOOL TO MAKE HIM CHOOSE BETWEEN HIS FRIENDS. I GUESS I'D BETTER--
ARGGGHH!

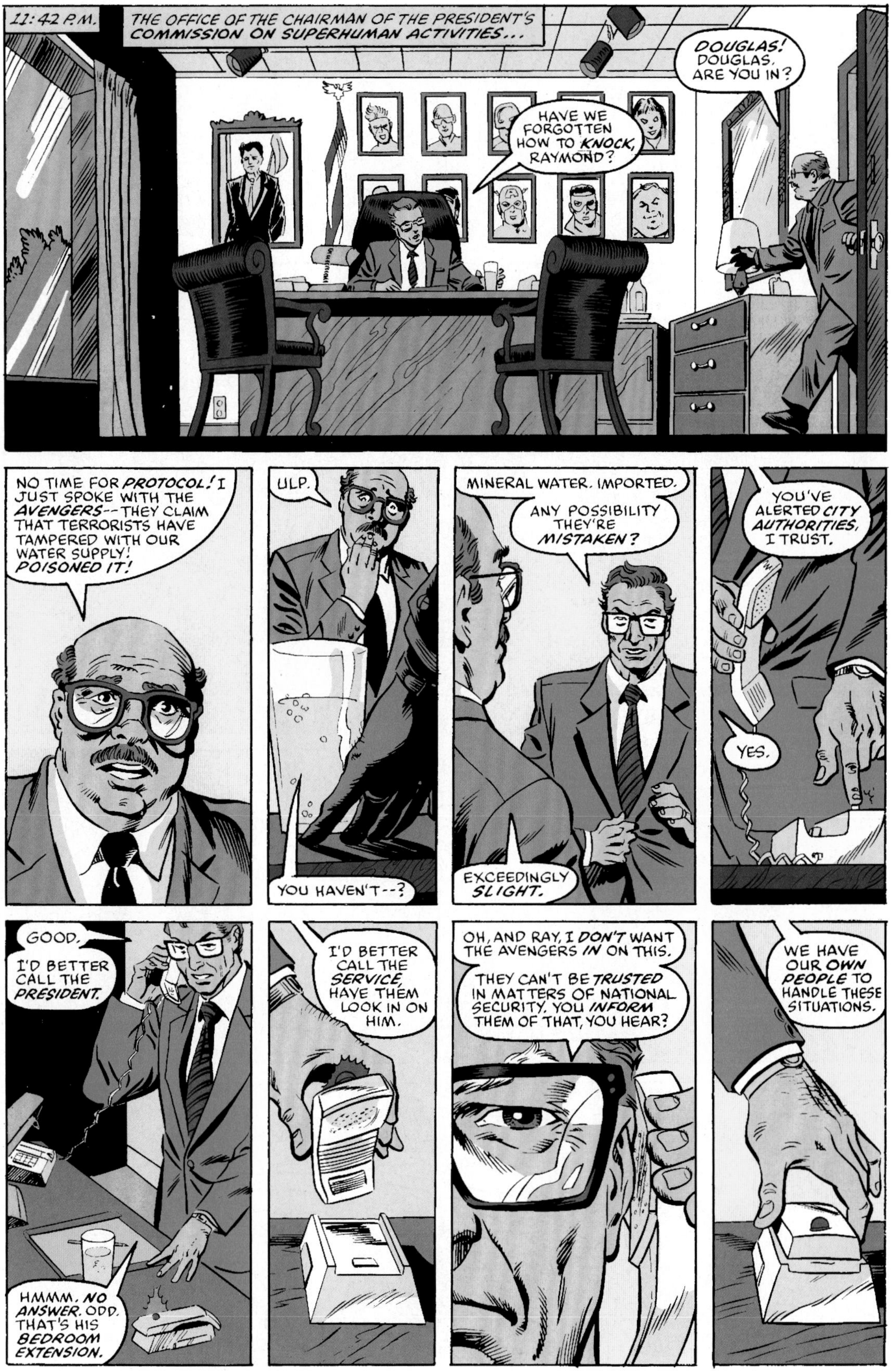
11:42 P.M.
THE OFFICE OF THE CHAIRMAN OF THE PRESIDENT'S COMMISSION ON SUPERHUMAN ACTIVITIES...
DOUGLAS! DOUGLAS. ARE YOU IN?
HAVE WE FORGOTTEN HOW TO KNOCK, RAYMOND?
NO TIME FOR PROTOCOL! I JUST SPOKE WITH THE AVENGERS--THEY CLAIM THAT TERRORISTS HAVE TAMPERED WITH OUR WATER SUPPLY! POISONED IT!
ULP.
YOU HAVEN'T--?
MINERAL WATER. IMPORTED.
ANY POSSIBILITY THEY'RE MISTAKEN?
EXCEEDINGLY SLIGHT.
YOU'VE ALERTED CITY AUTHORITIES, I TRUST.
YES.
GOOD.
I'D BETTER CALL THE PRESIDENT.
HMMM. NO ANSWER. ODD. THAT'S HIS BEDROOM EXTENSION.
I'D BETTER CALL THE SERVICE, HAVE THEM LOOK IN ON HIM.
OH, AND RAY, I DON'T WANT THE AVENGERS IN ON THIS.
THEY CAN'T BE TRUSTED IN MATTERS OF NATIONAL SECURITY. YOU INFORM THEM OF THAT, YOU HEAR?
WE HAVE OUR OWN PEOPLE TO HANDLE THESE SITUATIONS.

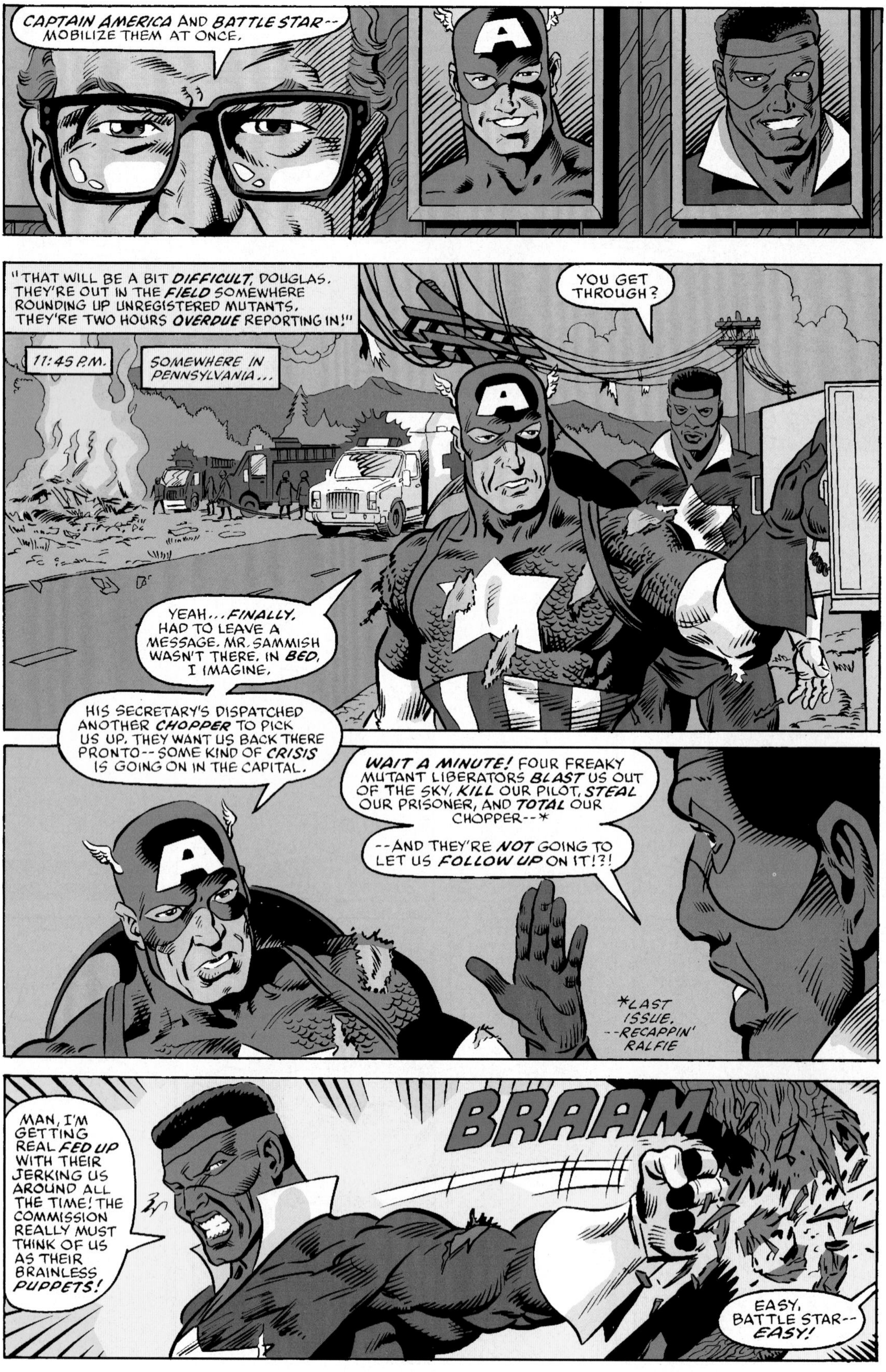
CAPTAIN AMERICA AND BATTLE STAR-- MOBILIZE THEM AT ONCE.
"THAT WILL BE A BIT DIFFICULT, DOUGLAS. THEY'RE OUT IN THE FIELD SOMEWHERE ROUNDING UP UNREGISTERED MUTANTS. THEY'RE TWO HOURS OVERDUE REPORTING IN!"
11:45 P.M.
SOMEWHERE IN PENNSYLVANIA...
YOU GET THROUGH?
YEAH...FINALLY. HAD TO LEAVE A MESSAGE. MR. SAMMISH WASN'T THERE. IN BED, I IMAGINE.
HIS SECRETARY'S DISPATCHED ANOTHER CHOPPER TO PICK US UP. THEY WANT US BACK THERE PRONTO--SOME KIND OF CRISIS IS GOING ON IN THE CAPITAL.
WAIT A MINUTE! FOUR FREAKY MUTANT LIBERATORS BLAST US OUT OF THE SKY, KILL OUR PILOT, STEAL OUR PRISONER, AND TOTAL OUR CHOPPER--*
--AND THEY'RE NOT GOING TO LET US FOLLOW UP ON IT!?!
*LAST ISSUE. --RECAPPIN' RALFIE
MAN, I'M GETTING REAL FED UP WITH THEIR JERKING US AROUND ALL THE TIME! THE COMMISSION REALLY MUST THINK OF US AS THEIR BRAINLESS PUPPETS!
BRAAM
EASY, BATTLE STAR-- EASY!

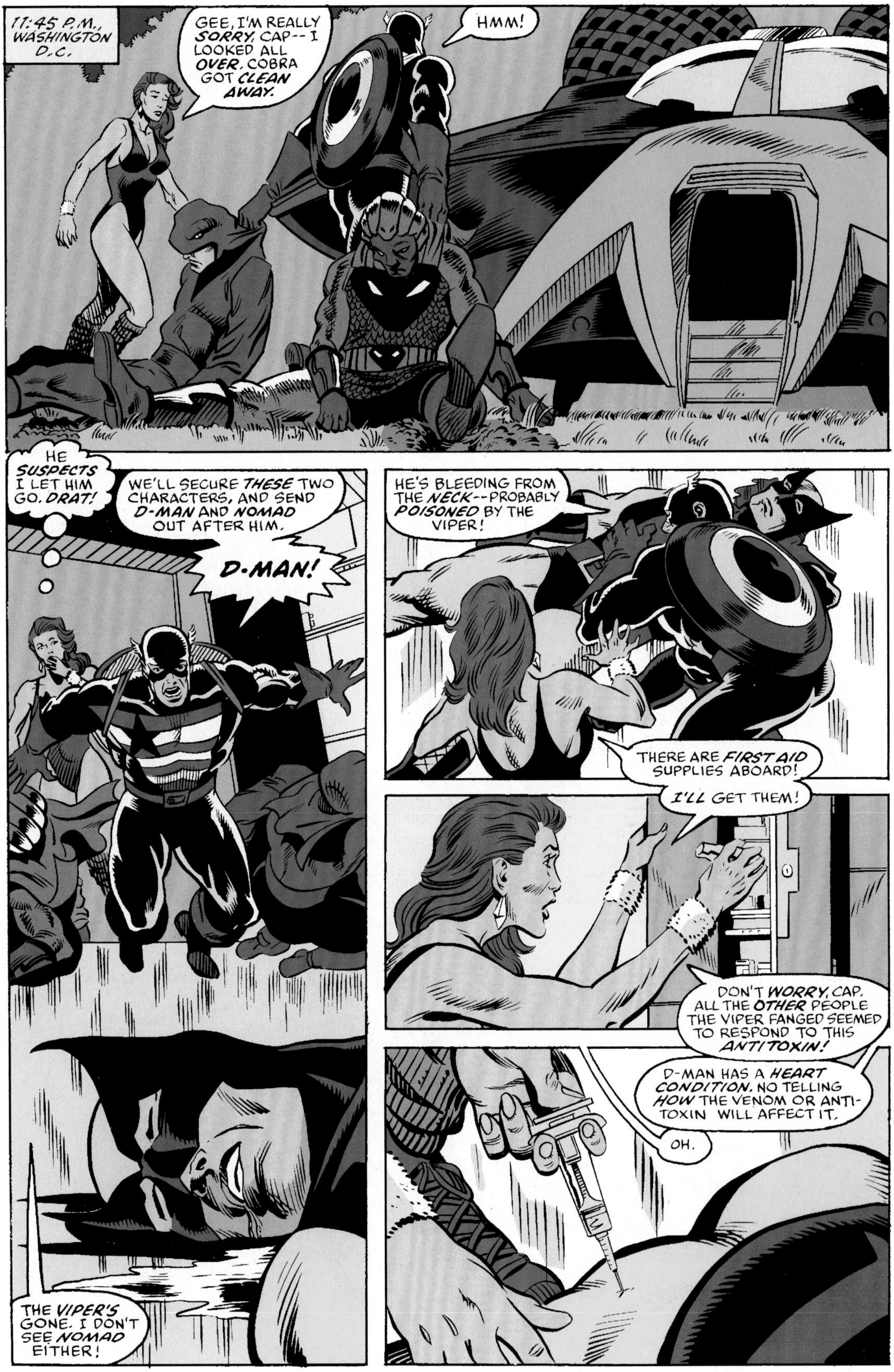

11:45 P.M., WASHINGTON D.C.
GEE, I'M REALLY SORRY, CAP-- I LOOKED ALL OVER. COBRA GOT CLEAN AWAY.
HMM!
HE SUSPECTS I LET HIM GO. DRAT!
WE'LL SECURE THESE TWO CHARACTERS, AND SEND D-MAN AND NOMAD OUT AFTER HIM.
D-MAN!
THE VIPER'S GONE. I DON'T SEE NOMAD EITHER!
HE'S BLEEDING FROM THE NECK--PROBABLY POISONED BY THE VIPER!
THERE ARE FIRST AID SUPPLIES ABOARD!
I'LL GET THEM!
DON'T WORRY, CAP. ALL THE OTHER PEOPLE THE VIPER FANGED SEEMED TO RESPOND TO THIS ANTITOXIN!
D-MAN HAS A HEART CONDITION. NO TELLING HOW THE VENOM OR ANTI-TOXIN WILL AFFECT IT.
OH.

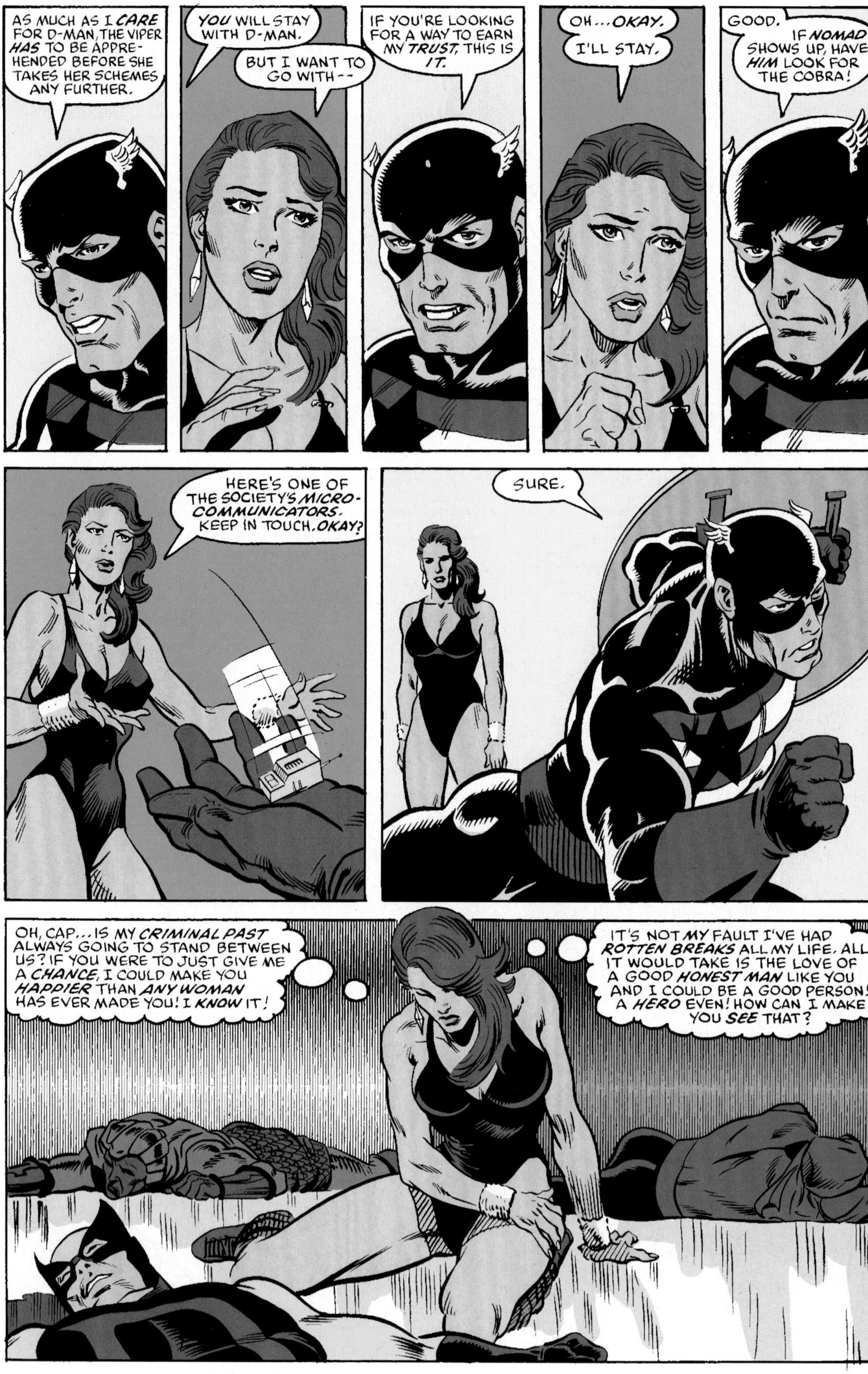

AS MUCH AS I CARE FOR D-MAN, THE VIPER HAS TO BE APPREHENDED BEFORE SHE TAKES HER SCHEMES ANY FURTHER.
YOU WILL STAY WITH D-MAN.
BUT I WANT TO GO WITH--
IF YOU'RE LOOKING FOR A WAY TO EARN MY TRUST, THIS IS IT.
OH... OKAY.
I'LL STAY.
GOOD.
IF NOMAD SHOWS UP, HAVE HIM LOOK FOR THE COBRA!
HERE'S ONE OF THE SOCIETY'S MICRO-COMMUNICATORS. KEEP IN TOUCH, OKAY?
SURE.
OH, CAP... IS MY CRIMINAL PAST ALWAYS GOING TO STAND BETWEEN US? IF YOU WERE TO JUST GIVE ME A CHANCE, I COULD MAKE YOU HAPPIER THAN ANY WOMAN HAS EVER MADE YOU! I KNOW IT!
IT'S NOT MY FAULT I'VE HAD ROTTEN BREAKS ALL MY LIFE. ALL IT WOULD TAKE IS THE LOVE OF A GOOD HONEST MAN LIKE YOU AND I COULD BE A GOOD PERSON! A HERO EVEN! HOW CAN I MAKE YOU SEE THAT?

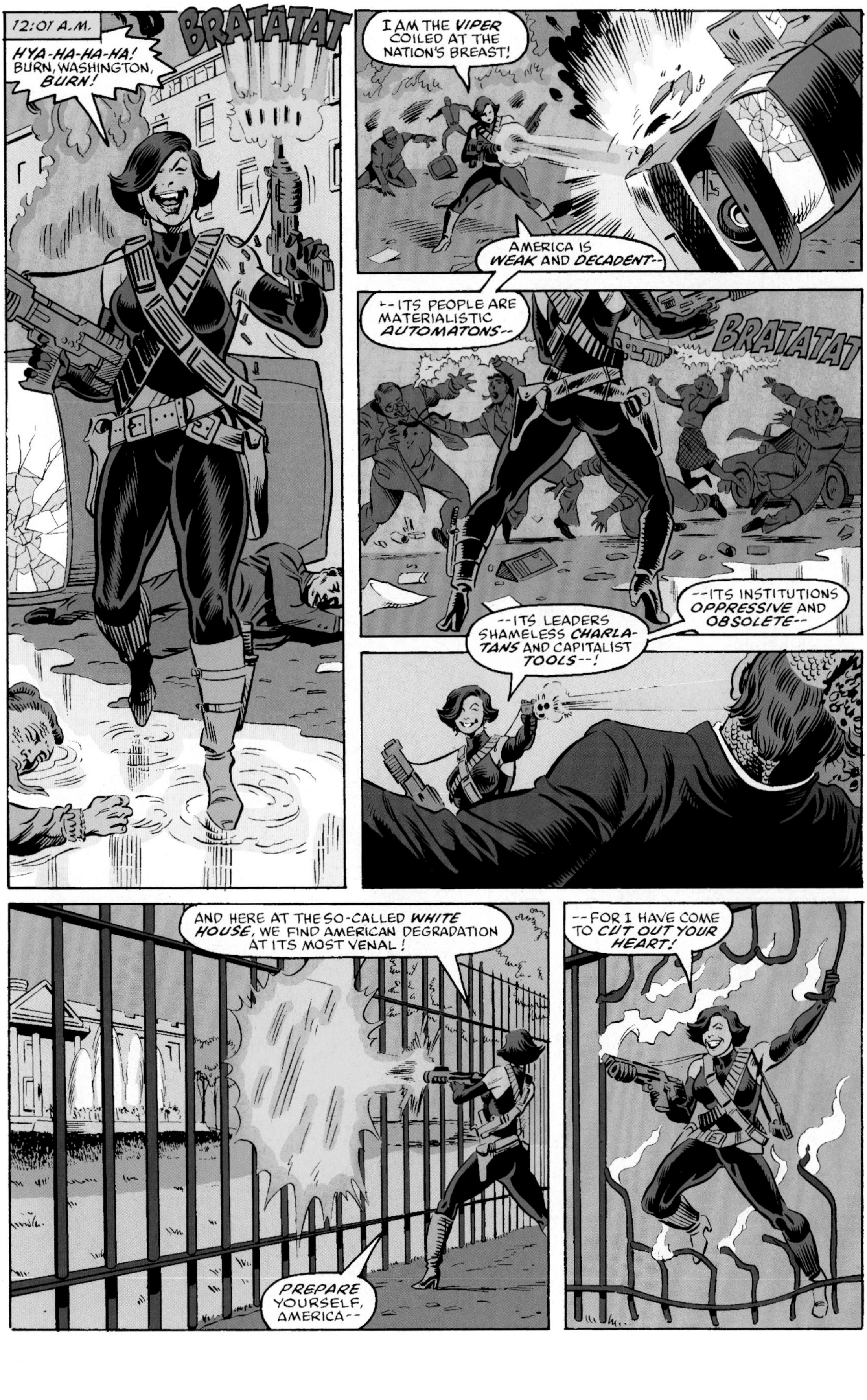

12:01 A.M.
BRATATAT
HYA-HA-HA-HA! BURN, WASHINGTON, BURN!
I AM THE VIPER COILED AT THE NATION'S BREAST!
AMERICA IS WEAK AND DECADENT--
--ITS PEOPLE ARE MATERIALISTIC AUTOMATONS--
BRATATAT
--ITS INSTITUTIONS OPPRESSIVE AND OBSOLETE--
--ITS LEADERS SHAMELESS CHARLATANS AND CAPITALIST TOOLS--!
AND HERE AT THE SO-CALLED WHITE HOUSE, WE FIND AMERICAN DEGRADATION AT ITS MOST VENAL!
PREPARE YOURSELF, AMERICA--
--FOR I HAVE COME TO CUT OUT YOUR HEART!

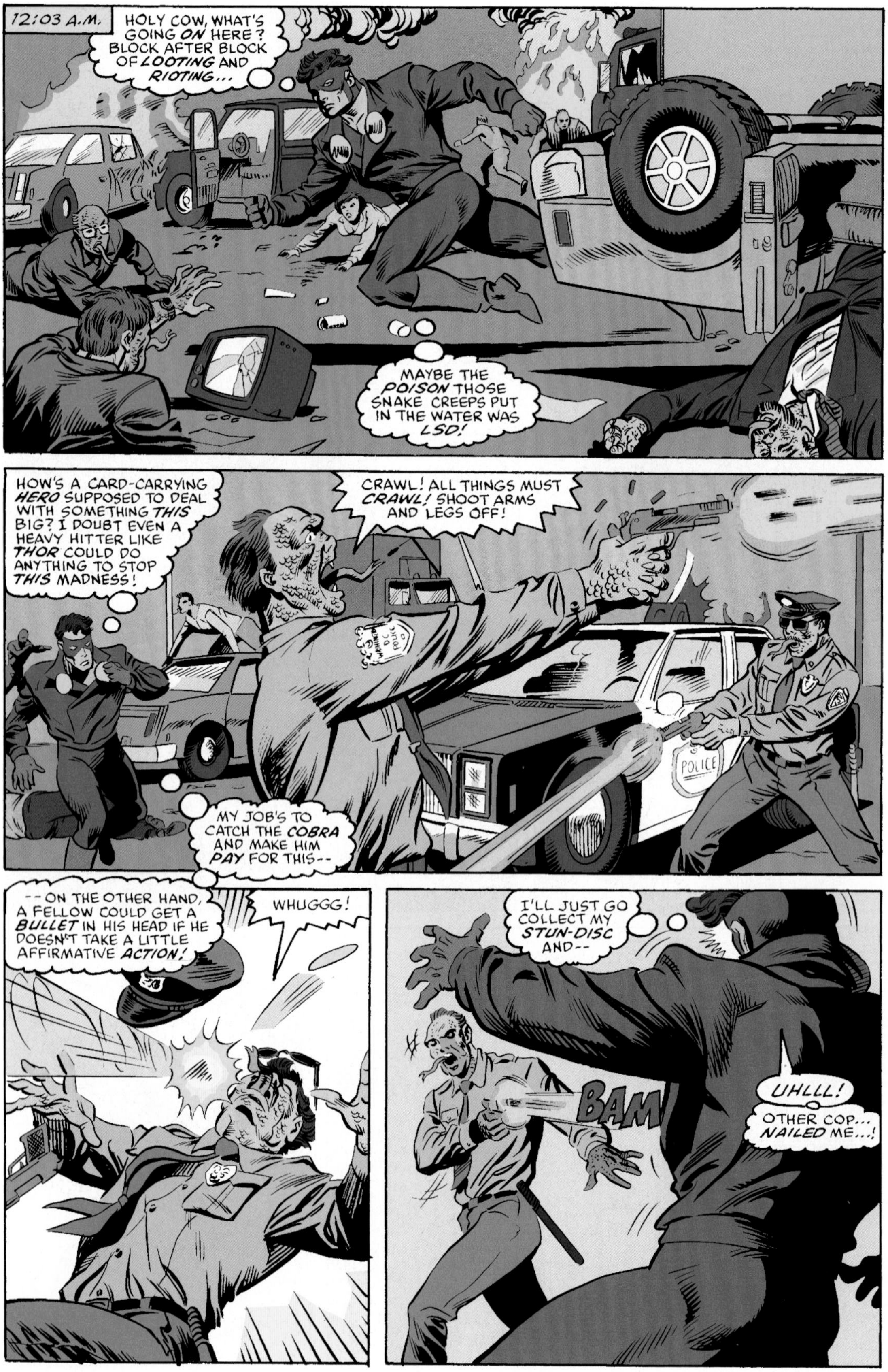

12:03 A.M.
HOLY COW, WHAT'S GOING ON HERE? BLOCK AFTER BLOCK OF LOOTING AND RIOTING...
MAYBE THE POISON THOSE SNAKE CREEPS PUT IN THE WATER WAS LSD!
HOW'S A CARD-CARRYING HERO SUPPOSED TO DEAL WITH SOMETHING THIS BIG? I DOUBT EVEN A HEAVY HITTER LIKE THOR COULD DO ANYTHING TO STOP THIS MADNESS!
CRAWL! ALL THINGS MUST CRAWL! SHOOT ARMS AND LEGS OFF!
POLICE
MY JOB'S TO CATCH THE COBRA AND MAKE HIM PAY FOR THIS--
--ON THE OTHER HAND, A FELLOW COULD GET A BULLET IN HIS HEAD IF HE DOESN'T TAKE A LITTLE AFFIRMATIVE ACTION!
WHUGGG!
I'LL JUST GO COLLECT MY STUN-DISC AND--
BAM
UHLLL!
OTHER COP... NAILED ME...!

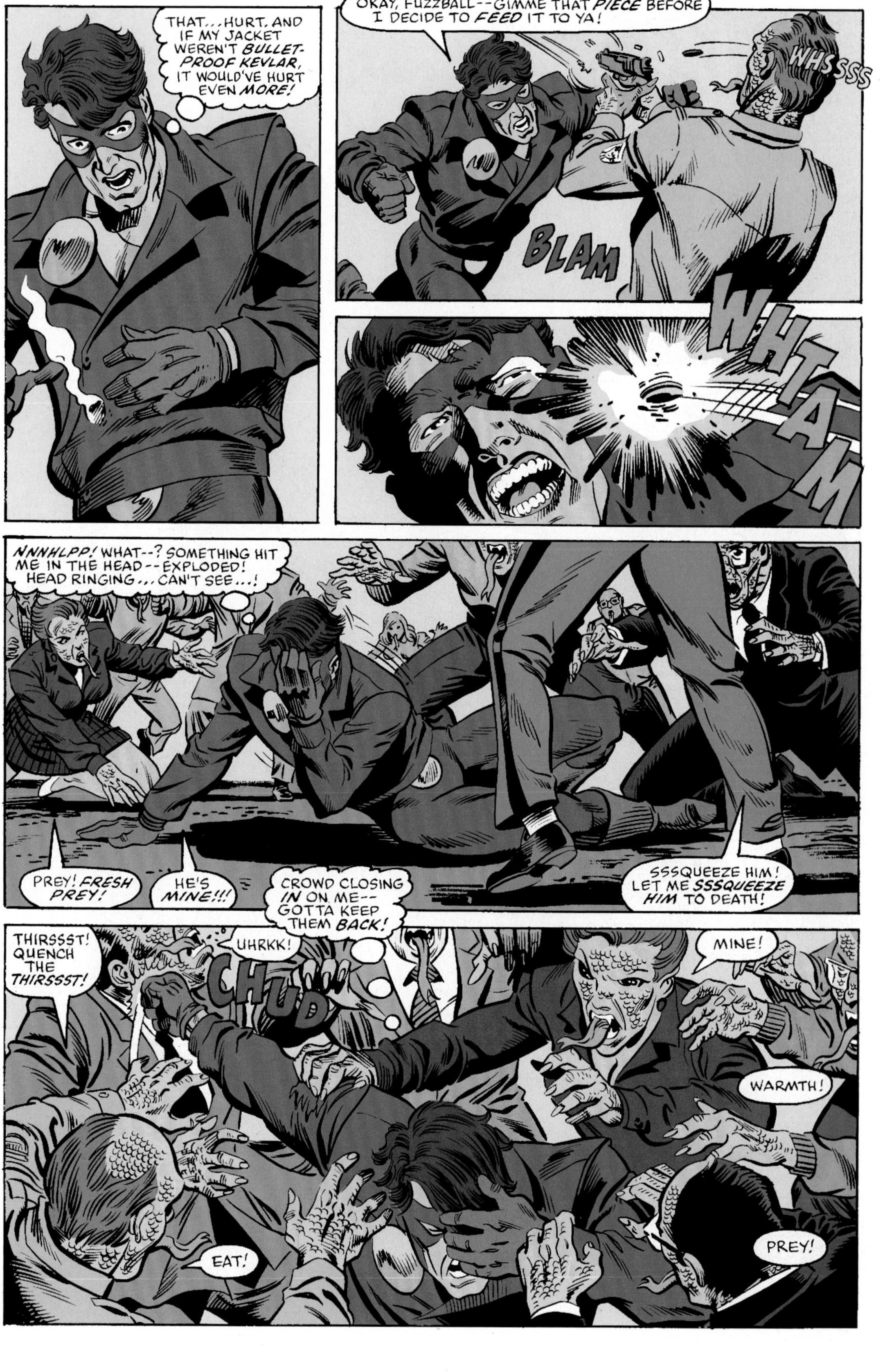
THAT... HURT. AND IF MY JACKET WEREN'T BULLET-PROOF KEVLAR, IT WOULD'VE HURT EVEN MORE!
OKAY, FUZZBALL--GIMME THAT PIECE BEFORE I DECIDE TO FEED IT TO YA!
WHSSSS
BLAM
WHTAM
NNNHLPP! WHAT--? SOMETHING HIT ME IN THE HEAD--EXPLODED! HEAD RINGING... CAN'T SEE...!
PREY! FRESH PREY!
HE'S MINE!!!
CROWD CLOSING IN ON ME-- GOTTA KEEP THEM BACK!
SSSQUEEZE HIM! LET ME SSSQUEEZE HIM TO DEATH!
THIRSSST! QUENCH THE THIRSSST!
UHRKK!
CHUD
MINE!
WARMTH!
EAT!
PREY!

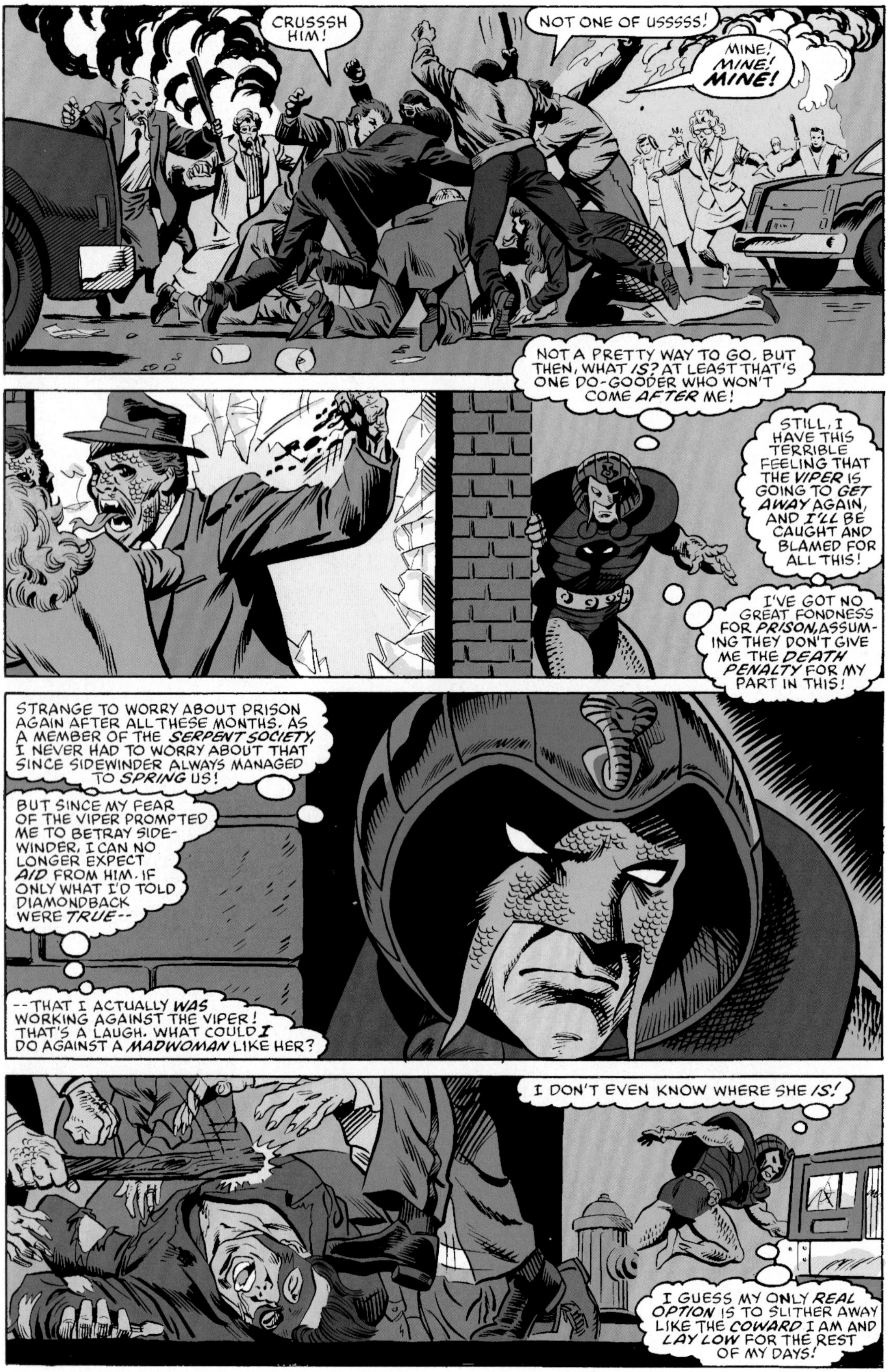

CRUSSSH HIM!
NOT ONE OF USSSSS!
MINE! MINE! MINE!
NOT A PRETTY WAY TO GO. BUT THEN, WHAT IS? AT LEAST THAT'S ONE DO-GOODER WHO WON'T COME AFTER ME!
STILL, I HAVE THIS TERRIBLE FEELING THAT THE VIPER IS GOING TO GET AWAY AGAIN, AND I'LL BE CAUGHT AND BLAMED FOR ALL THIS!
I'VE GOT NO GREAT FONDNESS FOR PRISON, ASSUMING THEY DON'T GIVE ME THE DEATH PENALTY FOR MY PART IN THIS!
STRANGE TO WORRY ABOUT PRISON AGAIN AFTER ALL THESE MONTHS. AS A MEMBER OF THE SERPENT SOCIETY, I NEVER HAD TO WORRY ABOUT THAT SINCE SIDEWINDER ALWAYS MANAGED TO SPRING US!
BUT SINCE MY FEAR OF THE VIPER PROMPTED ME TO BETRAY SIDE-WINDER, I CAN NO LONGER EXPECT AID FROM HIM. IF ONLY WHAT I'D TOLD DIAMONDBACK WERE TRUE--
--THAT I ACTUALLY WAS WORKING AGAINST THE VIPER! THAT'S A LAUGH. WHAT COULD I DO AGAINST A MADWOMAN LIKE HER?
I DON'T EVEN KNOW WHERE SHE IS!
I GUESS MY ONLY REAL OPTION IS TO SLITHER AWAY LIKE THE COWARD I AM AND LAY LOW FOR THE REST OF MY DAYS!

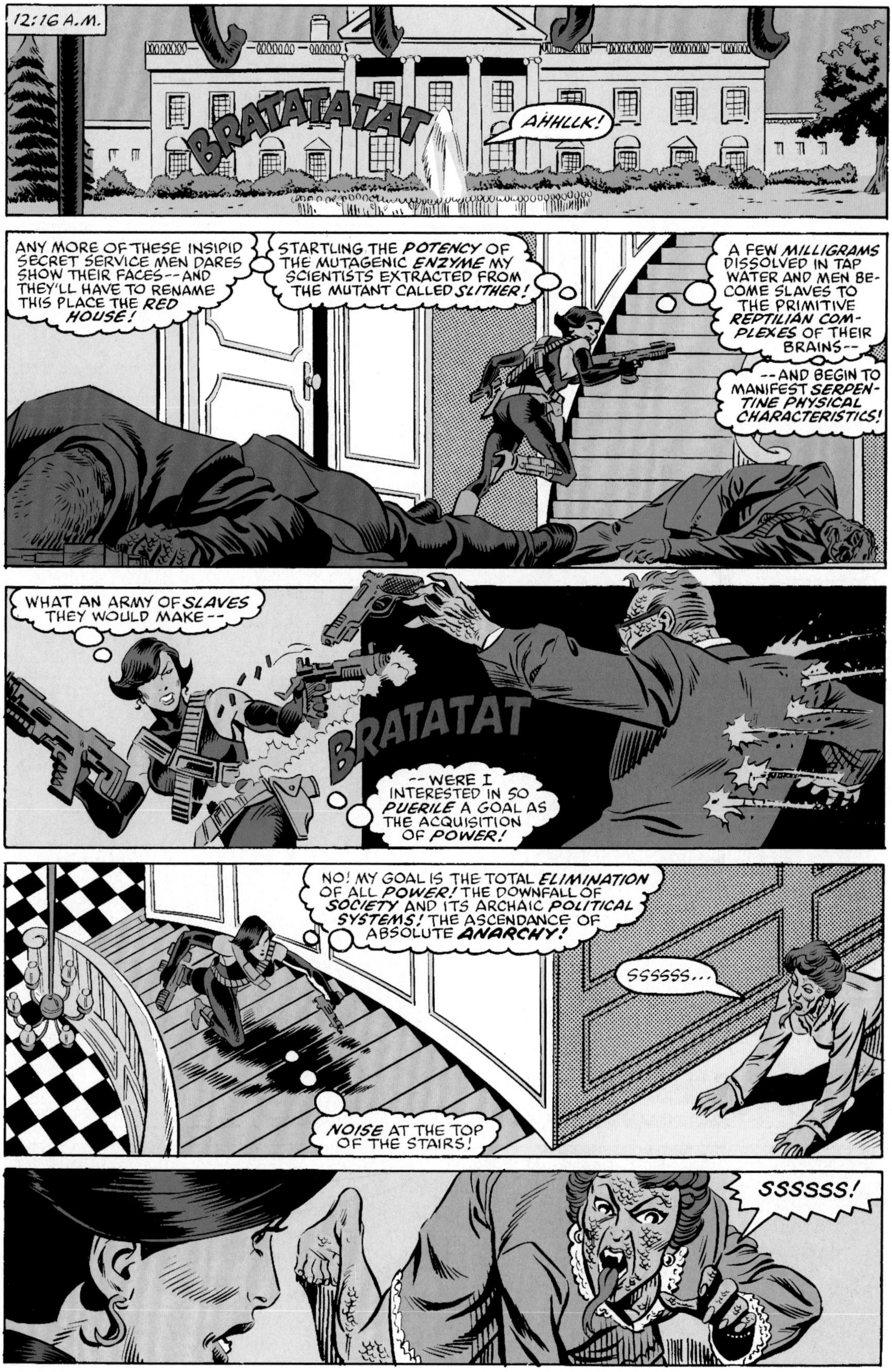
12:16 A.M.
BRATATATAT
AHHLLK!
ANY MORE OF THESE INSIPID SECRET SERVICE MEN DARES SHOW THEIR FACES--AND THEY'LL HAVE TO RENAME THIS PLACE THE RED HOUSE!
STARTLING THE POTENCY OF THE MUTAGENIC ENZYME MY SCIENTISTS EXTRACTED FROM THE MUTANT CALLED SLITHER!
A FEW MILLIGRAMS DISSOLVED IN TAP WATER AND MEN BECOME SLAVES TO THE PRIMITIVE REPTILIAN COMPLEXES OF THEIR BRAINS--
--AND BEGIN TO MANIFEST SERPENTINE PHYSICAL CHARACTERISTICS!
WHAT AN ARMY OF SLAVES THEY WOULD MAKE--
BRATATAT
--WERE I INTERESTED IN SO PUERILE A GOAL AS THE ACQUISITION OF POWER!
NO! MY GOAL IS THE TOTAL ELIMINATION OF ALL POWER! THE DOWNFALL OF SOCIETY AND ITS ARCHAIC POLITICAL SYSTEMS! THE ASCENDANCE OF ABSOLUTE ANARCHY!
SSSSSS...
NOISE AT THE TOP OF THE STAIRS!
SSSSSS!

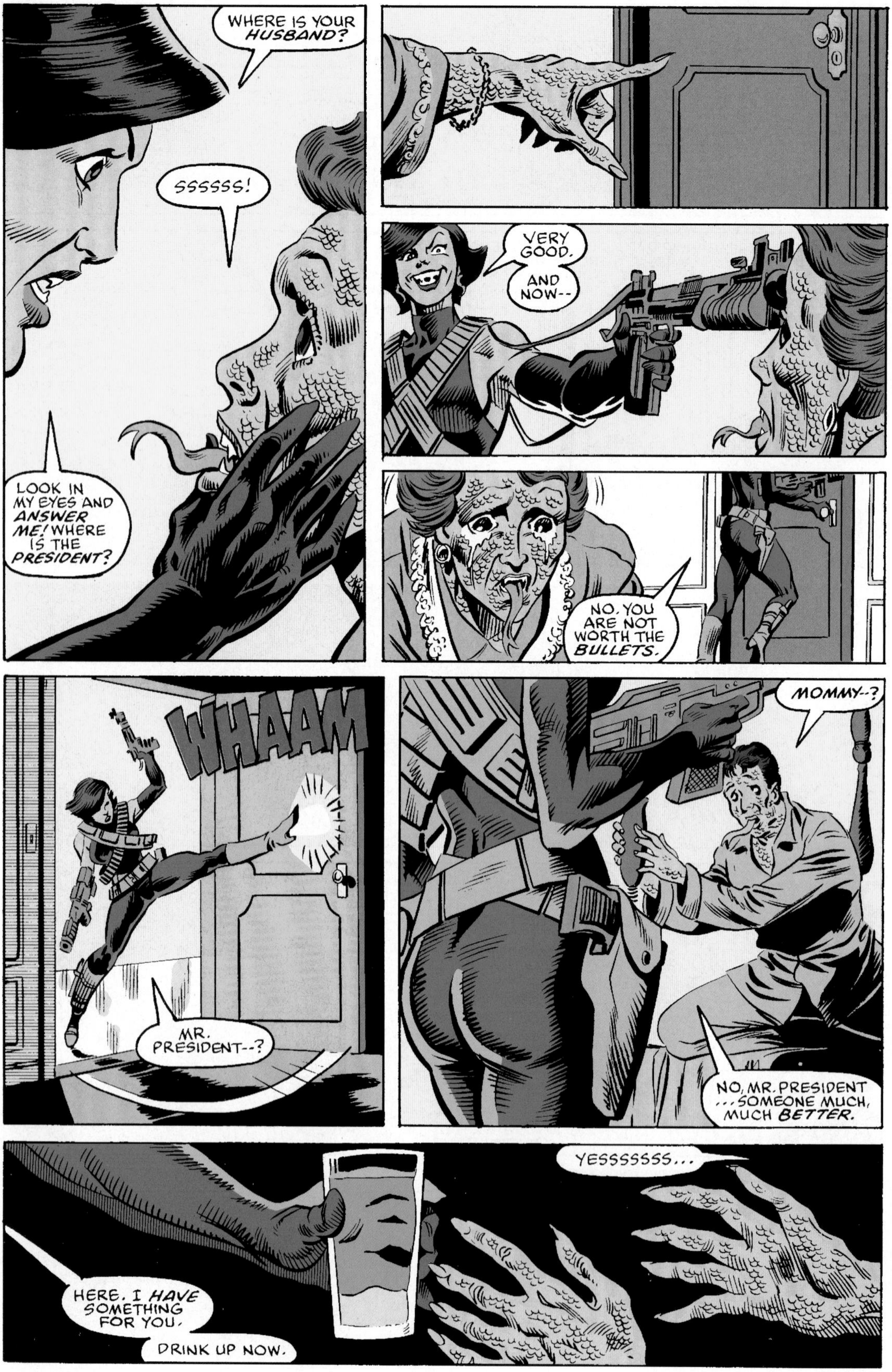
WHERE IS YOUR HUSBAND?
SSSSSS!
LOOK IN MY EYES AND ANSWER ME! WHERE IS THE PRESIDENT?
VERY GOOD.
AND NOW--
NO. YOU ARE NOT WORTH THE BULLETS.
WHAAM
MR. PRESIDENT--?
MOMMY--?
NO, MR. PRESIDENT ... SOMEONE MUCH, MUCH BETTER.
YESSSSSSS...
HERE. I HAVE SOMETHING FOR YOU.
DRINK UP NOW.

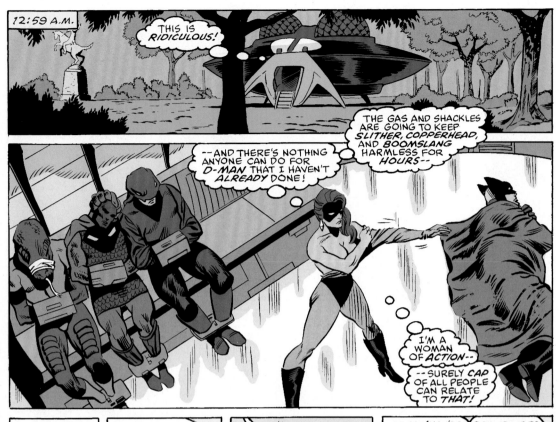

12:59 A.M.

THIS IS *RIDICULOUS!*

THE GAS AND SHACKLES ARE GOING TO KEEP *SLITHER, COPPERHEAD,* AND *BOOMSLANG* HARMLESS FOR *HOURS*—

—AND THERE'S NOTHING ANYONE CAN DO FOR *D-MAN* THAT I HAVEN'T *ALREADY* DONE!

I'M A WOMAN OF *ACTION*—

—SURELY *CAP* OF ALL PEOPLE CAN RELATE TO *THAT!*

IF NOT FOR *ME* PLACING THAT CALL TO CAP'S *HOTLINE,* CAP WOULDN'T HAVE FOUND OUT ABOUT THE *VIPER'S* CRAZINESS IN THE FIRST PLACE!

SURELY *THAT* ENTITLES ME TO MORE THAN *GUARD DUTY!*

CAPTAIN, THIS IS DIAMONDBACK, *COME IN PLEASE!*

NO ANSWER. THE BIG GOOF PROBABLY NEVER TURNED IT ON.

D-MAN? HEY, BIG FELLA, HOW YOU *DOING?*

NNNHH? OHH...KAYYY...

THINK YOU CAN HOLD DOWN THE FORT *YOURSELF?*

OHH... KAYYY...

GREAT! YOU'RE A REAL *SWEETIE,* D-MAN.

REMIND ME TO SHOW YOU A REAL *GOOD TIME* WHEN I GET BACK.

OHH... KAYYY...

NNNNHHHH...

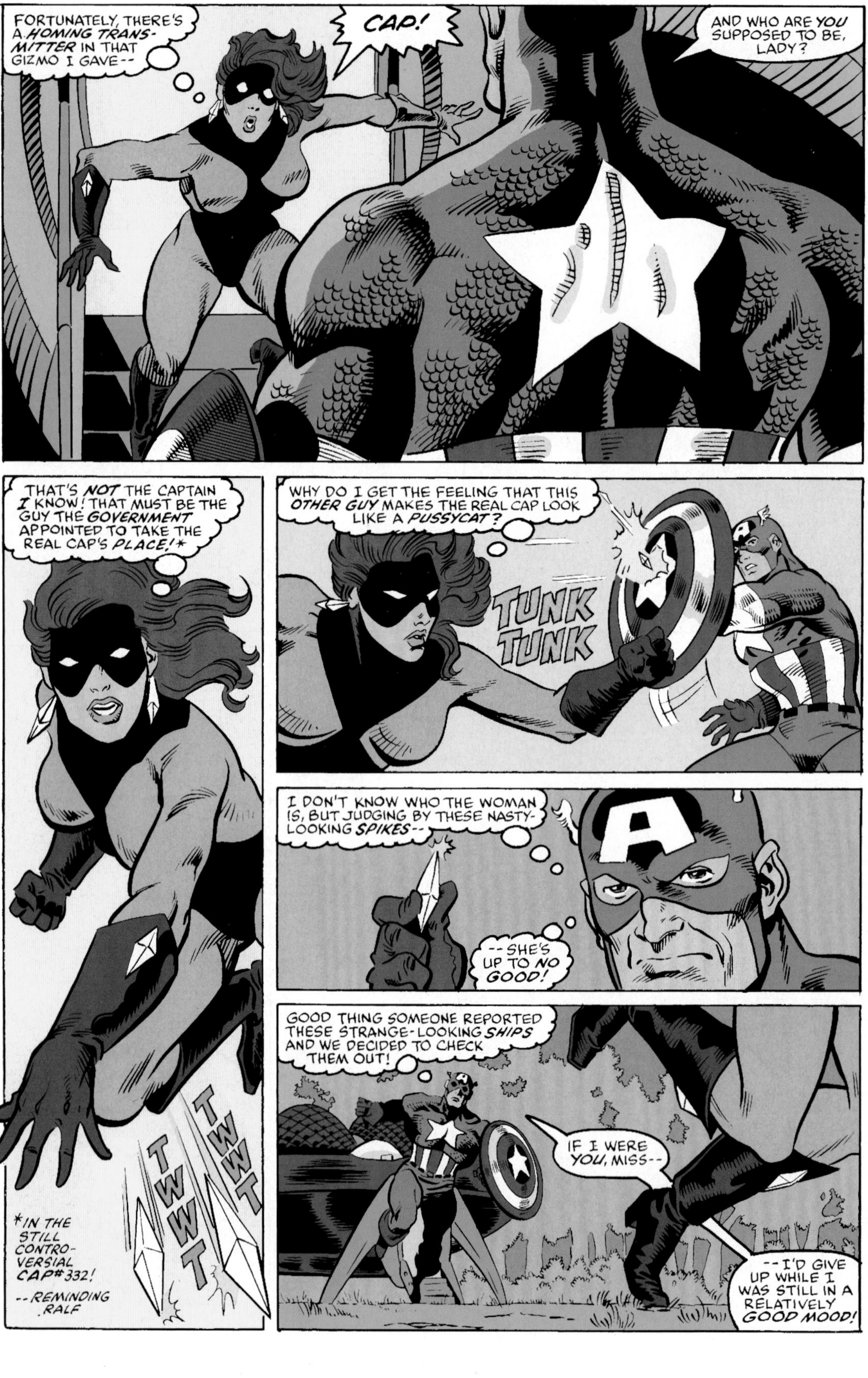
FORTUNATELY, THERE'S A HOMING TRANSMITTER IN THAT GIZMO I GAVE--
CAP!
AND WHO ARE YOU SUPPOSED TO BE, LADY?
THAT'S NOT THE CAPTAIN I KNOW! THAT MUST BE THE GUY THE GOVERNMENT APPOINTED TO TAKE THE REAL CAP'S PLACE!*
TWWT
TWWT
*IN THE STILL CONTROVERSIAL CAP#332! --REMINDING RALF
WHY DO I GET THE FEELING THAT THIS OTHER GUY MAKES THE REAL CAP LOOK LIKE A PUSSYCAT?
TUNK TUNK
I DON'T KNOW WHO THE WOMAN IS, BUT JUDGING BY THESE NASTY-LOOKING SPIKES--
--SHE'S UP TO NO GOOD!
GOOD THING SOMEONE REPORTED THESE STRANGE-LOOKING SHIPS AND WE DECIDED TO CHECK THEM OUT!
IF I WERE YOU, MISS--
--I'D GIVE UP WHILE I WAS STILL IN A RELATIVELY GOOD MOOD!

FIFTY FEET AWAY...

TWO OF THESE CRAZY *FLYING SAUCER* THINGS! *OUTRAGEOUS!* WHAT IF THERE ARE *ALIENS* INSIDE! WHAT'LL *I* SAY TO THEM?

"PARDON ME, BUT ARE YOU RESPONSIBLE FOR ALL THE RIOTING IN THE STREETS?" *HAH!*

WHEW! THESE GUYS DON'T *LOOK* LIKE ALIENS... EXCEPT MAYBE THAT *SNAKE-HEADED GUY* ON THE END. NAH... PROBABLY *LATEX.*

WONDER WHO KNOCKED THEM OUT AND CUFFED THEIR *HANDS* AND *FEET?* AND WHO'S THAT *BIG GUY* TAKING A *SNOOZE* ON THE FLOOR?

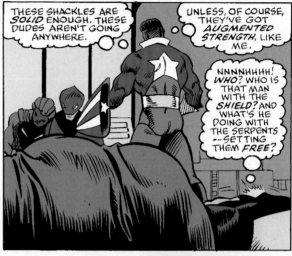

THESE SHACKLES ARE *SOLID* ENOUGH. THESE DUDES AREN'T GOING ANYWHERE.

UNLESS, OF COURSE, THEY'VE GOT *AUGMENTED STRENGTH,* LIKE ME.

NNNNHHHH! *WHO?* WHO IS THAT MAN WITH THE *SHIELD?* AND WHAT'S HE DOING WITH THE SERPENTS --SETTING THEM *FREE?*

I'VE GOT TO *STOP* HIM!

NO... I *CAN'T...* I FEEL TOO WEAK.

BETTER JUST LIE STILL, PLAY *'POSSUM,* LET HIM DO WHATEVER.

CAP WILL UNDERSTAND. WHAT COULD A *POISONED GUY* DO TO STOP ANYONE ANYWAY?

THIS!

I TOTALLY *DISGRACED* MYSELF BY DUCKING OUT OF A FIGHT THE OTHER WEEK...* BY GOD, POISON OR NO POISON, I'M *NOT* GOING TO *BACK DOWN* AGAIN!

HUH? THE GUY UNDER THE *BLANKET*--!

*CAP #340.

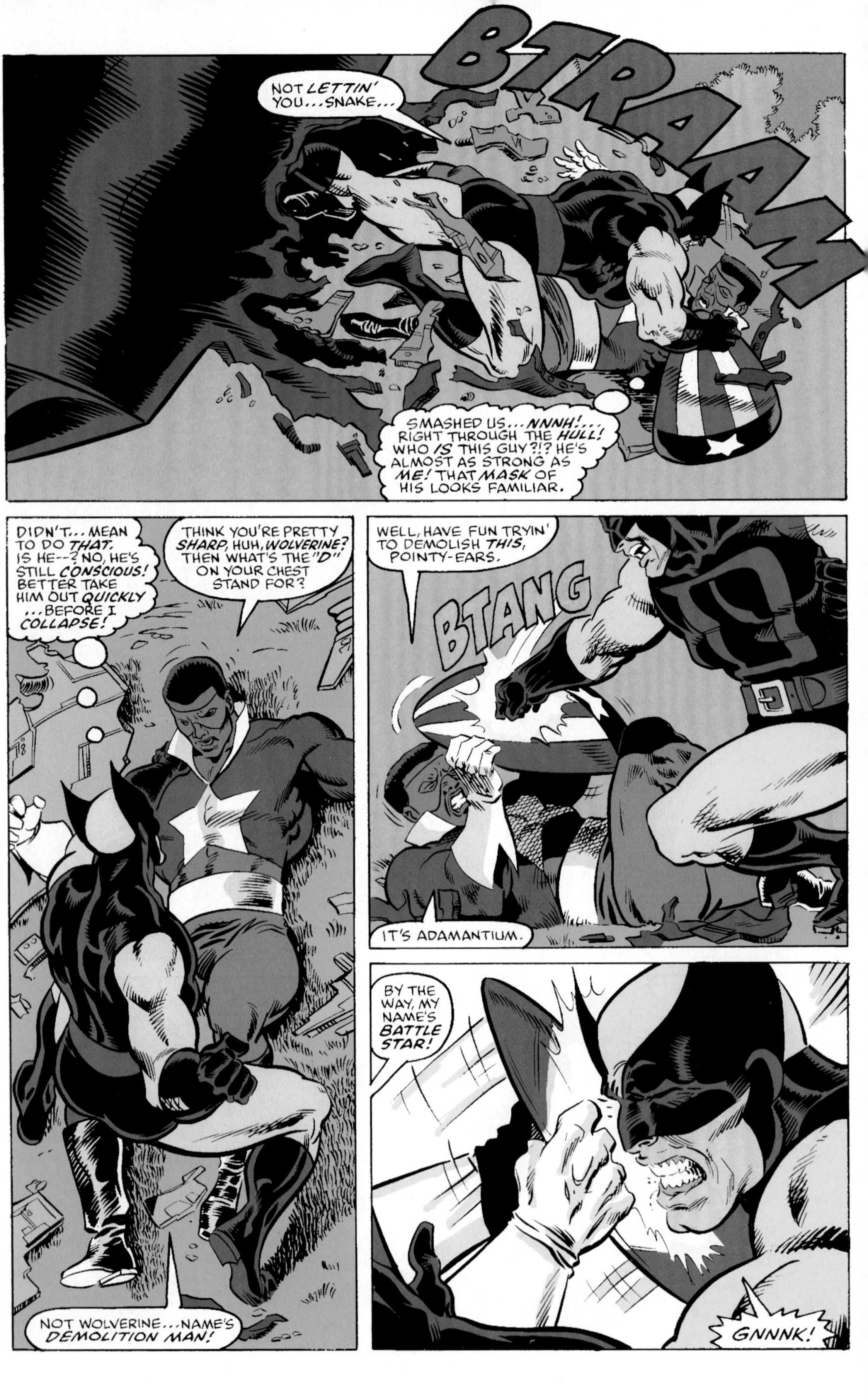
BTRAAM
NOT LETTIN' YOU... SNAKE...
SMASHED US... NNNH!... RIGHT THROUGH THE HULL! WHO IS THIS GUY?!? HE'S ALMOST AS STRONG AS ME! THAT MASK OF HIS LOOKS FAMILIAR.
DIDN'T... MEAN TO DO THAT. IS HE--? NO, HE'S STILL CONSCIOUS! BETTER TAKE HIM OUT QUICKLY ...BEFORE I COLLAPSE!
THINK YOU'RE PRETTY SHARP, HUH, WOLVERINE? THEN WHAT'S THE "D" ON YOUR CHEST STAND FOR?
NOT WOLVERINE... NAME'S DEMOLITION MAN!
WELL, HAVE FUN TRYIN' TO DEMOLISH THIS, POINTY-EARS.
BTANG
IT'S ADAMANTIUM.
BY THE WAY, MY NAME'S BATTLE STAR!
GNNNK!

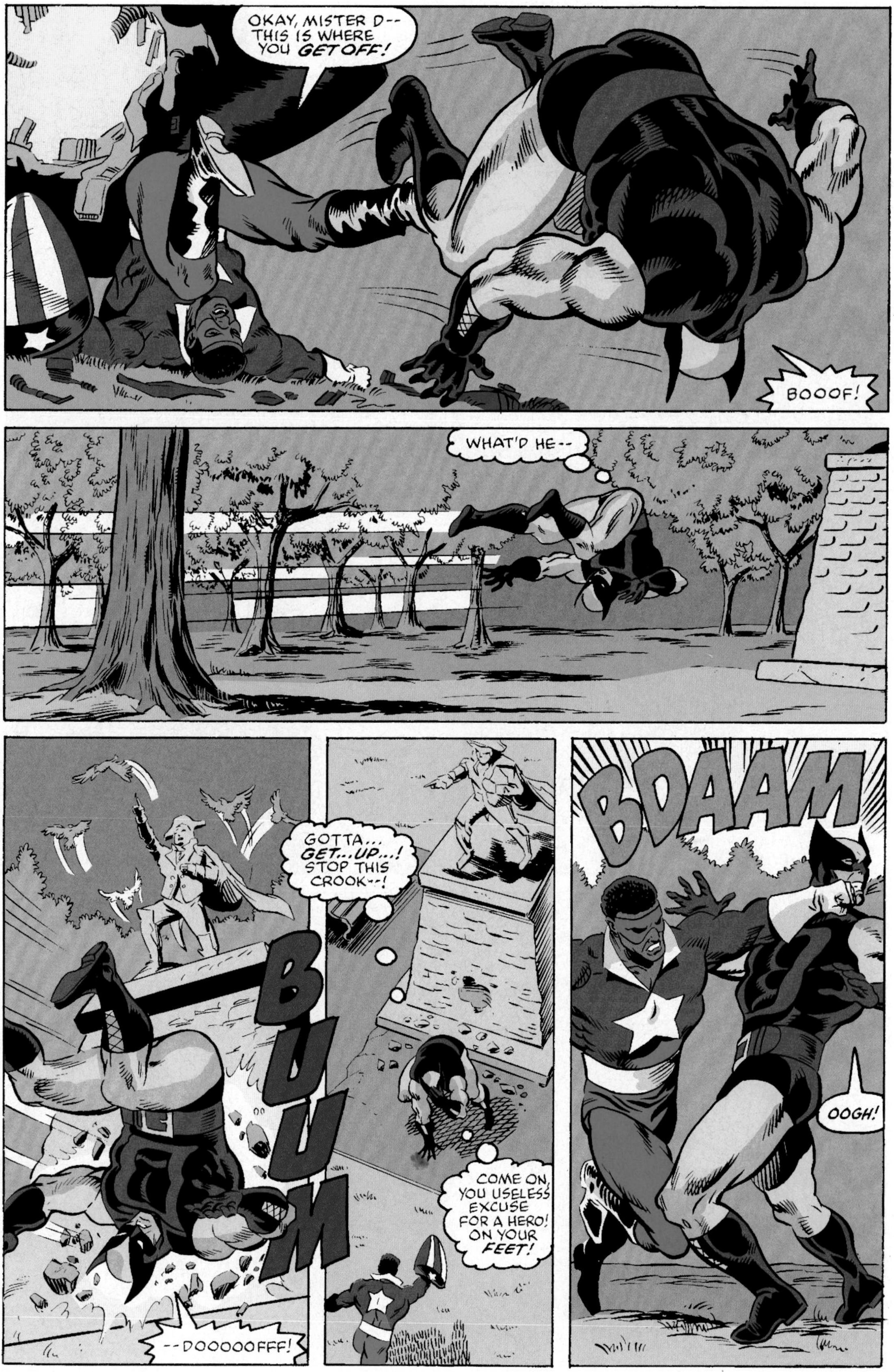
OKAY, MISTER D-- THIS IS WHERE YOU GET OFF!
BOOOF!
WHAT'D HE--
BDAAM
GOTTA... GET...UP...! STOP THIS CROOK--!
BUUM
--DOOOOOFFF!
COME ON, YOU USELESS EXCUSE FOR A HERO! ON YOUR FEET!
OOGH!

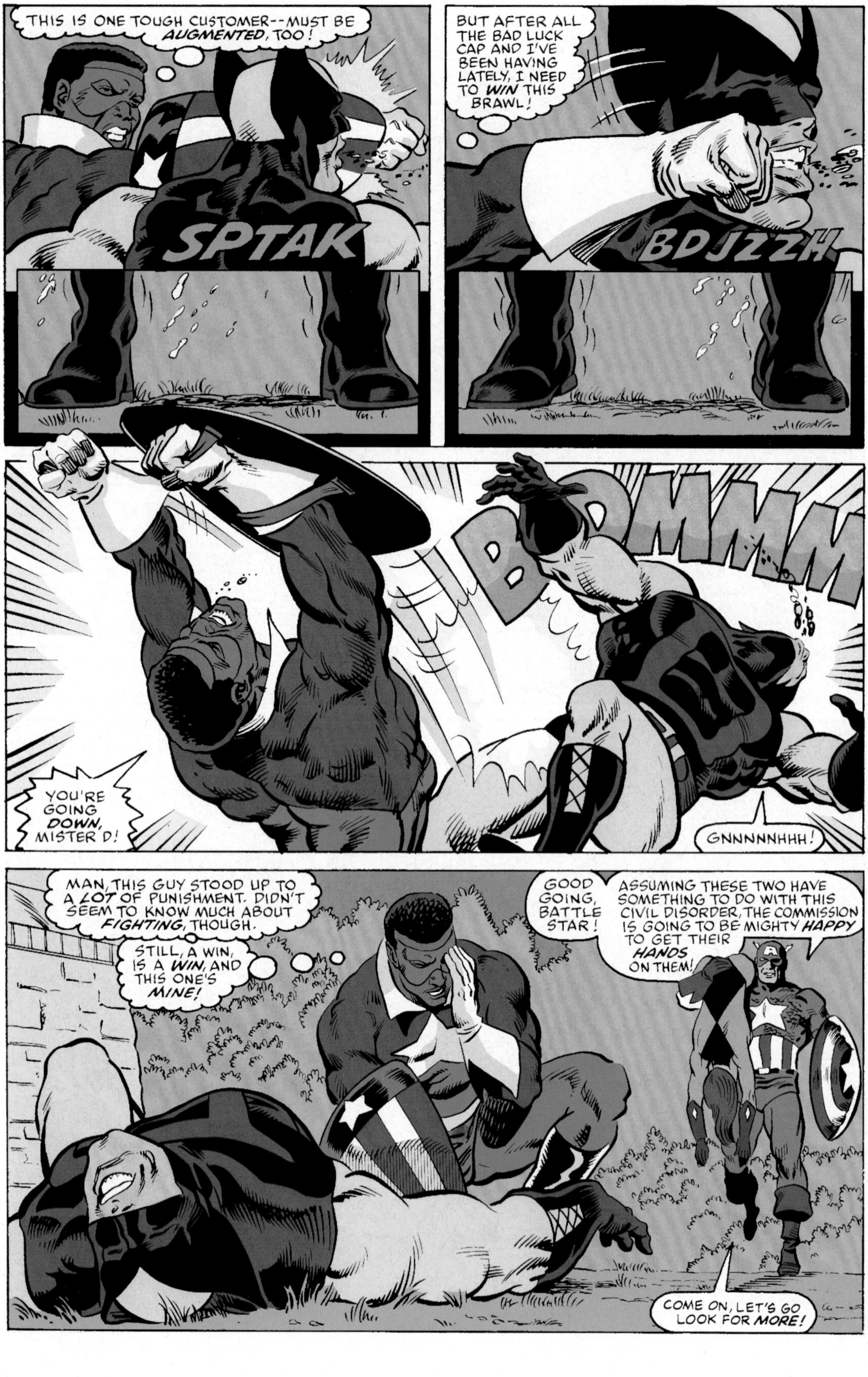

THIS IS ONE TOUGH CUSTOMER--MUST BE AUGMENTED, TOO!
SPTAK
BUT AFTER ALL THE BAD LUCK CAP AND I'VE BEEN HAVING LATELY, I NEED TO WIN THIS BRAWL!
BDJZZH
BOMMM
YOU'RE GOING DOWN, MISTER D!
GNNNNNHHH!
MAN, THIS GUY STOOD UP TO A LOT OF PUNISHMENT. DIDN'T SEEM TO KNOW MUCH ABOUT FIGHTING, THOUGH.
STILL, A WIN, IS A WIN, AND THIS ONE'S MINE!
GOOD GOING, BATTLE STAR!
ASSUMING THESE TWO HAVE SOMETHING TO DO WITH THIS CIVIL DISORDER, THE COMMISSION IS GOING TO BE MIGHTY HAPPY TO GET THEIR HANDS ON THEM!
COME ON, LET'S GO LOOK FOR MORE!

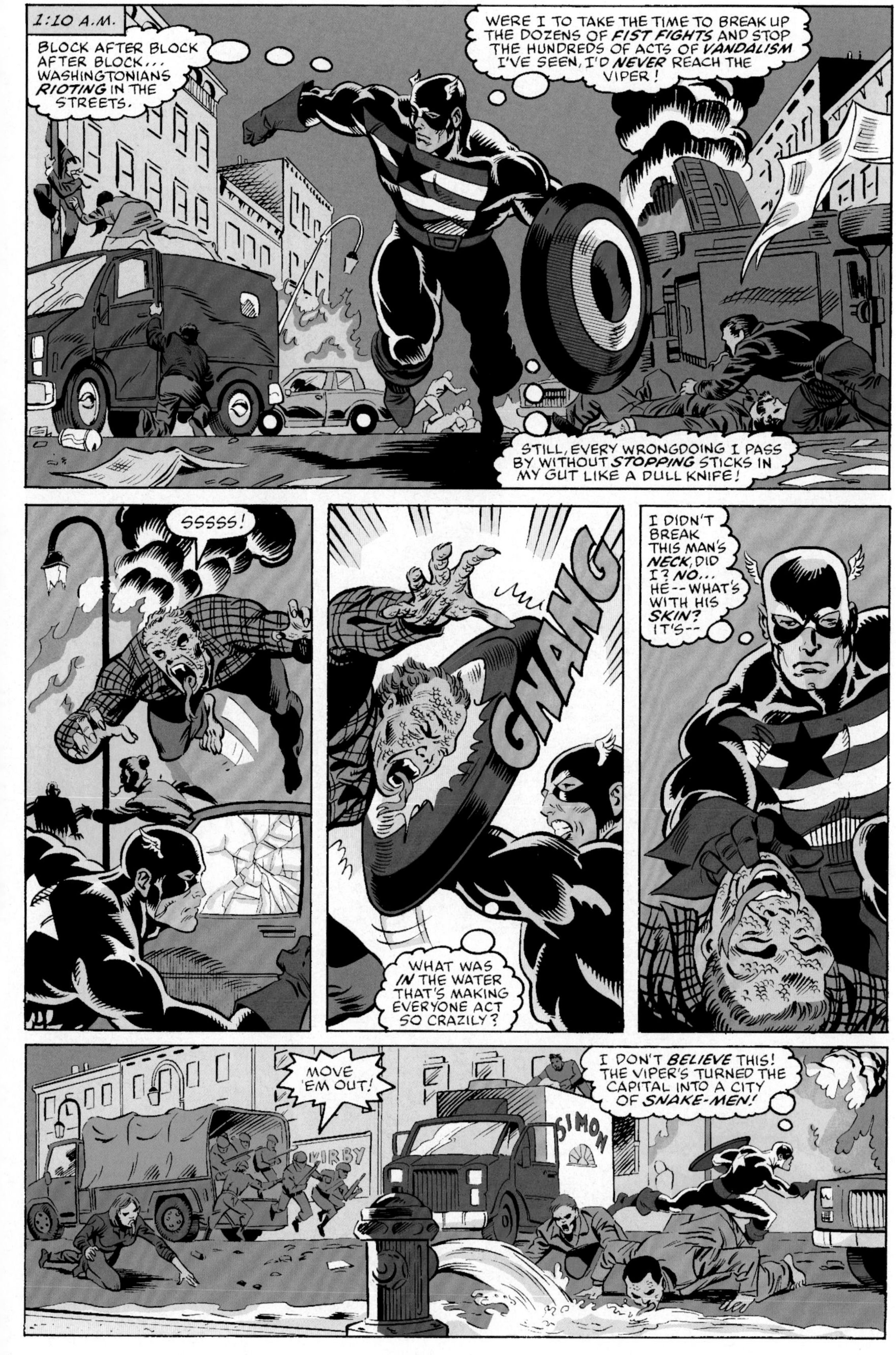
1:10 A.M.
BLOCK AFTER BLOCK AFTER BLOCK... WASHINGTONIANS RIOTING IN THE STREETS.
WERE I TO TAKE THE TIME TO BREAK UP THE DOZENS OF FIST FIGHTS AND STOP THE HUNDREDS OF ACTS OF VANDALISM I'VE SEEN, I'D NEVER REACH THE VIPER!
STILL, EVERY WRONGDOING I PASS BY WITHOUT STOPPING STICKS IN MY GUT LIKE A DULL KNIFE!
SSSSS!
GNANG
WHAT WAS IN THE WATER THAT'S MAKING EVERYONE ACT SO CRAZILY?
I DIDN'T BREAK THIS MAN'S NECK, DID I? NO... HE--WHAT'S WITH HIS SKIN? IT'S--
MOVE 'EM OUT!
I DON'T BELIEVE THIS! THE VIPER'S TURNED THE CAPITAL INTO A CITY OF SNAKE-MEN!
KIRBY
SIMON

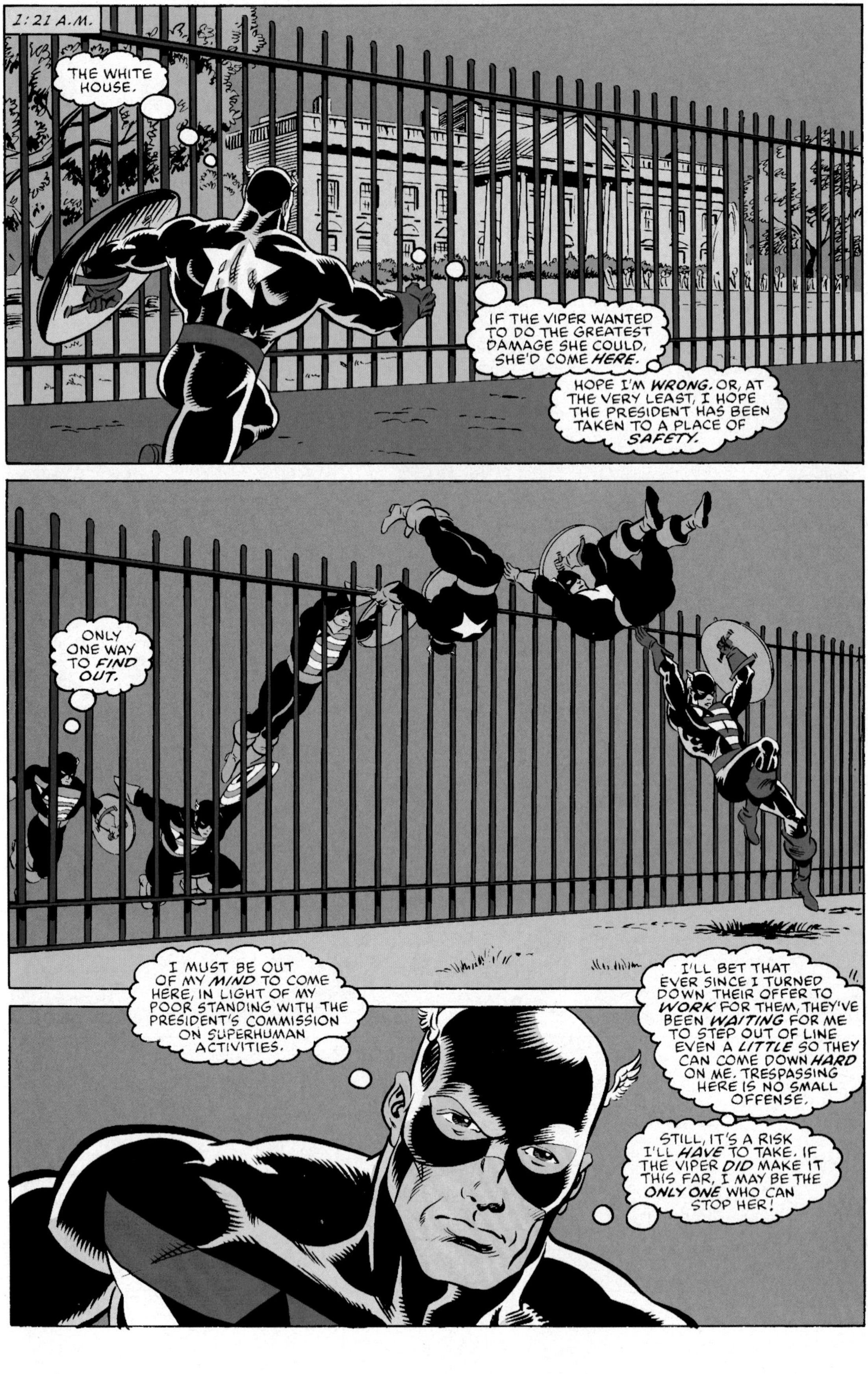

1:21 A.M.
THE WHITE HOUSE.
IF THE VIPER WANTED TO DO THE GREATEST DAMAGE SHE COULD, SHE'D COME HERE.
HOPE I'M WRONG. OR, AT THE VERY LEAST, I HOPE THE PRESIDENT HAS BEEN TAKEN TO A PLACE OF SAFETY.
ONLY ONE WAY TO FIND OUT.
I MUST BE OUT OF MY MIND TO COME HERE, IN LIGHT OF MY POOR STANDING WITH THE PRESIDENT'S COMMISSION ON SUPERHUMAN ACTIVITIES.
I'LL BET THAT EVER SINCE I TURNED DOWN THEIR OFFER TO WORK FOR THEM, THEY'VE BEEN WAITING FOR ME TO STEP OUT OF LINE EVEN A LITTLE SO THEY CAN COME DOWN HARD ON ME. TRESPASSING HERE IS NO SMALL OFFENSE.
STILL, IT'S A RISK I'LL HAVE TO TAKE. IF THE VIPER DID MAKE IT THIS FAR, I MAY BE THE ONLY ONE WHO CAN STOP HER!

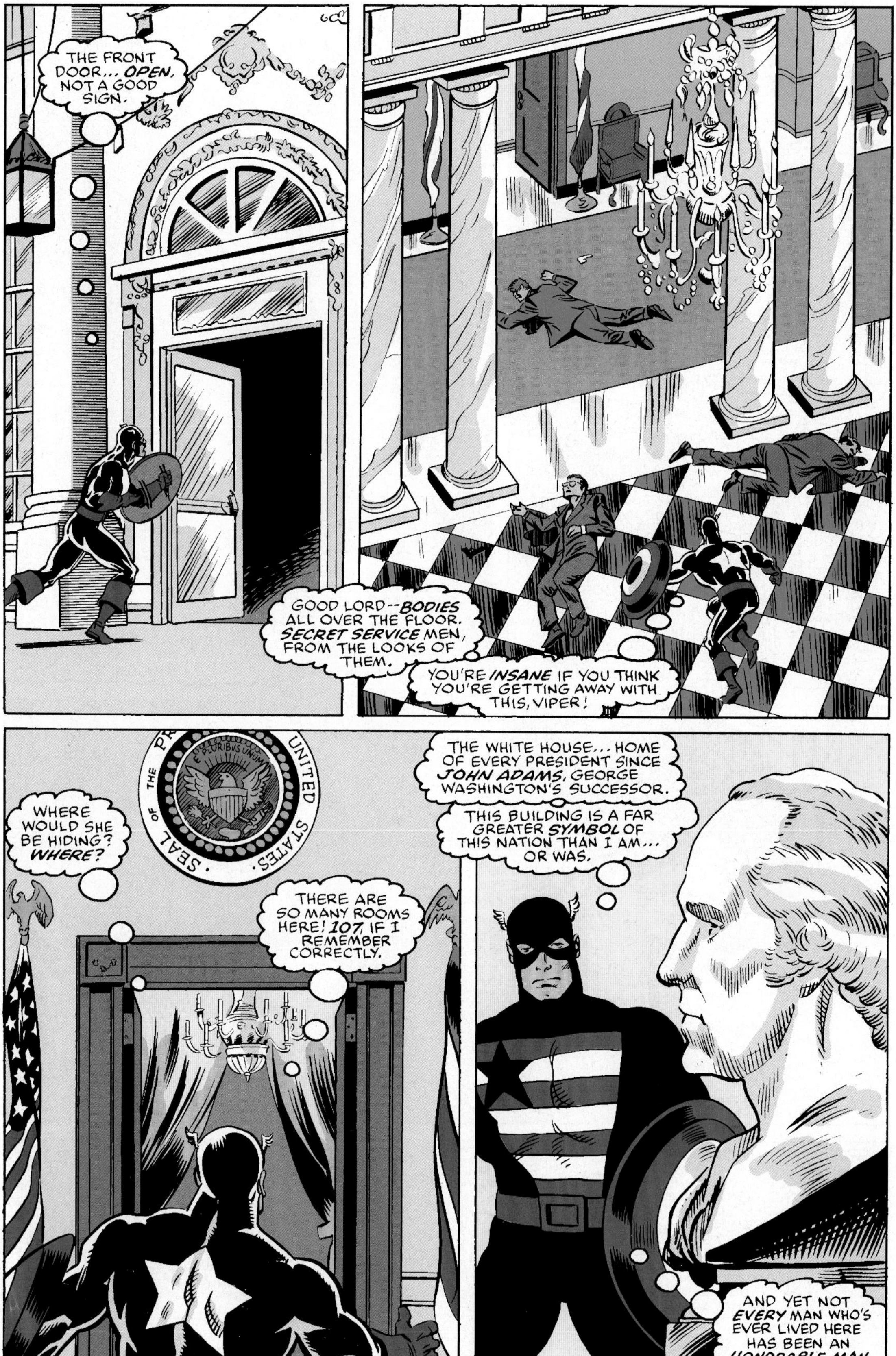
THE FRONT DOOR... OPEN. NOT A GOOD SIGN.
GOOD LORD--BODIES ALL OVER THE FLOOR. SECRET SERVICE MEN, FROM THE LOOKS OF THEM.
YOU'RE INSANE IF YOU THINK YOU'RE GETTING AWAY WITH THIS, VIPER!
SEAL OF THE PRESIDENT OF THE UNITED STATES
E PLURIBUS UNUM
WHERE WOULD SHE BE HIDING? WHERE?
THERE ARE SO MANY ROOMS HERE! 107, IF I REMEMBER CORRECTLY.
THE WHITE HOUSE... HOME OF EVERY PRESIDENT SINCE JOHN ADAMS, GEORGE WASHINGTON'S SUCCESSOR.
THIS BUILDING IS A FAR GREATER SYMBOL OF THIS NATION THAN I AM... OR WAS.
AND YET NOT EVERY MAN WHO'S EVER LIVED HERE HAS BEEN AN HONORABLE MAN.

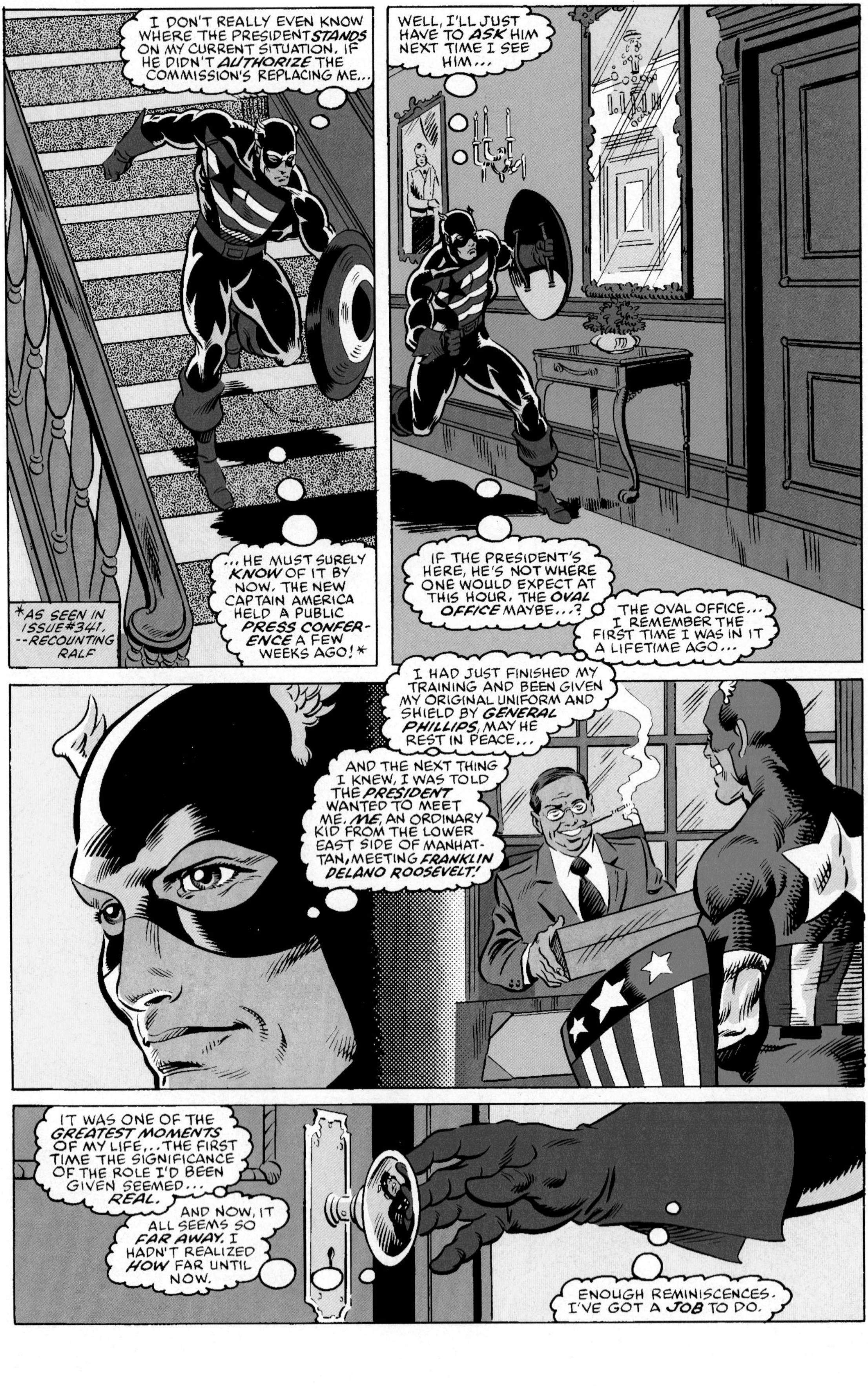
I DON'T REALLY EVEN KNOW WHERE THE PRESIDENT STANDS ON MY CURRENT SITUATION. IF HE DIDN'T AUTHORIZE THE COMMISSION'S REPLACING ME...
...HE MUST SURELY KNOW OF IT BY NOW. THE NEW CAPTAIN AMERICA HELD A PUBLIC PRESS CONFERENCE A FEW WEEKS AGO!*
*AS SEEN IN ISSUE #341. --RECOUNTING RALF
WELL, I'LL JUST HAVE TO ASK HIM NEXT TIME I SEE HIM...
IF THE PRESIDENT'S HERE, HE'S NOT WHERE ONE WOULD EXPECT AT THIS HOUR. THE OVAL OFFICE MAYBE...?
THE OVAL OFFICE... I REMEMBER THE FIRST TIME I WAS IN IT A LIFETIME AGO...
I HAD JUST FINISHED MY TRAINING AND BEEN GIVEN MY ORIGINAL UNIFORM AND SHIELD BY GENERAL PHILLIPS, MAY HE REST IN PEACE...
AND THE NEXT THING I KNEW, I WAS TOLD THE PRESIDENT WANTED TO MEET ME. ME, AN ORDINARY KID FROM THE LOWER EAST SIDE OF MANHATTAN, MEETING FRANKLIN DELANO ROOSEVELT!
IT WAS ONE OF THE GREATEST MOMENTS OF MY LIFE... THE FIRST TIME THE SIGNIFICANCE OF THE ROLE I'D BEEN GIVEN SEEMED... REAL.
AND NOW, IT ALL SEEMS SO FAR AWAY. I HADN'T REALIZED HOW FAR UNTIL NOW.
ENOUGH REMINISCENCES. I'VE GOT A JOB TO DO.

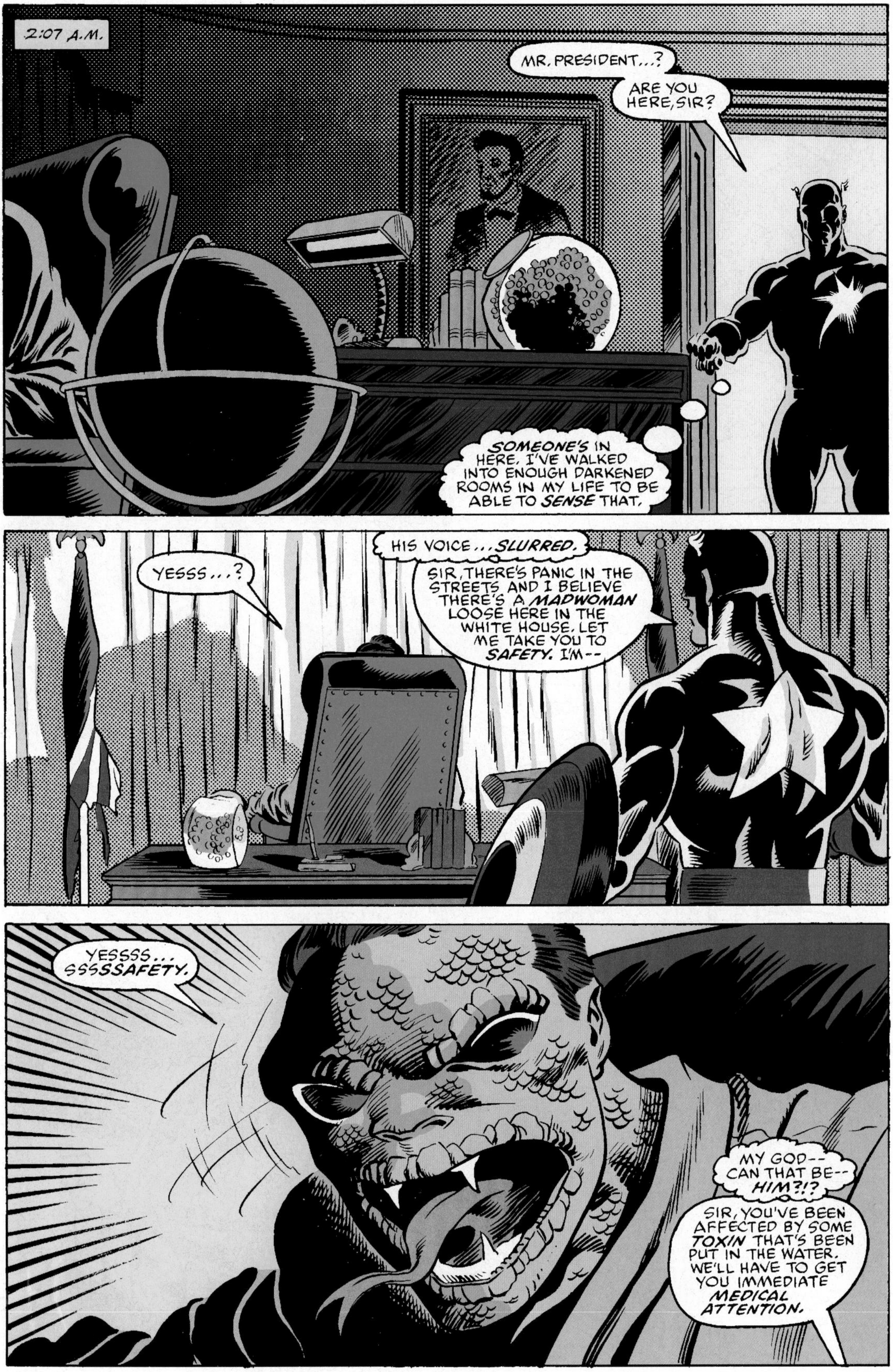
2:07 A.M.
MR. PRESIDENT...?
ARE YOU HERE, SIR?
SOMEONE'S IN HERE. I'VE WALKED INTO ENOUGH DARKENED ROOMS IN MY LIFE TO BE ABLE TO SENSE THAT.
YESSS...?
HIS VOICE... SLURRED.
SIR, THERE'S PANIC IN THE STREETS AND I BELIEVE THERE'S A MADWOMAN LOOSE HERE IN THE WHITE HOUSE. LET ME TAKE YOU TO SAFETY. I'M--
YESSSS... SSSSSSAFETY.
MY GOD-- CAN THAT BE-- HIM?!?
SIR, YOU'VE BEEN AFFECTED BY SOME TOXIN THAT'S BEEN PUT IN THE WATER. WE'LL HAVE TO GET YOU IMMEDIATE MEDICAL ATTENTION.

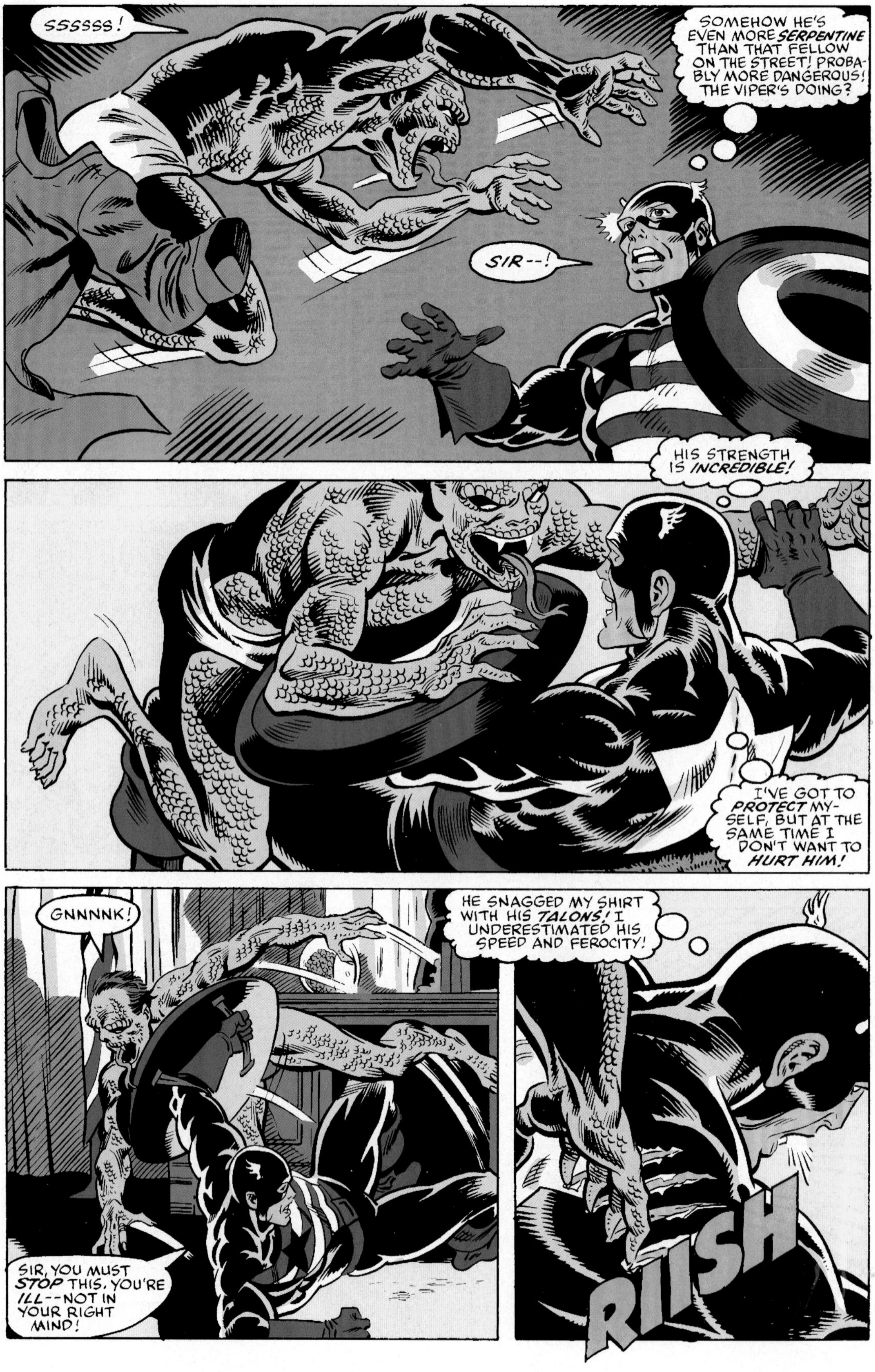
SSSSSS!
SOMEHOW HE'S EVEN MORE SERPENTINE THAN THAT FELLOW ON THE STREET! PROBABLY MORE DANGEROUS! THE VIPER'S DOING?
SIR--!
HIS STRENGTH IS INCREDIBLE!
I'VE GOT TO PROTECT MYSELF, BUT AT THE SAME TIME I DON'T WANT TO HURT HIM!
GNNNNK!
SIR, YOU MUST STOP THIS. YOU'RE ILL--NOT IN YOUR RIGHT MIND!
HE SNAGGED MY SHIRT WITH HIS TALONS! I UNDERESTIMATED HIS SPEED AND FEROCITY!
RIISH

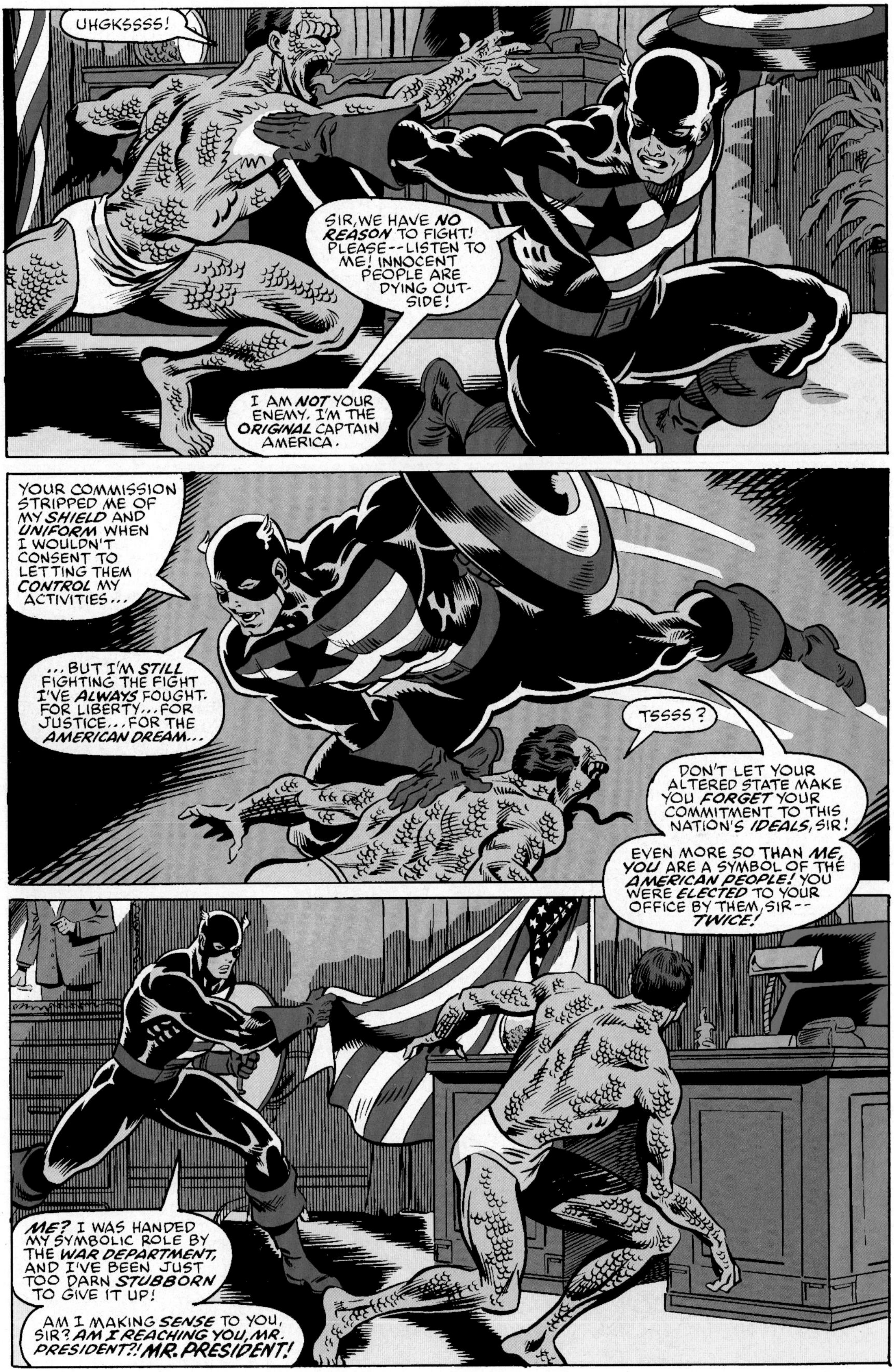
UHGKSSSS!
SIR, WE HAVE NO REASON TO FIGHT! PLEASE--LISTEN TO ME! INNOCENT PEOPLE ARE DYING OUT-SIDE!
I AM NOT YOUR ENEMY. I'M THE ORIGINAL CAPTAIN AMERICA.
YOUR COMMISSION STRIPPED ME OF MY SHIELD AND UNIFORM WHEN I WOULDN'T CONSENT TO LETTING THEM CONTROL MY ACTIVITIES...
...BUT I'M STILL FIGHTING THE FIGHT I'VE ALWAYS FOUGHT. FOR LIBERTY...FOR JUSTICE...FOR THE AMERICAN DREAM...
TSSSS?
DON'T LET YOUR ALTERED STATE MAKE YOU FORGET YOUR COMMITMENT TO THIS NATION'S IDEALS, SIR!
EVEN MORE SO THAN ME, YOU ARE A SYMBOL OF THE AMERICAN PEOPLE! YOU WERE ELECTED TO YOUR OFFICE BY THEM, SIR-- TWICE!
ME? I WAS HANDED MY SYMBOLIC ROLE BY THE WAR DEPARTMENT, AND I'VE BEEN JUST TOO DARN STUBBORN TO GIVE IT UP!
AM I MAKING SENSE TO YOU, SIR? AM I REACHING YOU, MR. PRESIDENT?! MR. PRESIDENT!

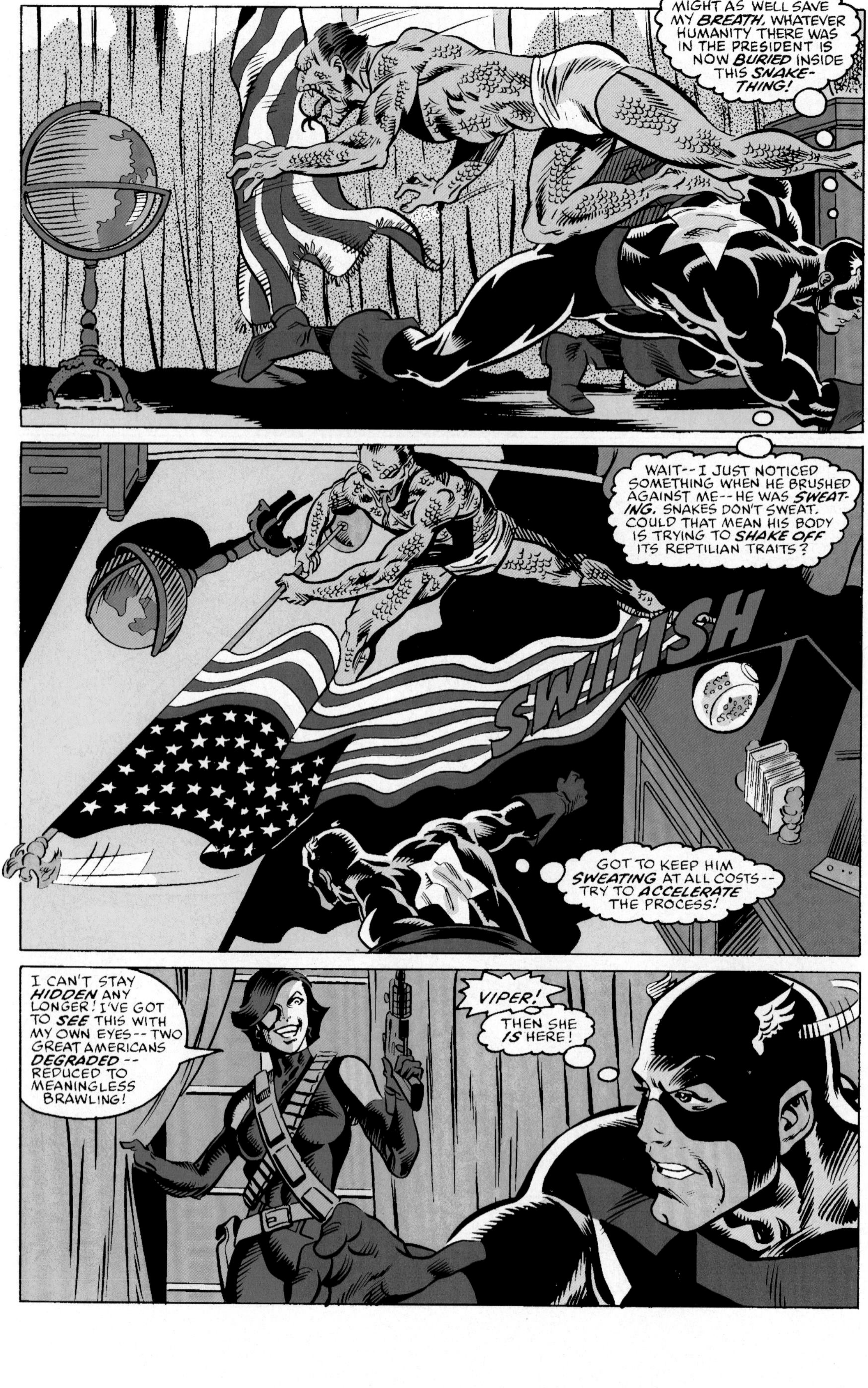
MIGHT AS WELL SAVE MY BREATH. WHATEVER HUMANITY THERE WAS IN THE PRESIDENT IS NOW BURIED INSIDE THIS SNAKE-THING!
WAIT-- I JUST NOTICED SOMETHING WHEN HE BRUSHED AGAINST ME-- HE WAS SWEATING. SNAKES DON'T SWEAT. COULD THAT MEAN HIS BODY IS TRYING TO SHAKE OFF ITS REPTILIAN TRAITS?
SWIIISH
GOT TO KEEP HIM SWEATING AT ALL COSTS-- TRY TO ACCELERATE THE PROCESS!
I CAN'T STAY HIDDEN ANY LONGER! I'VE GOT TO SEE THIS WITH MY OWN EYES-- TWO GREAT AMERICANS DEGRADED-- REDUCED TO MEANINGLESS BRAWLING!
VIPER!
THEN SHE IS HERE!

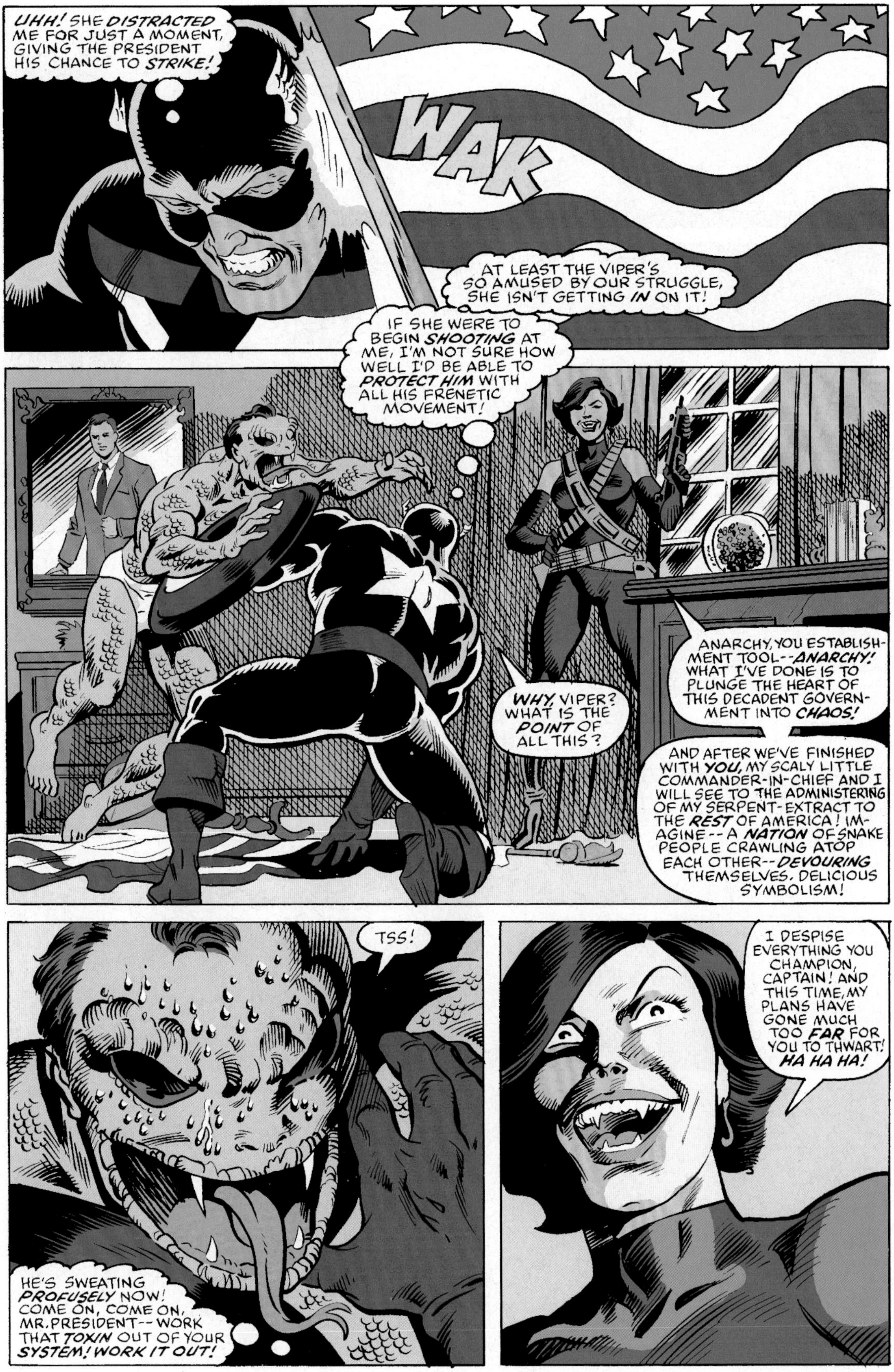
UHH! SHE DISTRACTED ME FOR JUST A MOMENT, GIVING THE PRESIDENT HIS CHANCE TO STRIKE!
WAK
AT LEAST THE VIPER'S SO AMUSED BY OUR STRUGGLE, SHE ISN'T GETTING IN ON IT!
IF SHE WERE TO BEGIN SHOOTING AT ME, I'M NOT SURE HOW WELL I'D BE ABLE TO PROTECT HIM WITH ALL HIS FRENETIC MOVEMENT!
WHY, VIPER? WHAT IS THE POINT OF ALL THIS?
ANARCHY, YOU ESTABLISHMENT TOOL--ANARCHY! WHAT I'VE DONE IS TO PLUNGE THE HEART OF THIS DECADENT GOVERNMENT INTO CHAOS!
AND AFTER WE'VE FINISHED WITH YOU, MY SCALY LITTLE COMMANDER-IN-CHIEF AND I WILL SEE TO THE ADMINISTERING OF MY SERPENT-EXTRACT TO THE REST OF AMERICA! IMAGINE--A NATION OF SNAKE PEOPLE CRAWLING ATOP EACH OTHER--DEVOURING THEMSELVES. DELICIOUS SYMBOLISM!
TSS!
HE'S SWEATING PROFUSELY NOW! COME ON, COME ON, MR. PRESIDENT--WORK THAT TOXIN OUT OF YOUR SYSTEM! WORK IT OUT!
I DESPISE EVERYTHING YOU CHAMPION, CAPTAIN! AND THIS TIME, MY PLANS HAVE GONE MUCH TOO FAR FOR YOU TO THWART! HA HA HA!

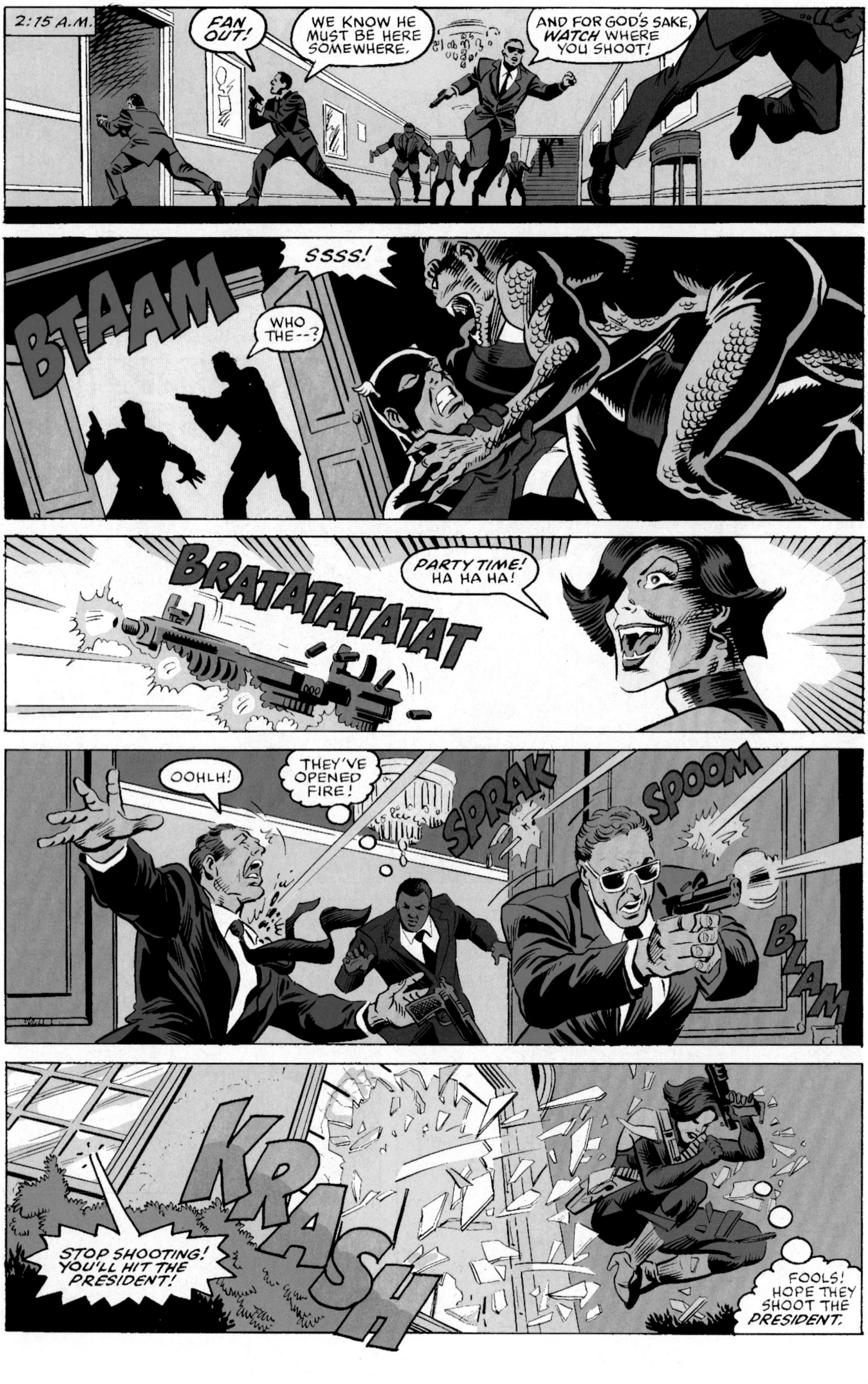
2:15 A.M.
FAN OUT!
WE KNOW HE MUST BE HERE SOMEWHERE.
AND FOR GOD'S SAKE, WATCH WHERE YOU SHOOT!
BTAAM
SSSS!
WHO THE--?
BRATATATATAT
PARTY TIME! HA HA HA!
OOHLH!
THEY'VE OPENED FIRE!
SPRAK
SPOOM
BLAM
KRASH
STOP SHOOTING! YOU'LL HIT THE PRESIDENT!
FOOLS! HOPE THEY SHOOT THE PRESIDENT.

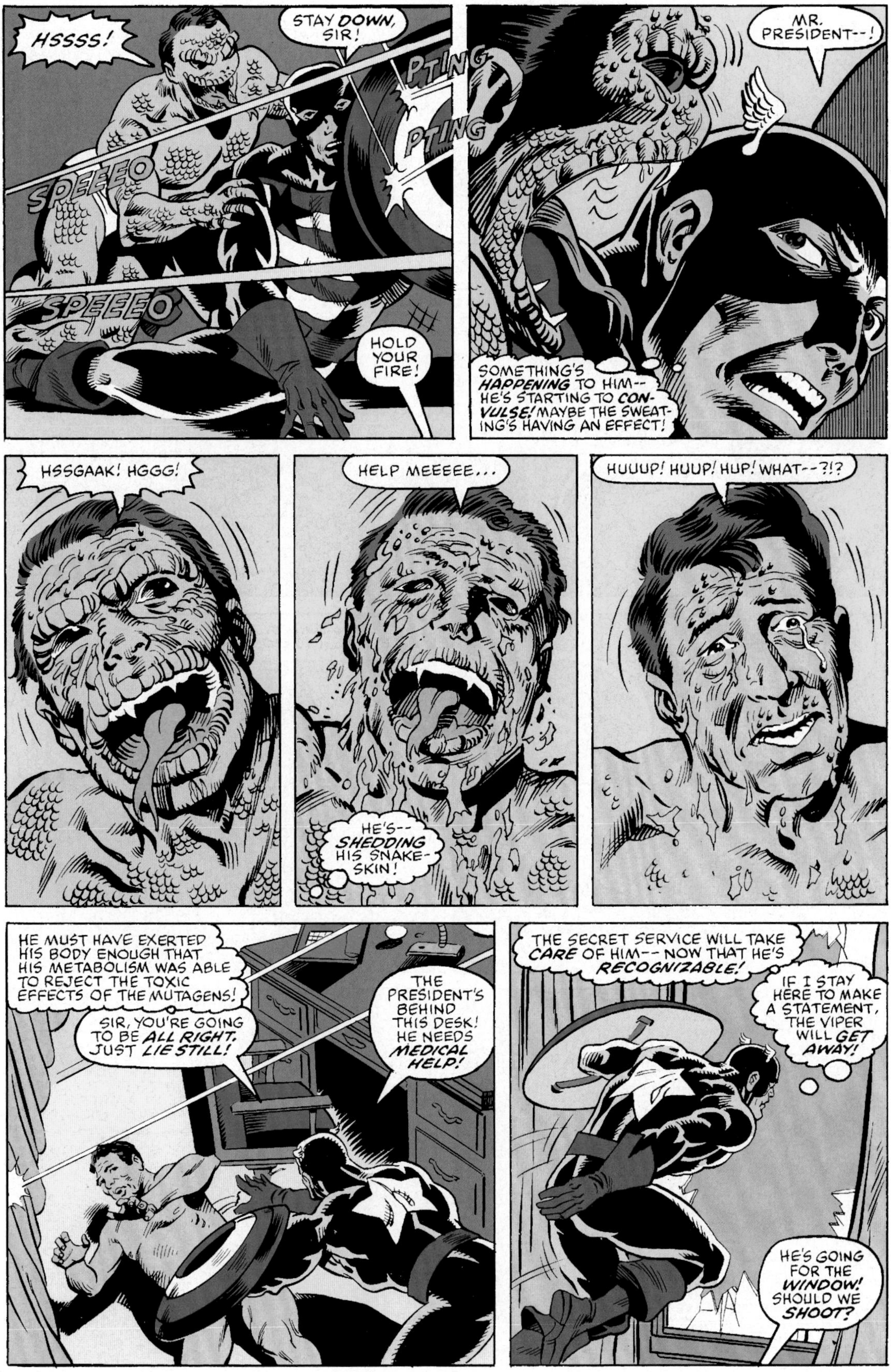
HSSSS!
STAY DOWN, SIR!
PTING
PTING
SPEEEO
SPEEEO
HOLD YOUR FIRE!
MR. PRESIDENT--!
SOMETHING'S HAPPENING TO HIM-- HE'S STARTING TO CONVULSE! MAYBE THE SWEATING'S HAVING AN EFFECT!
HSSGAAK! HGGG!
HELP MEEEEE...
HE'S-- SHEDDING HIS SNAKE-SKIN!
HUUUP! HUUP! HUP! WHAT--?!?
HE MUST HAVE EXERTED HIS BODY ENOUGH THAT HIS METABOLISM WAS ABLE TO REJECT THE TOXIC EFFECTS OF THE MUTAGENS!
SIR, YOU'RE GOING TO BE ALL RIGHT. JUST LIE STILL!
THE PRESIDENT'S BEHIND THIS DESK! HE NEEDS MEDICAL HELP!
THE SECRET SERVICE WILL TAKE CARE OF HIM-- NOW THAT HE'S RECOGNIZABLE!
IF I STAY HERE TO MAKE A STATEMENT, THE VIPER WILL GET AWAY!
HE'S GOING FOR THE WINDOW! SHOULD WE SHOOT?

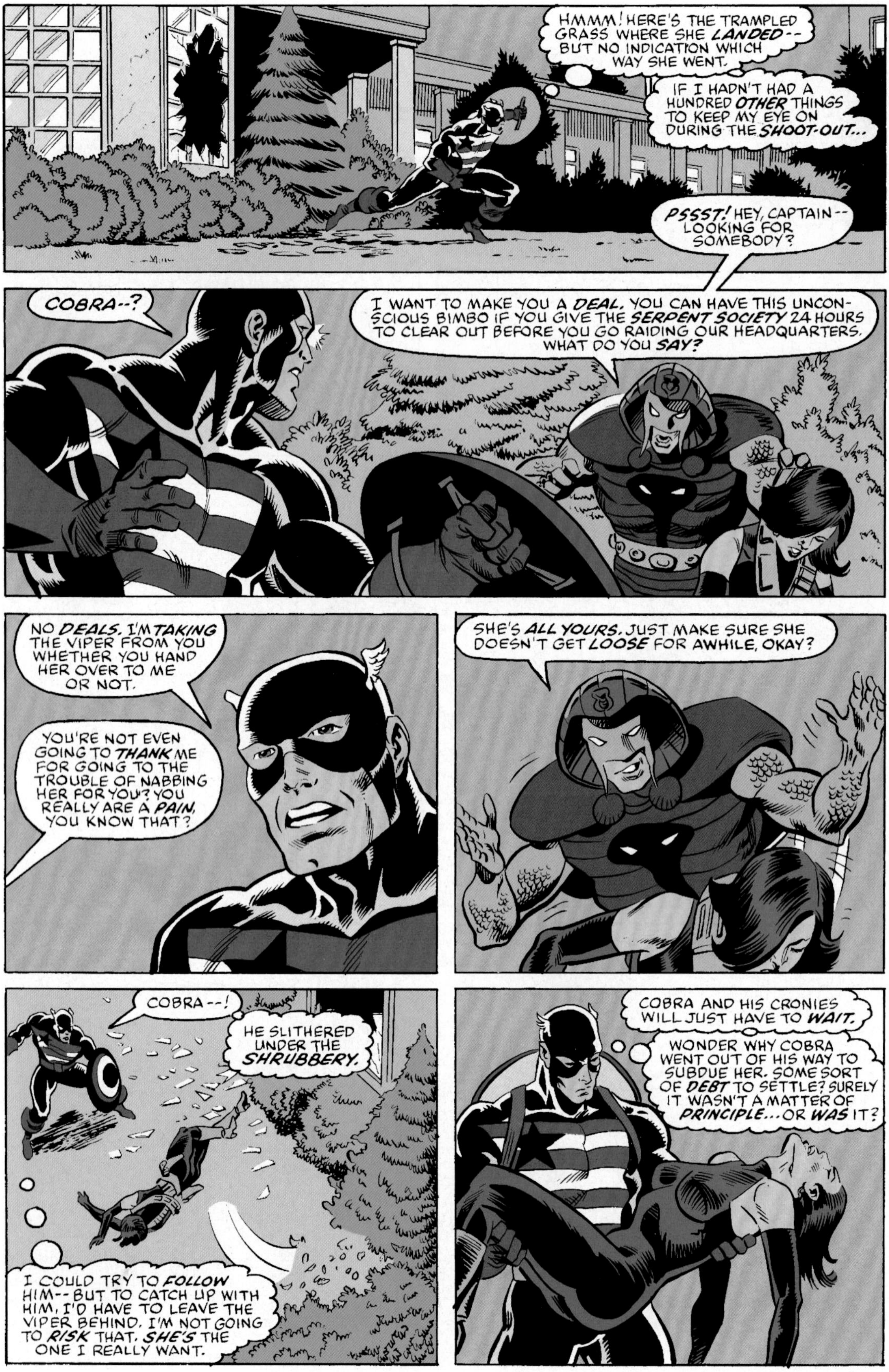
HMMM! HERE'S THE TRAMPLED GRASS WHERE SHE LANDED-- BUT NO INDICATION WHICH WAY SHE WENT.
IF I HADN'T HAD A HUNDRED OTHER THINGS TO KEEP MY EYE ON DURING THE SHOOT-OUT...
PSSST! HEY, CAPTAIN-- LOOKING FOR SOMEBODY?
COBRA--?
I WANT TO MAKE YOU A DEAL. YOU CAN HAVE THIS UNCONSCIOUS BIMBO IF YOU GIVE THE SERPENT SOCIETY 24 HOURS TO CLEAR OUT BEFORE YOU GO RAIDING OUR HEADQUARTERS. WHAT DO YOU SAY?
NO DEALS. I'M TAKING THE VIPER FROM YOU WHETHER YOU HAND HER OVER TO ME OR NOT.
YOU'RE NOT EVEN GOING TO THANK ME FOR GOING TO THE TROUBLE OF NABBING HER FOR YOU? YOU REALLY ARE A PAIN, YOU KNOW THAT?
SHE'S ALL YOURS. JUST MAKE SURE SHE DOESN'T GET LOOSE FOR AWHILE, OKAY?
COBRA--!
HE SLITHERED UNDER THE SHRUBBERY.
I COULD TRY TO FOLLOW HIM-- BUT TO CATCH UP WITH HIM, I'D HAVE TO LEAVE THE VIPER BEHIND. I'M NOT GOING TO RISK THAT. SHE'S THE ONE I REALLY WANT.
COBRA AND HIS CRONIES WILL JUST HAVE TO WAIT.
WONDER WHY COBRA WENT OUT OF HIS WAY TO SUBDUE HER. SOME SORT OF DEBT TO SETTLE? SURELY IT WASN'T A MATTER OF PRINCIPLE... OR WAS IT?

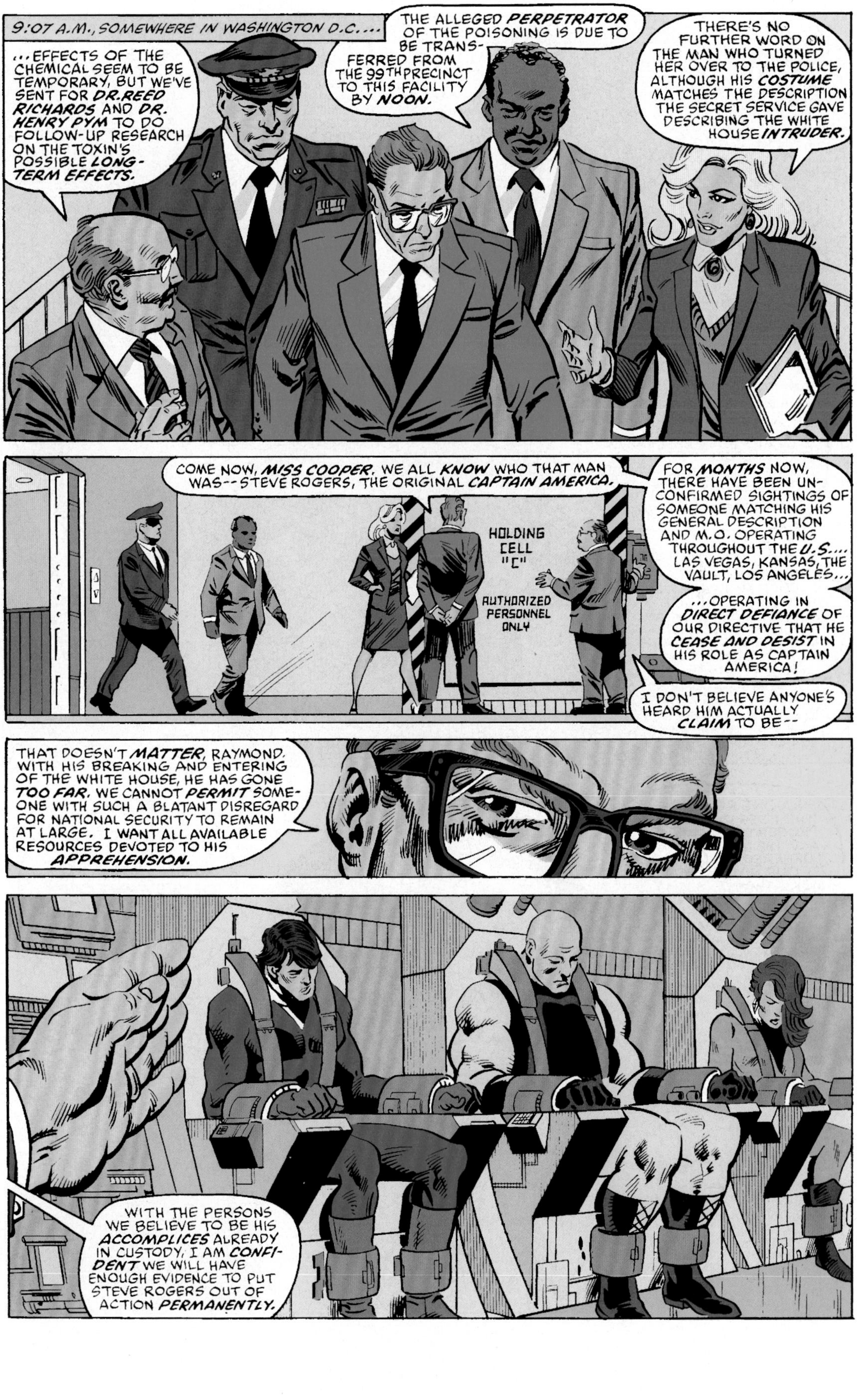
9:07 A.M., SOMEWHERE IN WASHINGTON D.C....
...EFFECTS OF THE CHEMICAL SEEM TO BE TEMPORARY, BUT WE'VE SENT FOR DR. REED RICHARDS AND DR. HENRY PYM TO DO FOLLOW-UP RESEARCH ON THE TOXIN'S POSSIBLE LONG-TERM EFFECTS.
THE ALLEGED PERPETRATOR OF THE POISONING IS DUE TO BE TRANSFERRED FROM THE 99TH PRECINCT TO THIS FACILITY BY NOON.
THERE'S NO FURTHER WORD ON THE MAN WHO TURNED HER OVER TO THE POLICE, ALTHOUGH HIS COSTUME MATCHES THE DESCRIPTION THE SECRET SERVICE GAVE DESCRIBING THE WHITE HOUSE INTRUDER.
COME NOW, MISS COOPER. WE ALL KNOW WHO THAT MAN WAS--STEVE ROGERS, THE ORIGINAL CAPTAIN AMERICA.
HOLDING CELL "C"
AUTHORIZED PERSONNEL ONLY
FOR MONTHS NOW, THERE HAVE BEEN UNCONFIRMED SIGHTINGS OF SOMEONE MATCHING HIS GENERAL DESCRIPTION AND M.O. OPERATING THROUGHOUT THE U.S.... LAS VEGAS, KANSAS, THE VAULT, LOS ANGELES...
...OPERATING IN DIRECT DEFIANCE OF OUR DIRECTIVE THAT HE CEASE AND DESIST IN HIS ROLE AS CAPTAIN AMERICA!
I DON'T BELIEVE ANYONE'S HEARD HIM ACTUALLY CLAIM TO BE--
THAT DOESN'T MATTER, RAYMOND. WITH HIS BREAKING AND ENTERING OF THE WHITE HOUSE, HE HAS GONE TOO FAR. WE CANNOT PERMIT SOMEONE WITH SUCH A BLATANT DISREGARD FOR NATIONAL SECURITY TO REMAIN AT LARGE. I WANT ALL AVAILABLE RESOURCES DEVOTED TO HIS APPREHENSION.
WITH THE PERSONS WE BELIEVE TO BE HIS ACCOMPLICES ALREADY IN CUSTODY, I AM CONFIDENT WE WILL HAVE ENOUGH EVIDENCE TO PUT STEVE ROGERS OUT OF ACTION PERMANENTLY.

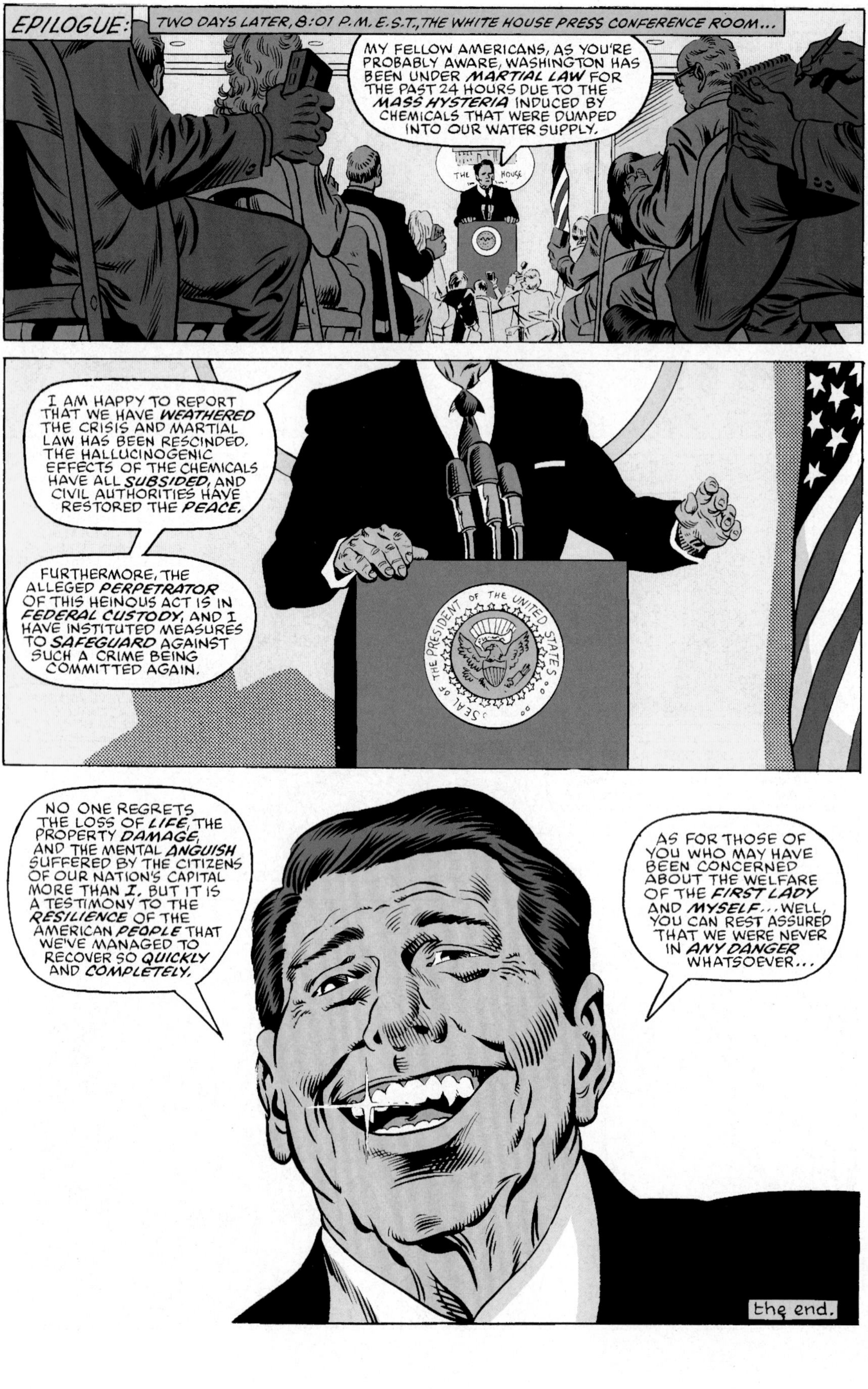
EPILOGUE:
TWO DAYS LATER, 8:01 P.M. E.S.T., THE WHITE HOUSE PRESS CONFERENCE ROOM...
MY FELLOW AMERICANS, AS YOU'RE PROBABLY AWARE, WASHINGTON HAS BEEN UNDER MARTIAL LAW FOR THE PAST 24 HOURS DUE TO THE MASS HYSTERIA INDUCED BY CHEMICALS THAT WERE DUMPED INTO OUR WATER SUPPLY.
I AM HAPPY TO REPORT THAT WE HAVE WEATHERED THE CRISIS AND MARTIAL LAW HAS BEEN RESCINDED. THE HALLUCINOGENIC EFFECTS OF THE CHEMICALS HAVE ALL SUBSIDED, AND CIVIL AUTHORITIES HAVE RESTORED THE PEACE.
FURTHERMORE, THE ALLEGED PERPETRATOR OF THIS HEINOUS ACT IS IN FEDERAL CUSTODY, AND I HAVE INSTITUTED MEASURES TO SAFEGUARD AGAINST SUCH A CRIME BEING COMMITTED AGAIN.
SEAL OF THE PRESIDENT OF THE UNITED STATES
NO ONE REGRETS THE LOSS OF LIFE, THE PROPERTY DAMAGE, AND THE MENTAL ANGUISH SUFFERED BY THE CITIZENS OF OUR NATION'S CAPITAL MORE THAN I. BUT IT IS A TESTIMONY TO THE RESILIENCE OF THE AMERICAN PEOPLE THAT WE'VE MANAGED TO RECOVER SO QUICKLY AND COMPLETELY.
AS FOR THOSE OF YOU WHO MAY HAVE BEEN CONCERNED ABOUT THE WELFARE OF THE FIRST LADY AND MYSELF... WELL, YOU CAN REST ASSURED THAT WE WERE NEVER IN ANY DANGER WHATSOEVER...
the end.

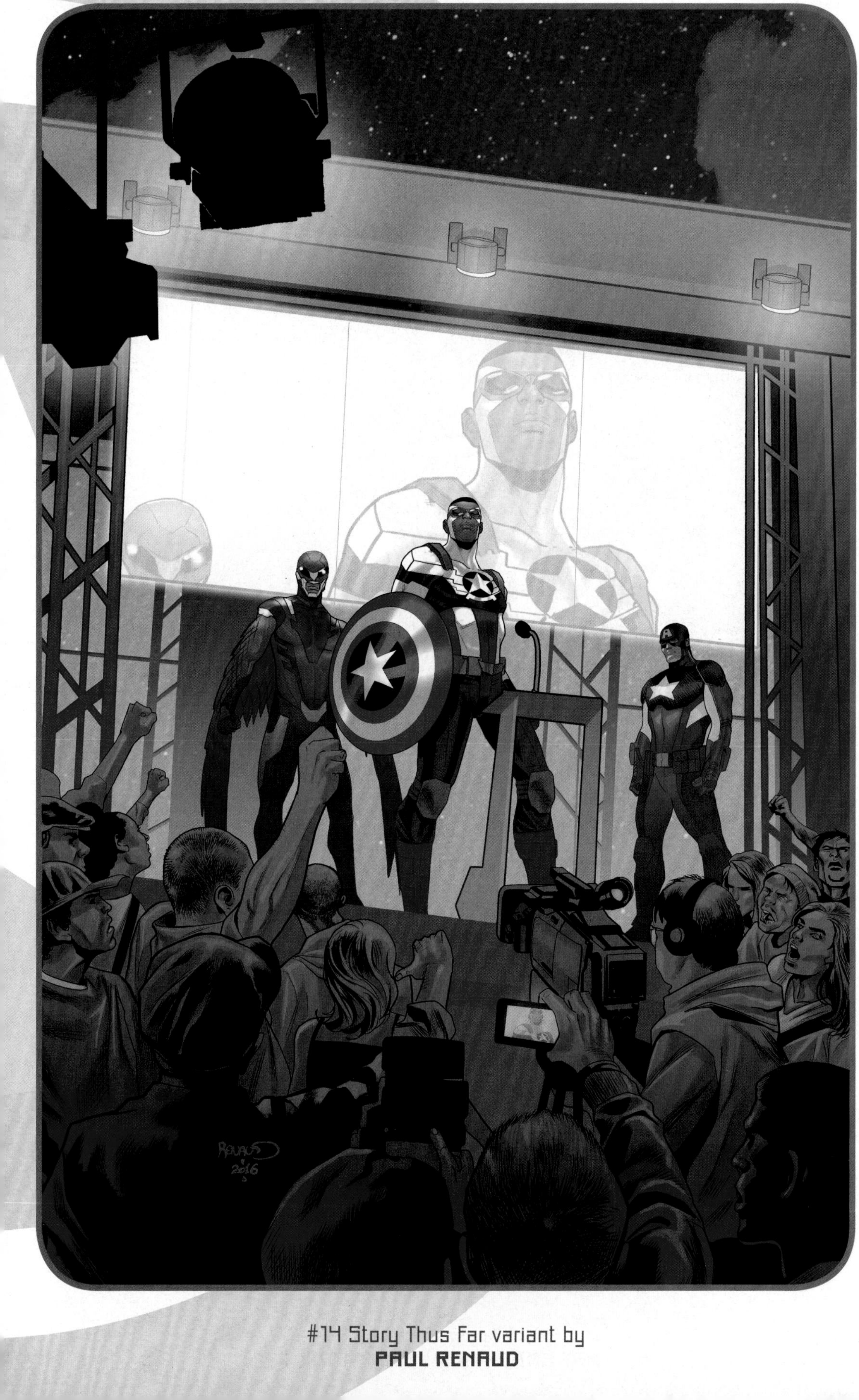

#14 Story Thus Far variant by
PAUL RENAUD

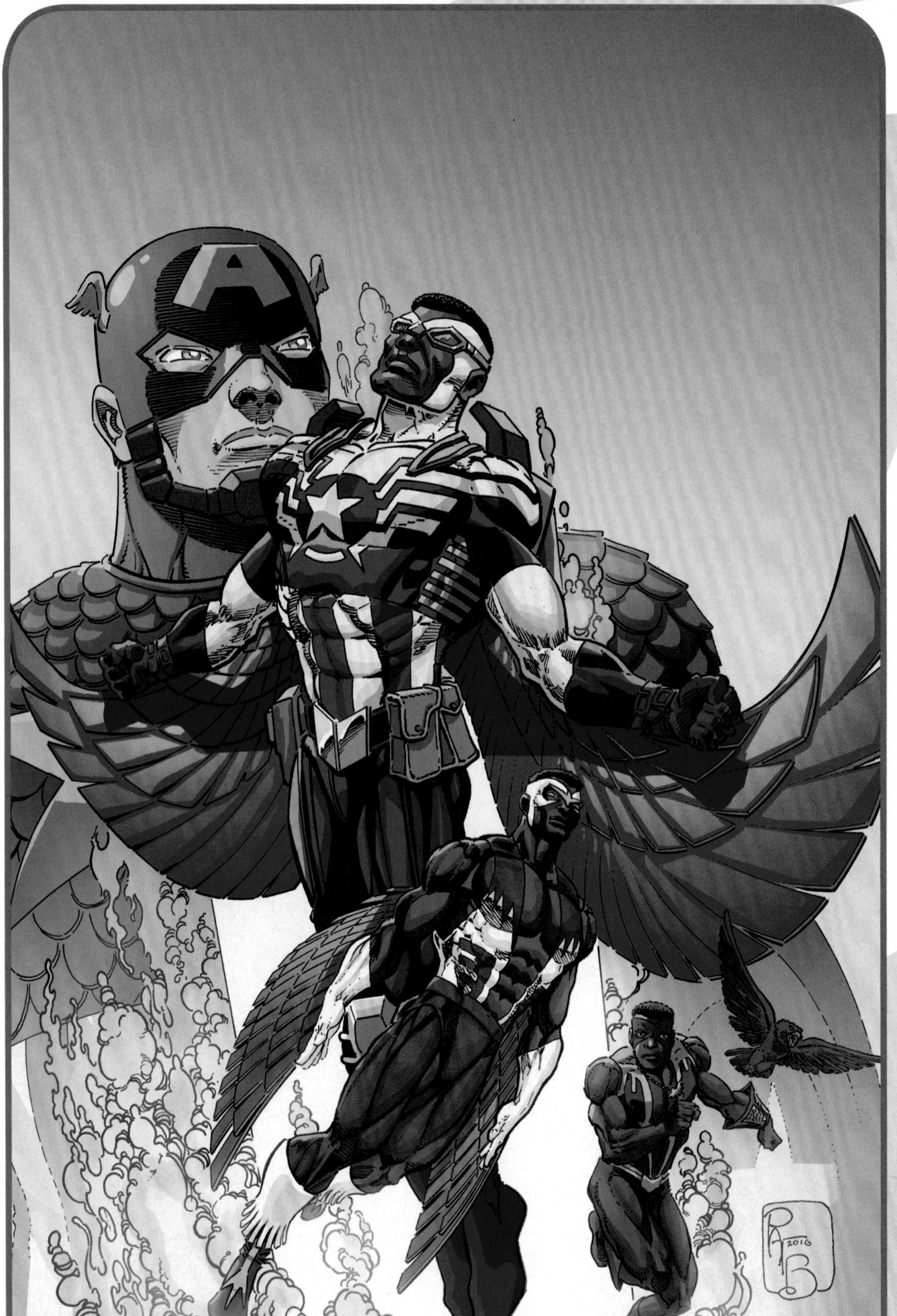

#14 variant by
PAT BRODERICK & ANDY TROY

character designs by **DANIEL ACUÑA**

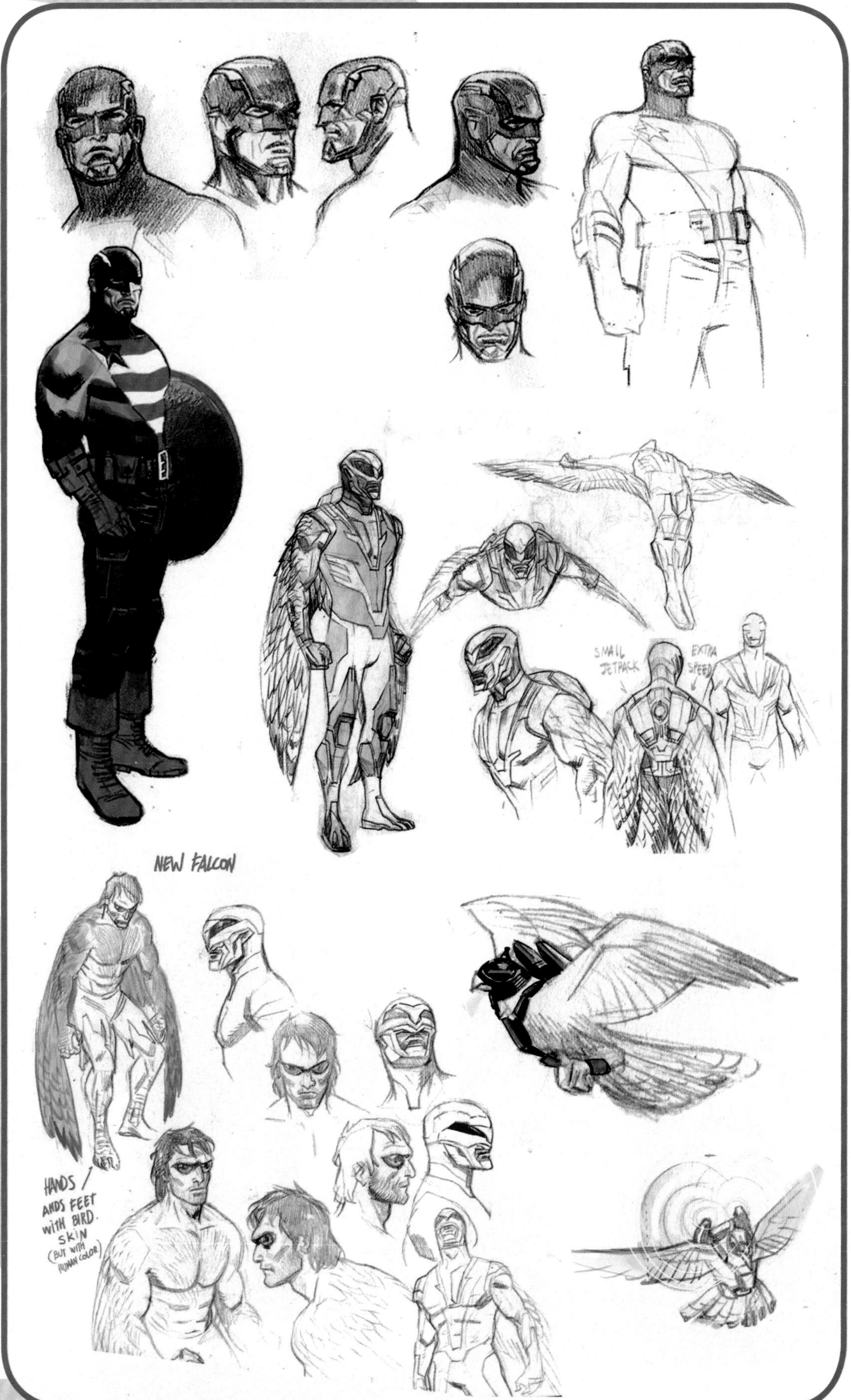
SMALL JETPACK
EXTRA SPEED
NEW FALCON
HANDS / ANDS FEET WITH BIRD SKIN (BUT WITH HUMAN COLOR)

character designs by **DANIEL ACUÑA**

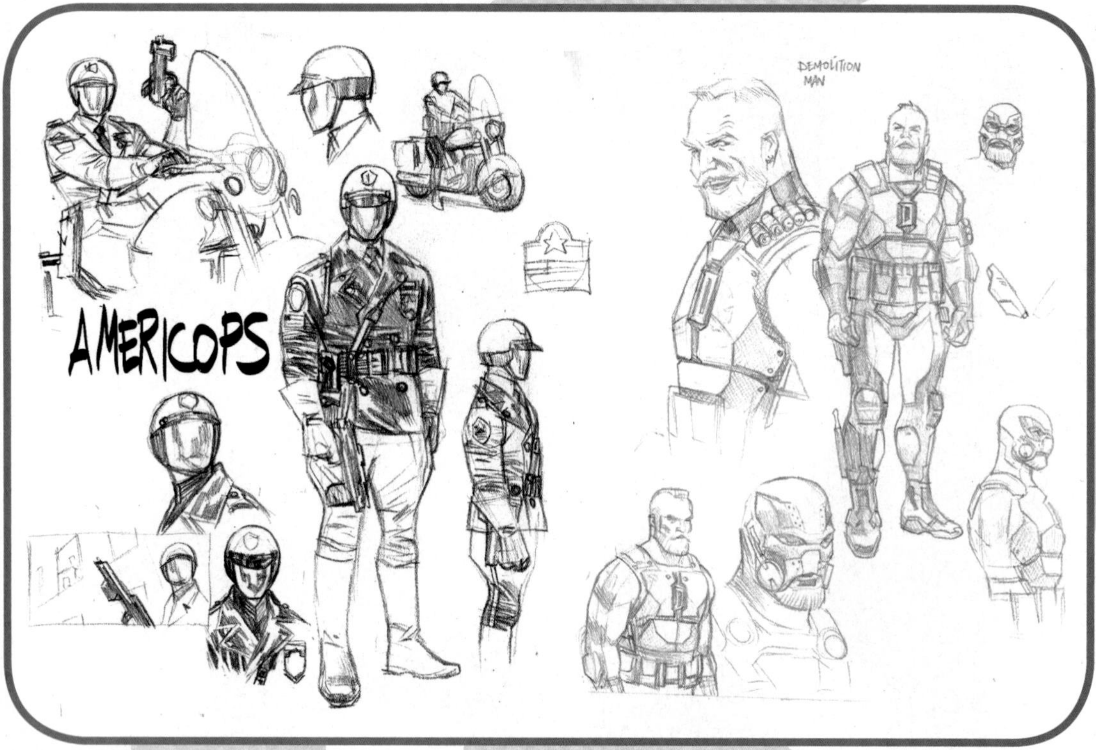
AMERICOPS
DEMOLITION MAN

character designs by **PAUL RENAUD**

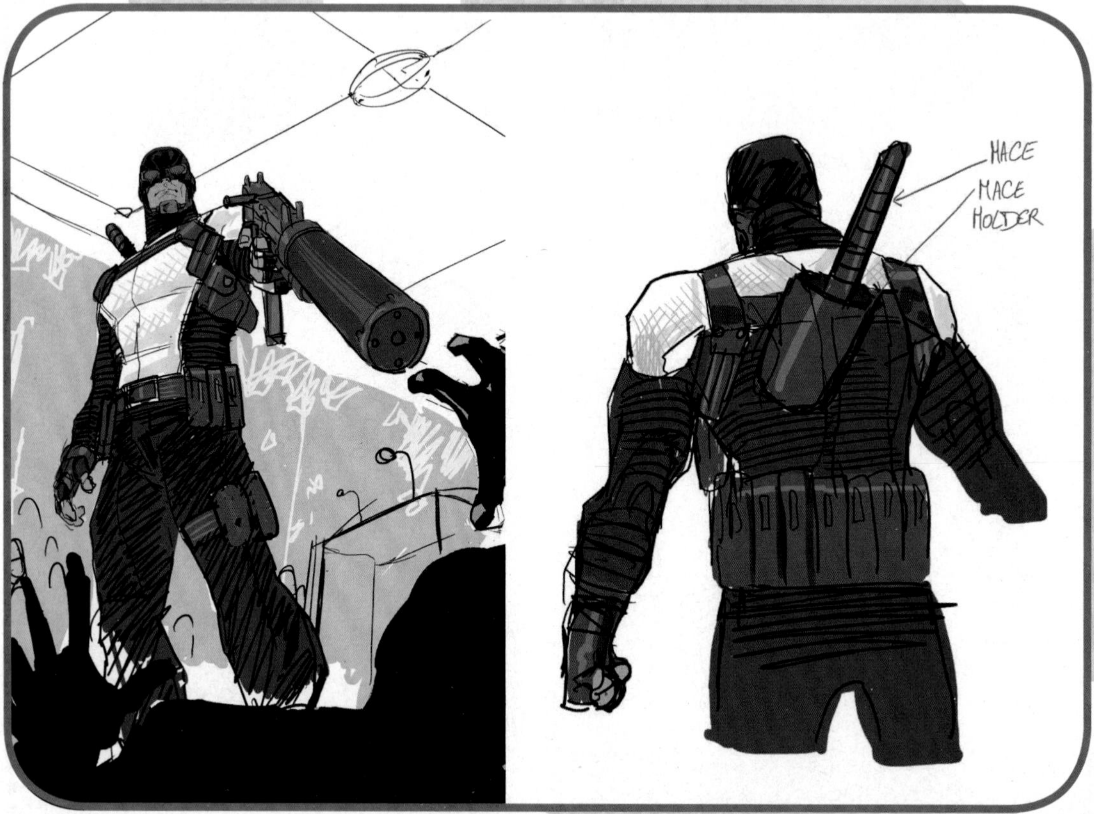
MACE
MACE HOLDER